THE LESSER EVIL

THOMAS CRANE PUBLIC LIBRARY
QUINCY MA

CITY APPROPRIATION

MICHAEL IGNATIEFF

THE LESSER EVIL

POLITICAL ETHICS IN
AN AGE OF TERROR

The Gifford Lectures

With a new preface by the author

PRINCETON UNIVERSITY PRESS   PRINCETON AND OXFORD

Copyright © 2004 by Michael Ignatieff
Requests for permission to reproduce material from this work should be sent to
Permissions, Princeton University Press

Published in the United States by Princeton University Press, 41 William Street,
Princeton, New Jersey 08540

All Rights Reserved

Fourth printing, and first paperback printing,
with a new preface by the author, 2005
Paperback ISBN-13: 978-0-691-12393-6
Paperback ISBN-10: 0-691-12393-4

The Library of Congress has cataloged the cloth edition of this book as follows

Ignatieff, Michael.
The lesser evil : political ethics in
an age of terror / Michael Ignatieff.
p.   cm.
Includes bibliographical references and index.
ISBN 0-691-11751-9 (cl. : alk. paper)
I. Title.
2003107023

This book has been composed in Palatino text types

Printed on acid-free paper. ∞

pup.princeton.edu

Printed in the United States of America

5   7   9   10   8   6

CONTENTS

Life's toughest choices are not between good and bad, but between bad and worse. We call these *choices between lesser evils*. We know that whatever we choose, something important will be sacrificed. Whatever we do, someone will get hurt. Worst of all, we *have* to choose. We cannot wait for better information or advice or some new set of circumstances. We have to decide now, and we can be sure that there will be a price to pay. If we do not pay it ourselves, someone else will.

These are the kinds of choices we face when dealing with terrorist threats. If we do too little, we will get attacked again. If we do too much, we will harm innocent people. In making these choices, we never have enough information. Some sources exaggerate the threat; others minimize it. Nothing we are told is reliable and nothing we do is ever likely to strike the right balance.

If we decide to round up potential terrorists, before they can strike, we do harm to established principles like the presumption of innocence, and if we detain them without trial, we do harm to the principle of detention only with due cause and judicial review. If we start interrogating them and they keep silent, we have to decide whether to put them under physical or psychological pressure, and once we do that, we can find ourselves on the downward slope to torture. If we do nothing, on the other hand, they may strike again.

It is naive to suppose that we do not have to make these choices. The belief that our existing rights and guarantees should never be suspended is a piece of moral perfectionism. Some of our freedoms are fine, but others leave us open to attack. Terrorists have exploited our openness, and it would be foolish to doubt that they will try again. To claim that there are no lesser evil choices to be made is to take refuge in the illusion that the threat of terrorism is exaggerated.

But there is an equal danger in the belief that the threat is so great that anything we do to fight terrorism can be justified: indefinite detention, assassination and coercive interrogation amounting to torture. Here lesser evil arguments slip into what the legal theorist Roberto Unger calls "false necessity."[1] We can allow exaggerated claims about terrorist threats to make us feel that we do not have any choices at all. We must do what we must do because our survival is at stake.

Thinking about the terrorist problem means escaping the trap of moral perfectionism on the one hand and false necessity on the other. A lesser evil approach—the one taken in this book—attempts to get beyond these alternatives. The book seeks a middle way, safeguarding the rights of persons while protecting us against those who respect no one's rights at all. This is usually supposed to mean balancing liberty against security. But the balancing metaphor is not honest enough about the difficulties. The reality is that we are bound to sacrifice some liberty for some security *and* some security for some liberty. We cannot ever be certain, in advance, how serious a terrorist threat is going to be. Inevitably we are going to make mistakes, sacrificing too much security *ex ante* and too much liberty *ex post*. Since we cannot avoid error, it is important that we learn from our mistakes quickly and correct them.

In choosing lesser evils in order to avoid greater ones, rules—like banning torture outright—do matter, but process matters more. Where mistakes are inevitable and we need to correct them quickly, it is vital that those who make the choices are forced, as often as possible, to justify their decisions, *ex ante* and *ex post*, and account for their mistakes. Democracy is better at correcting mistakes than any other form of rule. The checks and balances of a democratic system—legislature, executive, judiciary, and a free press—create multiple fora for "adversarial justification," where public authorities are forced to explain the balance they have drawn between liberty and security. The justifications are adversarial because the institutions compete for power with each other, and because the people who run these institutions are bound to disagree, often deeply, about how to draw these balances. At the heart of this book is a plea that we keep antiterrorist policy under the bright public light of "adversarial justification." This means defending a democratic system both against those who use false necessity arguments to justify secret government proceedings and those who use perfectionist arguments to claim that we need make no sacrifice of liberty.

It will be said that this approach is too trusting of our existing institutions. Anyone can assemble a depressing picture of democratic failure since 9/11: a cowed press, a timid legislature, an overly deferential judiciary, all unable to stop the relentless accumulation of secret power by the executive branch, and this in all of our democracies, not just the United States. This picture is true: indeed, the chief danger to democratic government posed by terrorist emergencies is that they favor secret, as opposed to open, government, and provide the justification for the accumulation of unchecked executive power. But if this is true, what is the solution? I can see only one: more democratic scrutiny, more adversarial justification, more open government, not less. The point is not that I trust our institutions but only that there are no real alternatives to making them work as best we can.

A lesser evil approach has been criticized by some on the left as providing "national self-justification" for the coercive measures taken by the United States and other democratic states since 9/11.[2] It is a doctrine, one critic charged, that "tells us how to do terrible things for a righteous cause and come away feeling good about it." It's not obvious to me why someone should think that the chief priority of this book was to make anyone feel better about making hard choices. The stress placed on the obligation to justify coercive measures in adversarial settings— court rooms, a free press, legislative hearing rooms, and free elections—assumes that some arguments for coercion, used by current politicians, were nothing better than feeble rationalizations, while others stood the test of scrutiny. The book's purpose is not to provide rationalizations for coercion, but to help citizens distinguish good reasons from bad ones in counterterrorism policy.

This is not to imply, again, that democracies work wonderfully well and all we need to do in a war on terrorism is to put our faith in the institutions we have. An enduring weakness of democracy is that citizens as a whole do not feel the impact of the civil liberties infringements imposed on vulnerable minorities. Democratic citizens do not actually have to balance *their* liberty against their security, but their security against the liberty of others, usually noncitizens. Decisions to abridge civil liberties for non-nationals have aroused little public resistance since 9/11, while measures aimed at citizens, like national identity cards or more intrusive security screenings at airports, have been stymied.[3] This bias of democracy against noncitizens is serious precisely because the terrorist threat is believed to come chiefly, if not exclusively, from them.

This is why a democracy's international obligations matter: national laws do not protect noncitizens well, and democratic institutions do a poor job giving their grievances a voice. Observing international law is the best way to correct the partiality that states feel toward their own citizens and to mitigate the discrimination that they mete out to noncitizens.

My emphasis on the necessity to balance national laws with observance of international human rights law and the laws of war has exposed me to criticism from conservative critics. They claim that the lesser evil approach denies that states faced with terrorist threats have a right to privilege the defense of their own nationals against the rights of non-nationals.[4] But the fact that our opponents are human beings and are entitled to basic standards of treatment if we capture them does not pre-empt our right to defend ourselves against them. A state should defend its own citizens robustly with lawful forms of preventive detention, surveillance, deportation, and military options abroad, including pre-emptive force. Like conservatives, I believe that a government is answerable, in the first instance, to the laws and institutions of its own people. The test that counterterrorist measures must meet is, first and foremost, the adversarial scrutiny of its own free institutions.

Yet democratic societies are not islands unto themselves, and the justifications they owe also extend to international society. A government that has ratified international agreements like the Torture Convention and the Geneva Convention is bound to comply with them. This obligation is both legal and moral: the requirement to accord minimum standards of decent treatment to noncitizens by virtue of their humanity. A state is entitled to balance its security obligations to its own citizens against these international obligations—i.e., to enter reservations explicitly limiting the application of these rules—but only in a manner consistent with the plain meaning of these agreements. The Torture Convention bans torture. It is not a text to be parsed, by ingenious legal casuists, into a permission for coercive interrogations that cross the line, as in the Abu Ghraib prison scandal, into gross and degrading physical abuse.[5] After Abu Ghraib and Guantanamo, the sovereignty doctrines of American conservatives seem both wrong in moral terms and dangerous to the security interests of the United States.[6] When a liberal democratic society like the United States starts believing—as conservatives have assiduously encouraged it to believe—that it owes no one but itself an account of how it treats non-nationals under its power, it can find itself creating a global detention and interrogation policy that manages the unique feat of incurring global obloquy without adding anything very obvious to the security of its own soldiers and citizens.

A final criticism—and the most justified—comes from fellow liberals who believe that in certain parts of the book I have failed to be sufficiently specific about how to craft legislative and institutional remedies.[7] This is true, but I am happy to defer to the expertise of others.[8] In any event, my purpose is different from theirs, not to propose specific measures but to articulate what values we are trying to defend from attack. My question is less "What must we do?"—but "Who and what are we trying to defend?" Knowing who we are—what democratic institutions are, why we need to strengthen adversarial justification, and why our identity as a free people is tied into the idea of respecting the basic rights of noncitizens—is a crucial first step in understanding what we must do. I hope the book will be helpful not only to those who have to make these choices, but also to those ordinary citizens whose patriotic duty it is to subject these choices to the adversarial review of a free society.

Cambridge, Massachusetts
June 2005

Notes

1. Roberto Unger, *False Necessity* (London: Verso, 2004).

2. Ronald Steel, "Fight Fire With Fire," *New York Times Book Review*, July 25, 2004.

3. This is a point made throughout David Cole's *Enemy Aliens* (New York: New Press, 2003).

4. Jeremy Rabkin, "The Lesser Evil is Not Good Enough," *Claremont Review of Books*, Winter 2004.

5. The preceding paragraph incorporates material to be found in "A Reply to Rabkin," to be published in the *Claremont Review of Books*, forthcoming, 2005. On Abu Ghraib, see Steven Strasser, ed., *The Abu Ghraib Investigations* (New York: Public Affairs, 2004); Mark Danner, "Torture and Truth," *New York Review of Books*, June 10, 2004.

6. P. J. Spiro, "The New Sovereigntists," *Foreign Affairs* 79, no. 6 (November/December 2000): 9–15.

7. Martha Minow, "But What Is the Greatest Evil?" *Harvard Law Review*, forthcoming, 2005.

8. Philip B. Heymann and Juliette N. Kayyem, "Preserving Security and Democratic Freedoms in the War on Terrorism" (Report of the Long-Term Legal Strategy Project, Harvard University, 2004).

I

When democracies fight terrorism, they are defending the proposition that their political life should be free of violence. But defeating terror requires violence. It may also require coercion, deception, secrecy, and violation of rights. How can democracies resort to these means without destroying the values for which they stand? How can they resort to the lesser evil, without succumbing to the greater? This book seeks to answer that question. While it is written under the impact of September 11, 2001, I have found inspiration in sources distant from our own time, from Euripides to Machiavelli, from Dostoevsky to Conrad, all of whom thought deeply about the moral hazard of using doubtful means to defend praiseworthy goals. This book brings together ideas from literature, law, ethics, philosophy, and history to help citizens and leaders make the hazardous choices that a successful struggle against terrorism requires.

There have been many valuable critiques of the measures taken by liberal democracies to defend themselves since September 11.[1] Instead of contributing yet another of these, I have tried to range more broadly, looking at the nineteenth- and twentieth-century history of attempts by states to deal with terrorist threats without sacrificing their constitutional identity. September 11 shadows the book, but while much of the discussion focuses on the dilemmas that America faces, I have tried to learn from terrorist emergencies in the United Kingdom, Canada, Italy, Germany, Spain, and Israel, as well as countries farther away, like Sri Lanka. I have also looked forward to consider the dark scenarios that open up when terrorists acquire chemical, nuclear, and biological weapons.

In the first chapter, "Democracy and the Lesser Evil," I explain why the use of coercive force in a liberal democracy, not just in

times of emergency, but in normal times as well, is regarded as
a lesser evil. This particular view of democracy does not prohibit
emergency suspensions of rights in times of terror. But it imposes an obligation on government to justify such measures
publicly, to submit them to judicial review, and to circumscribe
them with sunset clauses so that they do not become permanent.
Rights do not set impassable barriers to government action, but
they do require that all rights infringements be tested under adversarial review.

I try to chart a middle course between a pure civil libertarian
position which maintains that no violations of rights can ever be
justified and a purely pragmatic position that judges antiterrorist measures solely by their effectiveness. I argue that actions
which violate foundational commitments to justice and dignity—torture, illegal detention, unlawful assassination—should
be beyond the pale. But defining these limits in theory is not
hard. The problem is to protect them in practice, to maintain the
limits, case by case, where reasonable people may disagree as
to what constitutes torture, what detentions are illegal, which
killings depart from lawful norms, or which preemptive actions
constitute aggression. Neither necessity nor liberty, neither public danger nor private rights constitute trumping claims in deciding these questions. Since good democrats will disagree
about these questions, it is crucial that they agree at least to
strengthen the process of adversarial review that decides these
matters. When democrats disagree on substance, they need to
agree on process, to keep democracy safe both from our enemies
and from our own zeal.

The second chapter, "The Ethics of Emergency," examines the
impact of emergency suspensions of civil liberties on the rule of
law and human rights. The issue at stake here is whether emergency derogations of rights preserve or endanger the rule of law.
I take the position that exceptions do not destroy the rule but
save it, provided that they are temporary, publicly justified, and
deployed only as a last resort.

The larger question is what role human rights should play in
deciding public policy during terrorist emergencies. Most

human rights conventions allow for the derogation or suspension of some rights in times of emergency. Suspending rights is a lesser evil solution, but it compromises the status of human rights as a set of unchanging benchmarks. Once you admit that human rights can be suspended in times of emergency, you are accepting that human rights are not a system of indivisible absolutes; their application requires balancing liberty and necessity, pure principle and prudence. This does not reduce them to instruments of political expediency. On the contrary, realistic rights constraints are more likely to be effective than unrealistic ones. International human rights conventions serve to remind democracies at war with terror that even their enemies have rights, which are not dependent upon reciprocity or good conduct. Such conventions also remind states that their actions need to conform not just to national standards but to international ones too. But rights can fulfill this function only if they are flexible enough to allow some compromise with absolute standards when political necessity or emergency requires.

The third chapter, "The Weakness of the Strong," seeks to explain why liberal democracies consistently overreact to terrorist threats, as if their survival were in jeopardy. Why are liberal democracies so quick to barter away their liberty? The historical record suggests, disturbingly, that majorities care less about deprivations of liberty that harm minorities than they do about their own security. This historical tendency to value majority interests over individual rights has weakened liberal democracies. They usually survive the political challenge presented by terrorism but in the process of doing so they have inflicted enduring damage to their own rights framework. Far from being an incidental menace, terrorism has warped democracy's institutional development, strengthening secret government at the expense of open adversarial review.

In the fourth chapter, "The Strength of the Weak," the focus shifts to terrorism itself. The chief claim used to justify terrorism is that if oppressed groups were required to abstain from violence directed at civilians, their political cause would be condemned to failure. In the face of oppression and superior force, terrorism rationalizes itself as the only strategy that can lead the oppressed to victory. This argument from weakness presents liberal democrats with a special challenge, since liberal democratic theory has always admitted the right of the oppressed to take up arms as a last resort, when their cause is just and peaceful means are certain to fail. The way to meet the challenge of terrorism, I will argue, is to ensure that the oppressed always have peaceful political means of redress at their disposal. Where such means are denied, it is inevitable that violence will occur. Terrorists exploit injustice and claim to represent just causes. Hence a counterterror strategy that fails to address injustice, that fails to maintain political channels for redress of grievance, cannot succeed by purely military means. The key dilemma is to address injustice politically without legitimizing terrorists.

The fifth chapter, "The Temptations of Nihilism," examines the darker possibility that in a struggle between a liberal constitutional state and a terrorist enemy both sides will be tempted to descend into pure nihilism, that is, violence for violence's sake. High principle and moral scruple may lose their purchase on the interrogators in the state's secret prisons or the fighters in a guerrilla or insurgent struggle. Both sides may start with high ideals, and end, step by step, in their betrayal. A critic of a lesser evil morality would argue that anyone who traffics in evil, even with the best intentions, is likely to end up succumbing to nihilism. The chapter considers how this declension occurs and how it can be avoided.

The final chapter, "Liberty and Armageddon," addresses the acquisition by terrorist groups of weapons of mass destruction. If this were to occur, the state's ultimate powers of violence would pass into private hands, either those of a terrorist internationale like Al Qaeda, or those of a superempowered loner, a lonely citizen with a grudge and the capability to hold his entire nation hostage. These scenarios would take us into a new world, in which terrorism might transmute from an eternal but manageable challenge to liberal democracy into a potentially lethal foe. The book ends, therefore, by thinking the worst, in order to pose, as starkly as possible, the questions with which the book began: whether our democracies are strong enough to cope with these dangers and how to strengthen the institutions we are committed to defend.

II

This book began its life as six Gifford Lectures, delivered in the Playfair Library at the University of Edinburgh in January 2003. The Playfair Library is a long, high-ceilinged room, built at the turn of the nineteenth century, with white marble busts of the leading luminaries of the Scottish Enlightenment in its columned recesses. The august setting and the example of the preceding Gifford lecturers made it an inspiring experience. I owe that first audience an especial debt though I doubt that they will recognize anything but broad outlines of the original lectures in this book, since I have reworked and rethought all of my initial hypotheses.

I remain deeply grateful to the committee, especially Professor Timothy O'Shea and Professor Leslie Brown, who did me the honor of inviting me to give the lectures. One member of that committee, Nicholas Phillipson, has been my friend for twenty-five years, and I thank him for his support, hospitality, and affection. I also want to acknowledge Paul McGuire, who did so much to make the Gifford experience a pleasure. My appreciation also goes out to Stephen Neff, John Haldane, Duncan Forrester, and Vicki Bruce for their comments on the lectures.

After their life in the Gifford Lectures, the thoughts in this book were developed further in front of audiences at Macalester College, Amherst College, the Law School at the University of Chicago, the University of Manitoba, the University of Saskatchewan, and the University of Regina. I want to thank the audiences and academic commentators for pressing me to improve my arguments. Denise Rheaume, Cass Sunstein, Bernadine Dohrn, and Martha Nussbaum provided especially useful criticisms. I also delivered versions of these ideas at the Center for Ethics and the Professions at the Kennedy School, Harvard, and at a seminar on terrorism organized by the Harvard University

Committee for Human Rights. I want to thank Sandy Jencks, Jacqueline Bhabha, Philip Heymann, Arthur Applbaum, Louise Richardson, Jessica Stern, Dan Squires, and Michael Blake for their comments and suggestions.

At the Carr Center, Abena Asare, my devoted research assistant, led me to many sources and references I would have missed, and responded gamely to a constant stream of requests for books, articles, and half-remembered quotations, and to other research demands as the book took final shape. Jill Clarke helped keep the rest of the world at bay while I was writing. I want to thank Jill, Abena, and all of the staff at the Carr Center—under the leadership of Michelle Greene—for their unfailing good company as this project took shape. Samantha Power, my colleague at the Center, provided mordant commentary on some of my ideas and helped me to see the forest for the trees.

Ian Malcolm of Princeton University Press and Jackie Jones of Edinburgh University Press brought the book swiftly to publication. I am especially grateful to Ian Malcolm for his enthusiasm for the project and his detailed editorial suggestions. Lauren Lepow's editing significantly improved the text. I owe a special debt to the anonymous reader, assigned to the manuscript by Princeton University Press, whose eighteen pages of commentary proved invaluable in taking the analysis further in the final version. This anonymous benefactor displayed a rare intellectual generosity, and I believe the book is the better for it. I also want to thank Derek Johns of AP Watt and Michael Levine of Goodmans for shrewd advice.

The book is dedicated to my wife, Suzanna Zsohar, who has lived with it in all its incarnations and improved it, as she always does.

The Carr Center for Human Rights Policy
Kennedy School of Government
Harvard University
January 2004

CHAPTER ONE

DEMOCRACY AND
THE LESSER EVIL

On the appointed day the unarmed crowd of the Gothic youth was
carefully collected in the square or forum; the streets and avenues
were occupied by the Roman troops, and the roofs of the houses were
covered with archers and slingers. At the same hour, in all the cities
of the East, the signal was given of indiscriminate slaughter; and the
provinces of Asia were delivered, by the cruel prudence of Julius, from
a domestic enemy, who in a few months might have carried fire and
sword from the Hellespont to the Euphrates. The urgent consideration
of the public safety may undoubtedly authorize the violation of every
positive law. How far that or any other consideration may operate to
dissolve the natural obligations of humanity and justice is a doctrine
of which I still desire to remain ignorant.

—*Edward Gibbon*, The Decline and Fall of the
Roman Empire *(1776), 2.36*

I

What lesser evils may a society commit when it believes it faces
the greater evil of its own destruction? This is one of the oldest
questions in politics and one of the hardest to answer. The old
Roman adage—the safety of the people is the first law—set few
limits to the claims of security over liberty. In the name of the
people's safety, the Roman republic was prepared to sacrifice all
other laws. For what laws would survive if Rome itself per-
ished? The suspension of civil liberties, the detention of aliens,
the secret assassination of enemies: all this might be allowed, as
a last resort, if the life of the state were in danger. But if law must
sometimes compromise with necessity, must ethics surrender
too? Is there no moral limit to what a republic can do when its
existence is threatened? As Edward Gibbon retold the story of
how the Romans slaughtered defenseless aliens in their eastern
cities in 395 C.E. as a preemptive warning to the barbarians mass-

ing at the gates of their empire, he declined to consider whether actions that political necessity might require could still remain anathema to moral principle. But the question must not only be asked. It must be answered.

If the society attacked on September 11, 2001, had been a tyranny, these ancient questions might not be relevant. For a tyranny will allow itself anything. But the nation attacked on that bright morning was a liberal democracy, a constitutional order that sets limits to any government's use of force. Democratic constitutions do allow some suspension of rights in states of emergency. Thus rights are not always trumps. But neither is necessity. Even in times of real danger, political authorities have to prove the case that abridgments of rights are justified. Justifying them requires a government to submit them to the test of adversarial review by the legislature, the courts, and a free media. A government seeking to respond to an attack or an expected danger is required to present the case for extraordinary measures to a legislature, to argue for them with reasons that might convince a reasonable person, and to alter the measures in the face of criticism. Even after extraordinary measures receive legislative approval, they will still come under review by the courts.

The first challenge that a terrorist emergency poses to democracy is to this system of adversarial justification. The machinery of legislative deliberation and judicial review grinds slowly. Emergencies demand rapid action. Hence they require the exercise of prerogative. Presidents and prime ministers have to take action first and submit to questions later. But too much prerogative can be bad for democracy itself.

In emergencies, we have no alternative but to trust our leaders to act quickly, when our lives may be in danger, but it would be wrong to trust them to decide the larger question of how to balance liberty and security over the long term. For these larger questions, we ought to trust to democratic deliberation through our institutions. Adversarial justification is an institutional response, developed over centuries, to the inherent difficulty of making appropriate public judgments about just these types of conflicts of values.[1] Citizens are bound to disagree about how far the government is entitled to go in any given emergency. Because we disagree deeply about these matters, democracy's institutions provide a resolution, through a system of checks and balances, to ensure that no government's answer has the power to lead us either straight to anarchy or to tyranny.

In a terrorist emergency, we disagree, first of all, about the facts: chiefly, what type and degree of risk the threat of terrorism actually presents. It would make life easy if these facts were clear, but they rarely are. Public safety requires extrapolations about future threats on the basis of disputable facts about present ones. Worse, the facts are never presented to the public simply as neutral propositions available for dispassionate review. They come to us packaged with evaluation. They are usually stretched to justify whatever case for action is being made. Those who want coercive measures construe the risk to be great; those who oppose them usually minimize the threat. The disagreements don't end there. Even when we agree about the facts, we may still disagree whether the risks justify abridgments of liberty.

These disagreements extend to the very meaning of democracy itself. For most Americans, democracy simply means what Abraham Lincoln said it was: government of the people, by the people, for the people. In this account, democracy is a synonym for majority rule. Popular sovereignty, through elected representatives, has to be the final arbiter of what the government can be allowed to get away with when it is trying to defend our freedoms and our lives. Democracies do have bills of rights but these exist to serve vital majority interests. When the executive branch of government suspends rights, for example, it does so in the interest of the majority of citizens. The public interests that these rights defend are defined by the elected representatives of the people, and courts must interpret what these rights mean in obedience to what legislatures and the people say the rights mean.[2] Defending a right of an individual, for example, to freedom of association in times of safety protects the liberty of all. But protecting that same individual in a time of emergency may do harm to all. A terrorist emergency is precisely a case where allowing individual liberty—to plan, to plot, to evade detection—may threaten a vital majority interest. A democracy has no more important purpose than the protection of its members, and rights exist to safeguard that purpose. Civil liberty, the chief justice of the U.S. Supreme Court has written, means the liberty of a citizen, not the abstract liberty of an individual in a state of nature.[3] Such freedom, therefore, must depend on the survival of government and must be subordinate to its preservation.

What prevents such a system from falling prey to the tyranny of the majority is the system of checks and balances and, more broadly, the democratic process of adversarial justification itself. While injustice can always be justified if you have to justify it only to yourself, it is less easy when you have to justify it to other democratic institutions, like courts and legislatures or a free press. Thus presidents or prime ministers may not see anything wrong in a stringent measure, but if they know that this measure will have to get by the courts and the legislature, they may think twice.

Besides these constitutional checks and balances, there would also be the democratic check of competing social, religious, and political interests in the nation at large. One of the most lucid versions of this argument is to be found in *Federalist* No. 51, where in discussing the federal system's balance of federal and state power, the authors go on to say that while all authority in the United States will be derived from the power of the majority,

> the society itself will be broken into so many parts, interests, and classes of citizens, that the rights of individuals, or of the minority, will be in little danger from interested combinations of the majority. In a free government, the security for civil rights must be the same as that for religious rights. It consists in the one case in the multiplicity of interests and sects; and this may be presumed to depend on the extent of country and the number comprehended under the same government.[4]

Against this *pragmatic* view there is a *moral* view of democracy which maintains that it is something more than majority rule disciplined by checks and balances. It is also an order of rights that puts limits to the power of the community over individuals. These limits are not there just for prudential reasons, to prevent governments from riding roughshod over individuals. The rights are also there to express the idea that individuals matter intrinsically. Democracies don't just serve majority interests, they accord individuals intrinsic respect. This respect is expressed in the form of rights that guarantee certain freedoms. Freedom matters, in turn, because it is a precondition for living in dignity. Dignity here means simply the right to shape your life as best you can, within the limits of the law, and to have a voice, however small, in the shaping of public affairs. Government for the people, in other words, is something more than government for the happiness and security of the greatest number. The essential constraint of democratic government is that it must serve majority interests without sacrificing the freedom and dignity of the individuals who comprise the political community to begin with and who on occasion may oppose how it is governed. Rights certainly owe their origin to the sovereignty of the people, but the people—and their representatives—must steer majority interests through the constraints of rights.

Aharon Barak, president of Israel's Supreme Court, describes these two conceptions of democracy as "formal" and "substantive."[5] Other scholars have contrasted a "pragmatic" reading of the U.S. Constitution with a "moral" reading.[6] In normal times, these two meanings of democracy—one stressing popular sovereignty, the other stressing rights; one privileging collective interests, the other privileging individual dignity—are interdependent. You can't have a democracy without rights, and rights cannot be secure unless you have democracy. But in terrorist emergencies, their relation breaks apart. What makes security appear to trump liberty in terrorist emergencies is the idea—certainly true—that the liberty of the majority is utterly dependent upon their security. A people living in fear are not free. Hence the safety of the majority makes an imperative claim. On this view, rights are political conveniences a majority institutes for its defense and is therefore at liberty to abridge when necessity demands it. Those who defend a rights-based definition of democracy will then argue that rights lose all effect, not just for the individuals at risk, but for the majority as well if they are revocable in situations of necessity.

Both sides then appeal to history and seek vindication of their claims. Those who think of democracy primarily in terms of majority interest point to the frequent abridgments of liberty in national emergencies past—from Lincoln's suspension of habeas corpus during the Civil War to the detention of illegal aliens after 9/11—and argue that democracies survive in part because they do not let rights stand in the way of robust measures. Moreover, robust measures do not prevent rights' returning in times of safety. Temporary measures are just that and they need not do permanent damage to a democracy's constitutional fabric. Those who put rights first will reply that yes, democracy survives, but rights infringements needlessly compromise the democracy's commitment to dignity and freedom. The detention of Japanese Americans during World War II would qualify as an example of majoritarian tyranny and misuse of executive prerogative, driven by fear and racial bias.[7] One side in the debate worries that caring overmuch about rights will tie the hands of a democracy, while the other insists that if rights are abridged, even for a few individuals, then democracy betrays its own identity.

Civil libertarians think civil liberties define what a democracy is. But the recurrently weak and shallow public support for civil liberties positions suggests that many Americans disagree. They believe that the majority interest should trump the civil liberties of terrorist suspects.[8] For these democrats, rights are prudential limits on government action, revocable in times of danger; for civil libertarians, they are foundational commitments to individual dignity that ought to limit government action in times of safety and danger alike. For one side, what matters fundamentally is that democracies prevail. For the other, what matters more is that democracies prevail without betraying what they stand for.

A further disagreement arises over the question of whether a country facing a terrorist emergency should base its public policy exclusively on its own constitution and its own laws, or whether it has any duty to pay attention to what other states have to say and what international agreements and conventions require. Some maintain that a democracy's commitments to dignity are confined to its own citizens, not its enemies. Others point out that a democracy is not a moral island, sufficient unto itself. Thus, as many scholars have pointed out, the U.S. Constitution extends its protections to "persons" and not just to citizens.[9] Hence aliens have rights under U.S. law—as well as, of course, under international conventions to which the United States is a signatory. Enemy combatants have rights under the Geneva Conventions, and even terrorists retain their *human* rights, since these are inherent in being human and hence irrevocable. Others think this approach values consistency more than justice. Justice—to the victims of terrorist outrages—requires that terrorists be treated as "enemies of the human race" and hunted down without any regard to their human rights.[10]

When citizens of a democracy insist that what matters most in a terrorist emergency is the safety of the majority, they are usually saying that rights are at best a side constraint, at worst a pesky impediment to robust and decisive action. Those who think this are also likely to believe that international agreements, like the Geneva Conventions or the Torture Convention, should not limit what the United States can do in a war on terror. Since the threat is primarily directed at the United States, it must respond according to its own system of law, not according to anyone else's standards. To take this position, however, is also to assume that the lives of your own citizens matter more than the lives of people in other countries. It is, as Ronald Dworkin has pointed out, to base policy on the premise that Americans come first.[11] Those who disagree will usually be committed to the idea that a democracy's ethical commitments are universal and apply both to its own citizens and to its enemies.

These debates are also about whether some measures are just plain wrong. Consequentialists argue that measures which aim to save lives and preserve the security of the citizens cannot be wrong if they actually succeed in doing so. They are wrong only if they don't work—that is, if they produce a chain of further harms, like more terrorist attacks. Most civil libertarians take the view that some actions remain wrong even if they work. So torturing someone to divulge terrorist actions is wrong, no matter what useful information is extracted, and hence no democracy should ever have anything to do with torture. A third position lies between the two. It maintains that consequences can matter so much, for example, saving thousands of people from terrorist attack, that it might be worth subjecting an individual to relentless—though nonphysical—interrogation to elicit critical information. But this style of interrogation, which would push suspects to the limits of their psychological endurance, would remain a violation of their dignity. It would be a lesser evil than allowing thousands of people to die, but its necessity would not prevent it from remaining wrong.

This third position—which gives this book its title—maintains that necessity may require us to take actions in defense of democracy which will stray from democracy's own foundational commitments to dignity. While we cannot avoid this, the best way to minimize harms is to maintain a clear distinction in our minds between what necessity can justify and what the morality of dignity can justify, and never to allow the justifications of necessity—risk, threat, imminent danger—to dissolve the morally problematic character of necessary measures. Because the measures are morally problematic, they must be strictly targeted, applied to the smallest possible number of people, used as a last resort, and kept under the adversarial scrutiny of an open democratic system.

A lesser evil position holds that in a terrorist emergency, neither rights nor necessity should trump. A democracy is committed to both the security of the majority and the rights of the individual. Neither a morality of consequences nor a morality of dignity can be allowed exclusive domain in public policy decisions. If each of these ethical principles has legitimate claims, the resulting framework is going to be complex, to say the least. In it, there are no trump cards, no table-clearing justifications or claims. What works is not always right. What is right doesn't always work. Rights may have to bow to security in some instances, but there had better be good reasons, and there had better be clear limitations to rights abridgments; otherwise, rights will soon lose all their value. At the same time, a constitution is not a suicide pact: rights cannot so limit the exercise of authority as to make decisive action impossible. Finally, international standards matter. Nations are not moral islands: they should conform to international standards, both to comply with the treaties and conventions that nations have signed and to pay what Thomas Jefferson called "decent respect for the opinions of mankind."

A lesser evil morality is designed for skeptics, for people who accept that leaders will have to take decisive action on the basis of less than accurate information; who think that some sacrifice of liberty in times of danger may be necessary; who want a policy that works but are not prepared to make what works the sole criterion for deciding what to do. Such an ethics is a balancing act: seeking to adjudicate among the claims of risk, dignity, and security in a way that actually addresses particular cases of threat. An ethics of balance cannot privilege rights above all, or dignity above all, or public safety above all. This is the move—privileging one to the exclusion of the other—that produces moral error. They are all important principles—all must be weighed in the balance equally—and nothing trumps.

This is an ethics of prudence rather than first principle, one that assesses what to do in an emergency with a conservative bias against infringements of established standards of due process, equal protection, and basic dignity. A conservative bias assumes that in terrorist emergencies, the first response is usually wrong. Tried and tested standards of due process should not be hastily discarded. These standards are more than procedures, anchored in legal tradition. They reflect important commitments to individual dignity. Protection of the law means, concretely, that no one should be held indefinitely, without charge, without access to counsel or judicial review. Moreover, persons can be detained only for what they have done, not for who they are or for what they think, profess, or believe. A key conservative principle would be that blanket detentions and broad roundups of suspects are always a mistake, because they violate the law's principle of the individuality of guilt. It is invariably wrong to arrest or detain on the principle of guilt by association, based on race, ethnicity, or religious affiliation. Any detention policy must be targeted to individuals against whom probable cause can eventually be demonstrated. By these standards, the United States failed the test in its detention of nearly five thousand aliens, mostly single males of Muslim or Arab origin, after September 11. None have been found to merit charging with terrorist offenses. In retrospect, the whole exercise seems to have been as unnecessary as it was unjust.[12]

While a conservative bias will enable us to see through most of the overhasty reactions to terrorist emergencies, it may not be adequate when we have to face terrorists who control weapons of mass destruction. If the threat is sufficiently great, preemptive detention of suspects, together with military or police action to disarm, disable, or neutralize the threat, may be necessary. It is unrealistic to think that commitments to dignity, coupled with a conservative bias against departing from tried legal standards, will be sufficient to cope with any eventuality in the future. In the wake of another mass casualty terrorist attack, on or above the scale of September 11, most bets—and gloves—would be off. Even extreme necessity, however, cannot override democratic processes and the obligation to balance strong measures with basic commitments to full public justification.

If a war on terror may require lesser evils, what will keep them from slowly becoming the greater evil? The only answer is democracy itself. Liberal democracy has endured because its institutions are designed for handling morally hazardous forms of coercive power. It puts the question of how far government should go to the cross fire of adversarial review. Adversarial review procedures do not just pit one branch of government against another. Within each branch, there are, or should be, checks and balances, fire walls that guarantee the independence of institutions that perform intra-agency review. The General Accounting Office, for example, keeps the spending propensities of other federal agencies of the U.S. government in check. One branch of the Justice Department has recently criticized another branch's handling of administrative detainees after September 11, and that branch has changed its practices.[13]

In this process of adversarial review the test of reason is not the test of perfection. Citizens usually accept the decisions that result, not because they are right but because they are reasonable, and because democratic review affords a genuinely adversarial and open contest of opinions. Of course, even the most open process may produce perverse results. Senator Joseph McCarthy harassed and defamed individuals suspected of Communist sympathies in the full glare of publicity, and with the support, for a time, of majority opinion. While open proceedings are fallible, they at least create the possibility for correcting error. If McCarthy persecuted innocent people in open proceedings, he was also brought down by open proceedings.[14] Ultimately, if open proceedings fail to produce answers that command the assent of citizens, it is up to citizens themselves to force the institutions—through public criticism and the electoral process—to come up with better answers. What is striking about democracy is the role of distrust in keeping the system honest. The system of checks and balances and the division of powers assume the possibility of venality or incapacity in one institution or the other. The ultimate safety in a democracy is that decisions filtered down through this long process stand less of a chance of being wrong than ones decided, once and for all, at the top.

The war waged against terror since September 11 puts a strain on democracy itself, because it is mostly waged in secret, using means that are at the edge of both law and morality. Yet democracies have shown themselves capable of keeping the secret exercise of power under control. So long as "a decision for secrecy should not itself be secret," secrecy can be controlled.[15] Legislatures can take hearings on sensitive intelligence matters in camera; judges can demand that state prosecutors justify secret hearings or the withholding of information from the defense. The redlines should be clear: it is never justified to confine or deport an alien or citizen in secret proceedings. Openness in any process where human liberty is at stake is simply definitional of what a democracy is. The problem is not defining where the redline lies, but enforcing it. A democracy in which most people don't vote, in which many judges accord undue deference to executive decisions, and in which government refuses open adversarial review of its measures is not likely to keep the right balance between security and liberty. A war on terror is not just a challenge to democracy; it is an interrogation of the vitality of its capacity for adversarial review.

II

Having laid out the rudiments of a lesser evil approach to a war on terror, I need to say something about the word *evil*. First of all, not all evil is done by evil people or with evil design. Some of the worst things done to human beings are done with the best will in the world. The evil that is characteristic of democracies usually results from the blindness of good intentions. The evil I have in mind is committed by the officials of liberal democratic states who know they are not supposed to do wrong and who serve institutions that are created to guard against it. They may do wrong, nonetheless, believing these actions are justified because they forestall still greater harms, or, given the scale of modern bureaucracy, because they hardly know the consequences of their actions at all.

But why should democracies have anything to do with evil? Why expose their servants to such moral hazard? Why not stay safely on the side of pure legality? The answer is that we are faced with evil people, and stopping them may require us to reply in kind. If so, how do we keep lesser evils from slipping into greater ones?

Let me admit that the very process of justifying an act as a lesser of two evils is an exercise in moral risk. We can legitimately do so only if we actually know what we are doing and do not try to pretend that the necessary character of an evil act excuses its morally dubious character. Thus killing an innocent person to save the lives of hundreds of others might be a lesser evil, but the act would still be wrong. The law might accept a plea in mitigation but it would not excuse the act's criminal character. The Israeli Supreme Court has ruled that an agent of the state may make a defense of necessity if accused of torturing someone: this excuse might mitigate the penalty for violating the law, but it would not excuse the torture itself, which remains criminal.[16]

I do not want to minimize the moral hazard of resort to evil means. Sometimes we can accurately predict this hazard but more often we cannot. Choosing a lesser evil to ward off a greater one may bring the greater one to pass nonetheless. When escalating a military conflict, for example, a commander may choose the lowest possible increase in the gradient of force out of a desire to minimize harms and to secure a military objective at the lowest possible cost. But this may only redouble an opponent's willingness to resist, with the unintended result that the conflict costs more lives, possibly to both sides, than a short, sharp escalation would have done.[17] Bad consequences are not always predictable, and so in choosing the lesser evil course, we may have to take a shot in the dark, knowing, unfortunately, that good intentions cannot exempt us from blame when bad consequences result.

A further reason why any recourse to a lesser evil is bound to be morally hazardous is that human beings are so adept at inventing good intentions, coming up with plausible excuses for atrocious consequences. The ancient Greek playwright Euripides gives us a particularly unsparing account of this in *Medea*. It is a play about a woman who kills her two children, in order, so she claims, to spare them the horror of being killed by strangers:

> Women, my task is fixed as quickly as I may
> To kill my children, and start away from this land,
> And not, by wasting time, to suffer my children
> To be slain by another hand less kindly to them.

Force every way will have it they must die, and since
This must be so, then I, their mother, shall kill them.[18]

But since she also wants revenge on the father of the children, who has abandoned her, it is impossible to see Medea in an unqualified moral light. She may be sparing her children, but she may also be sacrificing them to her own fury. She even admits this:

I know indeed what evil I intend to do,
But stronger than all my afterthoughts is my fury,
Fury that brings upon mortals the greatest of evils.

Moreover, from the standpoint of her children, who is to say that being murdered at the hands of your own mother is a mercy compared to being murdered at the hands of strangers? Only if we can be certain that they would be tortured, abused, and then killed by strangers can we justify her act as a lesser evil. Because Euripides is a great playwright, he leaves us—the audience—uncertain about this issue, which is why, two thousand years later, we still leave the theater wondering whether she is a self-justifying monster or a tragic angel of mercy.

As Euripides shows us, human beings can justify anything as a lesser evil if they have to justify it only to themselves. In Medea's case, the audience sees more clearly than Medea ever does, even if they cannot disentangle her motives. In this play, evil appears as the incapacity to take any distance—through reason—from the primal force of feeling, so that all strong emotion becomes automatically self-justifying.

Evil can also appear in rational form, in the careful and deliberate choice to do harm, motivated by a rational but mistaken calculation of anticipated good. Either way, in hysterical grief or in cold calculation, the course of the lesser evil can lead to tragedy or to crime. But as Euripides insists, these choices are unavoidable elements of human experience. A war on terror presents leaders with such choices: harming some to save others, deceiving some to entrap others, killing some to preserve the freedom of others. Democracy is designed to cope with tragic choice, and it does so by understanding that if anyone can justify anything, provided they only justify it to themselves, they are less likely to be able to carry it out if they are forced to do so in adversarial proceedings before their fellow citizens.

But this does not mean that democrats do not sometimes commit evil. No system of politics is capable of saving us from moral hazard. Indeed, as Machiavelli understood a long time ago, dubious decisions are not just accidental incidents in political life; they are intrinsic to political action. Machiavelli famously insisted that the moral qualities we admire in private life—probity, honesty, forbearance—can be liabilities in public life, and that to apply private scruples to the decisions that have to be taken when a republic's security is at stake might be to condemn the republic to disaster.[19] Thanks to Machiavelli, we are familiar with the irony that a politician who, in private life, would condemn acts of killing, must not hesitate to order his armed forces to kill the republic's enemies en masse. The same political leader who would be ashamed to lie to his own family must not hesitate to dissemble in the legislature when the public safety requires that a secret mission to protect the republic be concealed from scrutiny.

If Machiavelli says that all political life necessarily entails lesser evils, he does not ask whether democracy imposes particular limits on the kinds of evils that democrats can contemplate. While international law sets standards for states regardless of whether they are free or tyrannical, well or ill governed, it seems evident that democratic states will hold themselves to higher standards of dignity and due process.

They do so because liberal states seek both to create a free space for democratic deliberation and to set strict limits to the coercive and compulsory powers of government.[20] This is the double sense in which democracies stand against violence: positively, they seek to create free institutions where public policy is decided freely, rather than by fear and coercion; negatively, they seek to reduce, to a minimum, the coercion and violence necessary to the maintenance of order among free peoples.

This is not true of democracy's other twentieth-century competitors. In Hitler's Germany or Stalin's Russia, law, politics, and culture were all ordered so as to eliminate the very idea that government violence was problematic. Far from being evils, Hitler's and Stalin's acts of extermination were heralded as necessary to the creation of a utopia: a world of class unity and social justice, or, in the case of the Thousand Year Reich, a nation purified of the racial enemy.[21] If such were the utopias that class warfare and racial extermination were supposed to serve, violence in their service could hardly be a crime. Hence the very idea that violence can be a lesser evil has meaning only in societies very different from these.

Thanks to the rights they entrench, the due process rules they observe, the separation of powers they seek to enforce, and the requirement of democratic consent, liberal democracies are all guided by a constitutional commitment to minimize the use of dubious means—violence, force, coercion, and deception—in the government of citizens. It is because they do so in normal times that they feel constrained to do so in times of emergency. Otherwise, these societies will not be true to who they are. When citizens consent to be ruled, they do so on the condition that the abridgment of their freedom, necessary to maintain a free and secure public realm, must be kept to a minimum. This implies that in a liberal democracy even government based on consent remains coercive. The coercions in question range from collection of taxes and the imposition of fines to punishment for criminal or civil liability. Coercion may be necessary to maintain social order, but in a democratic theory of government it is an evil, and it must be kept to a strict minimum.[22] Why else would a liberal society put such store in rights, if it did not seek to protect individuals from the abusive exercise of coercive power?

This account of a liberal democracy may sound strange to some, because it stresses the coercive powers of government and fails to emphasize its enabling role in creating public goods— schools, roads, public security, hospitals, and welfare services— that allow individuals to exercise their freedom. They are positive goods, created by the consent of the governed. Yet majority consent does not eliminate the problem of minority constraint. These positive goods are paid for by a coercive measure—taxation—which most, but not all, citizens accept for the sake of the greater good. Not all citizens will agree about how much of their private income should be taxed to support this public infrastructure, nor how extensive this infrastructure should be. Disputes about this constitute the largest part of public politics, and the arbitration of these disputes, by legislation and by elections, inevitably leaves some citizens convinced that their freedom has been unduly constrained. There is simply no consensus about the proper extent of public goods or about the proper extent of government's power. At the margins, the constraint intrinsic to government will be experienced, at least by some citizens, as a lesser evil, to be submitted to as a condition of public life.

It might be asked whether coercive yet necessary uses of government power deserve to be called an evil at all. Taxation may be unpopular but hardly counts as an evil. Yet other acts of government, like punishment, which inflict direct harm on individuals, do raise the specter of evil. Or at least they do in our type of society. Only liberal democracies have a guilty conscience about punishment. Totalitarian societies have enthusiastically embraced coercion as a positive social instrument to create desired social types, ideal workers, obedient citizens, enthusiastic party apparatchiks. Only in liberal societies have people believed that the pain and suffering involved in depriving people of their liberty must make us think twice about imposing this constraint even on those who justly deserve it.[23] The fact that it is necessary and the fact that it is just do not make it any less painful. It is necessary that criminals be punished, but the suffering that punishment causes remains an evil nonetheless.

It might be said that this example fails to distinguish necessary actions that cause harm from unnecessary actions caused by malice or gross negligence. Another way of saying the same thing is that a necessary evil cannot really be an evil at all, since it is a characteristic of evil that it is not necessary but gratuitous. I still want to hold on to the idea of the lesser evil, because it captures the idea, central to liberal theory, that necessary coercion remains morally problematic.

To insist that justified exercises of coercion can be defined as a lesser evil is to say that evil can be qualified. If two acts are evil, how can we say that one is the lesser, the other the greater? Qualifying evil in this way would seem to excuse it. Yet it is essential to the idea of a lesser evil that one can justify resort to it without denying that it is evil, justifiable only because other means would be insufficient or unavailable. Using the word *evil* rather than the word *harm* is intended to highlight the elements of moral risk that a liberal theory of government believes are intrinsic to the maintenance of order in any society premised upon the dignity of individuals.

Thus even in times of safety, liberal democracies seek to limit the use of force necessary to their maintenance. These limits seek to balance the conflict between the commitments to individual dignity incarnated in rights and the commitments to majority interest incarnated in popular sovereignty. In times of danger, this conflict of values becomes intense. The suppression of civil liberties, surveillance of individuals, targeted assassination, torture, and preemptive war put liberal commitments to dignity under such obvious strain, and the harms they entail are so serious, that, even if mandated by peremptory majority interest, they should be spoken of only in the language of evil.

In a war on terror, I would argue, the issue is not whether we can avoid evil acts altogether, but whether we can succeed in choosing lesser evils and keep them from becoming greater ones. We should do so, I would argue, by making some starting commitments—to the conservative principle (maintaining the free institutions we have), to the dignity principle (preserving individuals from gross harms)—and then reasoning out the consequences of various courses of action, anticipating harms and coming to a rational judgment of which course of action is likely to inflict the least damage on the two principles. When we are satisfied that a coercive measure is a genuine last resort, justified by the facts as we can understand them, we have chosen the lesser evil, and we are entitled to stick to it even if the price proves higher than we anticipated. But not indefinitely so. At some point—when we "have to destroy the village in order to save it"—we may conclude that we have slipped from the lesser to the greater. Then we have no choice but to admit our error and reverse course. In the situation of factual uncertainty in which most decisions about terrorism have to be taken, error is probably unavoidable.

It is tempting to suppose that moral life can avoid this slope simply by avoiding evil means altogether. But no such angelic option may exist. Either we fight evil with evil or we succumb. So if we resort to the lesser evil, we should do so, first, in full awareness that evil is involved. Second, we should act under a demonstrable state of necessity. Third, we should chose evil means only as a last resort, having tried everything else. Finally, we must satisfy a fourth obligation: we must justify our actions publicly to our fellow citizens and submit to their judgment as to their correctness.

III

The challenge in assessing which measures might be permissible is to find a viable position between cynicism and perfectionism. Cynicism would maintain that ethical reflection is irrelevant: the agents of the state will do what they will do, and the terrorists will do what they will do, and force and power alone will decide the outcome. The only question to ask about these means is whether they work. The cynics are wrong. All battles between terrorists and the state are battles for opinion, and in this struggle ethical justifications are critical, to maintain the morale of one's own side, to hold the loyalty of populations who might otherwise align with the terrorists, and to maintain political support among allies. A counterterror campaign probably can be run only by cynics, by professionals schooled in the management of moral appearances, but even cynics know that some moral promises have to be kept if they are to be believed at all. Preventive detention to withdraw suspicious aliens from the general population might disrupt terrorist networks, but it

might so enrage innocent groups that they would cease to cooperate with the police. Torture might break apart a network of
terrorist cells, but it would also engender hatred and resentment
among the survivors of the torture and further increase their
support among disaffected populations. There is simply no way
to disentangle the technical question of what works from the political question of what impact such methods will have on the
struggle for opinion that is the essence of any campaign against
terror. Extreme measures, like torture, preventive detention, and
arbitrary arrest, typically win the battle but lose the larger war.
Even cynics know that Pyrrhic victories are worse than useless.

As for moral perfectionism, this would be the doctrine that a
liberal state should never have truck with dubious moral means
and should spare its officials the hazard of having to decide between lesser and greater evils. A moral perfectionist position
also holds that states can spare their officials this hazard simply
by adhering to the universal moral standards set out in human
rights conventions and the laws of war.

There are two problems with a perfectionist stance, leaving
aside the question of whether it is realistic. The first is that artic-
ulating nonrevocable, nonderogable moral standards is relatively easy. The problem is deciding how to apply them in specific cases. What is the line between interrogation and torture,
between targeted killing and unlawful assassination, between
preemption and aggression? Even when legal and moral distinc-
tions between these are clear in the abstract, abstractions are less
than helpful when political leaders have to choose between
them in practice. Furthermore, the problem with perfectionist
standards is that they contradict each other. The same person
who shudders, rightly, at the prospect of torturing a suspect
might be prepared to kill the same suspect in a preemptive attack on a terrorist base. Equally, the perfectionist commitment
to the right to life might preclude such attacks altogether and
restrict our response to judicial pursuit of offenders through process of law. Judicial responses to the problem of terror have their
place, but they are no substitute for military operations when
terrorists possess bases, training camps, and heavy weapons. To

stick to a perfectionist commitment to the right to life when under terrorist attack might achieve moral consistency at the price of leaving us defenseless in the face of evildoers. Security, moreover, is a human right, and thus respect for one right might lead us to betray another.

A lesser evil morality is antiperfectionist in its assumptions. It accepts as inevitable that it is not always possible to save human beings from harm without killing other human beings; not always possible to preserve full democratic disclosure and transparency in counterterrorist operations; not always desirable for democratic leaders to avoid deception and perfidy; not always possible to preserve the liberty of the majority without suspending the liberties of a minority; not always possible to anticipate terrible consequences of well-meant acts, and so on. Far from making ethical reflection irrelevant, these dilemmas make ethical realism all the more essential to democratic reflection and good public policy. The fact that liberal democratic leaders may order the surreptitious killing of terrorists, may withhold information from their voters, may order the suspension of civil liberties need not mean that "anything goes." Even if liberties must be suspended, their suspension can be made temporary; if executives must withhold information from a legislature in public, they can be obliged to disclose it in private session or at a later date. Public disinformation whose sole purpose is to deceive the enemy might be justified, but deliberately misleading a democratic electorate with a view to exaggerating risk or minimizing hazard can never be. The same balancing act needs to be observed in other cases. If the targeted killing of terrorists proves necessary, it can be constrained by strict rules of engagement and subjected to legislative oversight and review. The interrogation of terrorist suspects can be kept free of torture. Drawing these lines means keeping in clear sight the question of whether these means reinforce or betray the democratic identity they are supposed to defend.

Keeping lesser evils from becoming greater ones is more than a matter of democratic accountability. It is also a matter of individual conscience. Hannah Arendt once argued that being able to think for yourself is a precondition for avoiding evil, especially in large bureaucracies where there is a premium against independent thought. She said that the one common denominator uniting opponents of Nazi rule in Germany was a capacity to ask, at all times, what kind of person one was or wished to be. Those who refused to kill others, she said, "refused to murder, not so much because they still held fast to the command 'Thou Shalt Not Kill', but because they were unwilling to live together with a murderer—themselves."[24]

No society can avoid official crimes and brutality unless this sense of responsibility is widely shared among public officials. Rules and procedures are not enough. Character is decisive, and there is some reason to think that democracies encourage the right kind of character. People who grow up in societies with constitutional rights are taught to believe that their opinions matter, that they are entitled to a certain fairness and due process in official dealings, and that they have a responsibility to the rights of others. But we cannot be sure that democracy teaches us all to do the right thing.

Moreover, no matter how good our moral learning we all stand in need of the scrutiny of good institutions. A war on terror puts these institutions under strain. It is not always possible to subject intelligence agents and Special Forces to full democratic scrutiny and control. Yet the agents themselves remain citizens, and their responsibility to the constitutional order they defend remains the tribunal of last resort to save them and us from a descent into barbarism. We depend for much of what we know about abuses of power on whistle-blowers, honest people who could not stand what they were being asked to do.[25] Any democracy that wants to fight a clean war on terror needs to safeguard the rights of whistle-blowers, in the most secret agencies of government, to tell the truth to elected officials and the media. The only way to prevent zones of impunity from opening up in our government is for legislatures to insist on their rights of oversight, for the media to continue to demand access, and for the law to sustain the rights of whistle-blowers to tell the truth.

But these are not the only moral checks on a war on terror. Internationally ratified human rights instruments, together with the UN Charter and the Geneva Conventions, widen the audience of justification beyond the electorates of democratic states under direct attack, to a broader network of states and international bodies, whose views must be taken into account. Their views matter because liberal democracies constitute a community of values as well as a community of interests, and successful joint action against terrorism will soon become impossible if states disregard their allies, ignore their objections to national policies, and seek unilateral advantage or exemption from international commitments.[26]

International standards matter but we must not assume that nations always agree about what they mean. European countries disagree with the United States about the legitimacy of the death penalty, and they have refused to extradite terrorist suspects to the United States, where capital punishment may be the penalty. International conventions prohibit torture, but the exact point at which intensive interrogation passes over the redline into torture is a matter of dispute. The Geneva Conventions protect the idea of civilian immunity, but who counts as a civilian remains controversial. International conventions set standards, but each country may interpret them differently. How political leaders do so depends on what their domestic electorates appear to allow. But a political standard is not necessarily an ethically normless or relativist one. Public opinion will not accept simply anything. The norms that govern a war on terror are not the monopoly of government. They are susceptible to influence by moral entrepreneurship. Human rights activists and members of civil liberties NGOs will seek to raise the barrier of the morally permissible, while groups representing the military and the police may want to lower it. In any liberal democracy, standards for a war on terror will be set by adversarial moral competition.

As a contribution to this process of standard setting, I would propose the following tests for policy makers. First, a democratic war on terror needs to subject all coercive measures to *the dignity test*—do they violate individual dignity? Foundational commit-

ments to human rights should always preclude cruel and unusual punishment, torture, penal servitude, and extrajudicial execution, as well as rendition of suspects to rights-abusing
countries. Second, coercive measures need to pass *the conservative test*—are departures from existing due process standards really necessary? Do they damage our institutional inheritance?
Such a standard would bar indefinite suspension of habeas corpus and require all detention, whether by civil or military authorities, to be subject to judicial review. Those deprived of
rights—citizens and noncitizens—must never lose access to
counsel. A third assessment of counterterror measures should
be consequentialist. Will they make citizens more or less secure
in the long run? This *effectiveness* test needs to focus not just on
the short term, but on the long-term political implications of
measures. Will they strengthen or weaken political support for
the state undertaking such measures? A further consideration is
the last resort test: have less coercive measures been tried and
failed? Another important issue is whether measures have
passed the test of *open adversarial review* by legislative and judicial bodies, either at the time, or as soon as necessity allows. Finally, "decent respect for the opinions of mankind," together
with the more pragmatic necessity of securing the support of
other nations in a global war on terror, requires any state fighting terrorism to respect its international obligations as well as
the considered opinions of its allies and friends. If all of this adds
up to a series of constraints that tie the hands of our governments, so be it. It is the very nature of a democracy that it not
only does, but should, fight with one hand tied behind its back.
It is also in the nature of democracy that it prevails against its
enemies precisely because it does.

CHAPTER TWO

THE ETHICS OF
EMERGENCY

Now in a well-ordered republic it should never be necessary to resort to extra-constitutional measures; for although they may for the time be beneficial, yet the precedent is pernicious, for if the practice is once established of disregarding the laws for good objects, they will in a little while be disregarded under that pretext for evil purposes. Thus no republic will ever be perfect if she has not by law provided for everything, having a remedy for every emergency and fixed rules for applying it.

—*Niccolò Machiavelli*

I

Terrorist states of emergency raise fundamental questions about the nature of the rule of law.[1] If laws can be abridged and liberties suspended in an emergency, what remains of their legitimacy in times of peace? If laws are rules, and emergencies make exceptions to these rules, how can their authority survive once exceptions are made? In this chapter, I consider the impact of emergency suspensions of civil liberties on the idea of the rule of law, and I ask a related question: what remains of the status of human rights if they can be abridged in times of public danger?

Roughly speaking, emergency legislation may take three forms: national, territorial, or selective. In *national* emergencies, martial law is substituted for civilian rule throughout a country for an indeterminate period of time. A state facing a terrorist insurgency will suspend the normal rule of law in order to give the military full authority to arrest, detain, search, and harass insurgents within a civilian population. In some Latin American countries—Colombia, for example—emergency suspensions of the constitution have been so frequent that they have replaced the rule of law as the norm.[2] In *territorial* emergencies, martial law is confined to special zones of the country, where terrorist or insurgent activity is underway and the state believes it needs the military to have powers of detention, search, and arrest without civilian constraint or review. In active combat zones in Sri Lanka, where the state is combating an insurgency, military, rather than civilian, law prevails. A special subcategory of emergency rule relates to zones of occupation. In the occupied territories under Israeli control, the civilian due process guarantees that obtain in Israel proper are suspended and the territories are governed by military rule, distinct from the Israeli judicial system. A further subvariety of territorial emergency legislation operates in Northern Ireland. The province is not under martial law, but the rule of law functions differently than in other parts of the United Kingdom: for example, in the operation of special courts that try terrorist cases without standard trial by jury. The third form of emergency legislation is piecemeal: no general state of emergency is proclaimed, no part of the country is removed from the normal rule of law, but portions of the law are suspended for terrorist suspects. This third—*selective*—kind of emergency has been manifested in the United States since September 11: preventive or investigative detention for certain detainees, either aliens or citizens; changes in their right of access to counsel and lawyer-client privilege; widening of police powers of search and seizure; increased wiretap authorizations and other forms of surveillance. Most of what I say here will focus on these piecemeal emergency measures. Some of these measures are limited by sunset clauses providing for their expiration, while others are permanent. Even a selective emergency, therefore, can turn into a constitutional way of life.

Emergencies, in the words of Kathleen Sullivan, raise the specter of a "constitutional black hole," a break in the continuity of law that contradicts the idea of a constitution as an unvarying arbiter of social and political disputes.[3] How can the rule of law be maintained if the law can be suspended as necessity dictates? How can the effectiveness of human rights as a guarantee of dignity be sustained, if rights are suspended in emergency?

Emergencies invariably entail the extraordinary use of executive prerogative. Prerogative, as John Locke defined it, is the "power to act according to discretion for the public good, without the prescription of the law and sometimes even against it."[4] Locke thought such powers necessary to the maintenance of a government in times of crisis, and in thinking this, he was sustaining a line of thought that went back to the Roman republic and to its system of temporary dictatorship. This kind of temporary, delegated dictatorship to save the constitution has always been a feature of republican thought.[5] Liberal theories of constitutional government, however, have always feared that an executive might use the pretext of emergency to seize power and abolish constitutional freedom. There is thus a conflict between a *republican* and a *liberal* theory of emergency powers.[6] A republican account could envisage a democratic rationale for rights abridgments in emergency based on the need for executive decisiveness to protect majority interests, while a liberal view would fear that such a majoritarian rationale would risk permanent damage both to rights and to the system of checks and balances.

One of the most pertinent defenses of this republican use of prerogative power and the necessity of emergency suspensions of liberties was made by Abraham Lincoln in a letter in 1863 justifying his suspension of habeas corpus and indefinite detention of opponents of the draft laws, during the American Civil War. Yes, Lincoln was talking about wartime, and terrorist emergencies are not the same as wartime ones. Still, his words remain relevant to our case, and I will quote at length, since Lincoln speaks directly to the central issue: whether temporary abridgments of freedom do permanent damage to constitutional liberty:

> The Constitution is not, in its application, in all respects the same, in case of rebellion or invasion involving the public safety, as it is in time of profound peace and public security. The Constitution itself makes the distinction; and I can no more be persuaded that the Government can take no strong measures in time of rebellion, because it can be shown that

the same could not be lawfully taken in time of peace, than
I can be persuaded that a particular drug is not good medicine for a sick man, because it can be shown not to be good
food for a well one. Nor am I able to appreciate the danger
apprehended by the meeting that the American people will,
by means of military arrests during the Rebellion, lose the
right of Public Discussion, the Liberty of Speech and the
Press, the Law of Evidence, Trial by Jury and Habeas Corpus, throughout the indefinite peaceful future, which I trust
lies before them, any more than I am able to believe that a
man could contract so strong an appetite for emetics during
temporary illness as to persist in feeding upon them during
the remainder of his healthful life.[7]

As Lincoln predicted, though he did not live to see the day,
habeas corpus returned in robust health after the Civil War. Its
temporary suspension in wartime did not erode its legitimacy
once peace returned. On the contrary, Lincoln's actions had the
effect of hardening judicial opinion against easy suspensions in
the future. In *Ex parte Milligan* in 1866, the U.S. Supreme Court
condemned Lincoln's suspension of habeas corpus in uncom-
promising language:

> No doctrine involving more pernicious consequences was
> ever invented by the wit of man than that any of the Consti-
> tution's provisions can be suspended during any of the
> great exigencies of government. Such a doctrine leads di-
> rectly to anarchy or despotism, but the theory of necessity
> on which it is based is false; for the government, within the
> Constitution, has all the powers granted to it which are nec-
> essary to preserve its existence.[8]

Yet the *Milligan* decision is not the last word on the long-term
impact of Lincoln's actions. Later Supreme Courts, especially
those sitting during the Second World War, sided more with Lincoln than with the judges in *Milligan*.[9] When Roosevelt established a military commission in 1942 to try German saboteurs
and the case went to the Supreme Court for review, Lincoln's

use of military commissions was cited by the government in justification.[10] When the Bush administration established military
tribunals to try terrorists and illegal combatants for crimes of
war and crimes against humanity, rather than putting them
through the federal court system, the Lincoln decision again
figured as a precedent.[11] So if in the short term Lincoln was
right—the remedies given a sick man are not those he craves
when well—in the longer term, the precedent he set has provided subsequent presidents with the warrant to abridge liberty
in emergencies.[12]

There are two types of question to ask about these emergency
circumstances. First, are they actually necessary? And second,
even if they are necessary, will they diminish respect for laws
and rights in the future? The two questions need to be distinguished: short-term benefits to order may entail long-term harm
to liberty. But there may also be a deeper conflict. A lesser evil
approach to a war on terror acknowledges a tension "of tragic
dimensions," as Oren Gross puts it, between what is necessary
and what is right.[13] Saying the choices are tragic is not meant to
excuse indecision—decisions will have to be made—but decisions in favor of necessity should be constrained by awareness
of the seriousness of the loss in terms of justice. Weighing loss
in this way implies the inadequacy of a solely pragmatic or utilitarian calculation of the balance between order and freedom. A
utilitarian calculus may be biased toward security, because it has
to value majority interest more than minority rights loss. Such a
calculus may also be too short-term, neglecting long-term losses
to the framework of rights.

In the previous chapter, I laid out a balanced position in which
neither necessity nor liberty should have trumping claims. Terrorist attack can justify abridgments of liberty only if suspensions of liberty do actually enhance security. If they do, it should
be lawful to detain suspects and hold them without trial, until
the nature of the risk they pose can be determined. At the same
time, detainees must retain the right to counsel and judicial review of their detention. A constitutional democracy should keep
rights abridgments to a strict minimum and limit their duration

with sunset clauses. When organizations are designated as terrorist, they should retain the right to judicial review of their proscription.[14] Withdrawing the rule of law from anyone in a democratic state can never be justified. No "constitutional black holes" should be allowed to develop in a war on terror, for they threaten to pull individuals down into realms beyond the control and the ken of other citizens.

Any strategy of preventive or investigative detention that targets a particular social group—say, Arab Americans or aliens of Muslim faith—potentially violates the constitutional norms of equal protection. Rule of law implies both invariance and equality, both unchanging standards of due process and equal ones for all persons. Selectively targeted detentions may be justified in situations of dramatic uncertainty, like the weeks following September 11, but once it became clear that there was no larger plot or further risk of attack, equality considerations alone would mandate the early release of specially targeted suspects, against whom probable cause cannot be demonstrated.

The second question about abridgments of liberty is long-term: what do they do to the status of law once an emergency is over? Lincoln insisted that emergency suspension of civil liberties did not endanger the constitutional fabric in peacetime, but civil libertarians point out that temporary suspensions have a way of becoming permanent.[15] Moreover, their ambit has a way of spreading: measures introduced to stop terrorists are then used, once the emergency is over, to catch criminals and other types of offenders. Terrorism becomes a widening wedge, in other words, that weakens due process protections for all. Even if emergency measures are eventually revoked, the very fact that the law is made more severe in a time of emergency, civil libertarians argue, does damage to respect for the law as an abiding set of standards. This is especially the case with national emergencies, which substitute some form of martial law for the rule of law throughout a whole country. There seems little doubt that emergency law, so frequently invoked in Latin America to create temporary military dictatorships, has made it more difficult for committed democrats to anchor the constitutional rule of law throughout their continent.[16] But even piecemeal emergencies may do significant damage to the rule of law.

The question that civil libertarians raise is the relation between legitimacy and invariance. Do legal rules have to be invariant in order for them to retain legitimacy? In some constitutions, the rules are written so as to exclude as much variance as possible. U.S. civil libertarians point out, for example, that the U.S. Constitution makes only one reference to emergencies, in the clause allowing the suspension of habeas corpus in "cases of rebellion or invasion" when "the public safety requires it."[17] This, in their view, compares favorably with more recent European constitutions that make elaborate provision for the imposition of emergency regulations in times of war or civil insurrection.[18] Clearly, civil libertarians prefer a constitution that allows the fewest possible opportunities for the exercise of emergency power.

The metaphor most often used to describe what is at stake in this discussion is the story of Ulysses and the Sirens in Homer's *Odyssey*. Ulysses, voyaging home from Troy, is warned by an oracle that death awaits him and his crew if they listen to the haunting voice of the Sirens, who will lure them and their ship onto the rocks. So Ulysses orders the crew to lash him to the mast, and he puts beeswax into the ears of his oarsmen; thus protected, they row safely past the Sirens, while Ulysses himself listens to their alluring cries.

Ulysses' conduct is often cited to help us understand law and rights as strategies of precommitment. Like Ulysses tying himself to the mast so that he will hear but not succumb to the Sirens' song, democratic states precommit themselves to respecting rights, knowing that they will be sorely tempted to abridge them in times of danger.[19] Ulysses commits himself in advance, knowing that when temptation is upon him, it will be too late. Rights, this story tells us, are like Ulysses' beeswax: devices of reason, designed in moments of tranquillity, to master temptation in times of danger.

Terrorism is a supreme test of a liberal society's ability to abide by these precommitments. For they are commitments to invariance and equality alike, and going back on these commitments is easy. Oppression by majorities comes at little direct cost to their own liberties and rights. As Ronald Dworkin has pointed out, the trade-off is not between *our* liberty and *our* security in times of terrorist threat, but between *our* security and *their* liberty, by which he means the freedoms of small suspect groups, like adult male Muslims and particularly the subset in violation of immigration regulations.[20] These abridgments of the rights of a few are easy to justify politically when the threat of terrorism appears to endanger the many.

The idea of rights as precommitments seeks to give special attention to the dignity claims of individuals who may be endangered by majority interest. Special attention here simply means that we cannot accord a trumping claim to the public order interests of the majority. We need to balance competing claims, and we should do so on the assumption that precommitments made in times of safety should be maintained, as far as possible, in times of danger.

II

Yet this preliminary outline of a lesser evil position is controversial, and to appreciate why, I need to contrast it with other possibilities. To the question "What do exceptions and emergencies do to the rule of law?" there appear to be three answers. A pragmatic answer is that the law's legitimacy has something to do with invariance, but much more to do with effectiveness. So if you have to choose between leaving laws unchanged and changing them to stop terrorists in their tracks, and your concern is to maintain the rule of law, far better to abridge a right than to let a concern for pure consistency stay your hand. Lincoln's justification of his use of emergency powers in 1861—"are all the laws, but one, to go unexecuted, and the government itself go to pieces, lest that one be violated?"—is the great standing defense of sacrificing invariance for the sake of effectiveness.[21] A second position, closest to pure civil libertarianism, would be that legitimacy—and, as a result, effectiveness—are tightly tied to invariance, to the idea that law should not bend to necessity, emergency, or political exigency. A third view, closest to the lesser evil position set out in this book, does not want to separate effectiveness, invariance, and legitimacy. According to this view, laws do derive some of their power from being difficult to change, and yet if they are completely unresponsive to emergency situations, they may be ineffective. Emergency alterations of legal protections like habeas corpus may be necessary, but there is a price to pay when you do. Habeas corpus is weakened because once it has been suspended, everyone then understands that an important guarantee of freedom is pliable and susceptible to political pressures.

It is not merely the legitimacy of the law that terrorist emergencies call into question, but the status of the moral standards encapsulated in the idea of human rights. Here the claim would be that the specific civil and political rights to be found in liberal democratic constitutions are not just a revocable privilege of citizenship, but reflect a constitutional commitment to respect the particular and equal moral status of human beings. One way to put this would be that beneath civil and political rights, enshrined in the particular constitutions of liberal democracies, stands an idea of human rights. This is a moral rather than a juridical claim: it does not imply that all liberal democratic states incorporate human rights norms into their constitutions in the same way. Some of these states may have signed on to international human rights conventions, and others, like the United States, may sign on only to some or sign on with reservations, but even if their relation to international human rights is ambivalent or ambiguous, their constitutional doctrine expresses a view of the protected moral status of human beings that is consonant with human rights.[22]

This commitment to respect the moral status of human beings means treating individuals equally and treating all with at least a minimum respect. Insisting on establishing the guilt of individuals beyond a reasonable doubt is one practical way that the law does this. Another is that the law is supposed to keep these commitments irrespective of the way its officers—policemen, judges, lawyers—may feel toward the prisoner in the dock.[23] This commitment—to respect individuals irrespective of conduct—distinguishes human rights from other rights. Some civil rights—like the right to vote—can be forfeited on commission of felony. They are conditional, therefore, on conduct. Others, like the right of judicial review of detention, might be revocable in emergencies if necessity dictates. But human rights are independent of conduct, circumstances, citizenship, desert, or moral worth. Humans have human rights simply because they are humans. Hence even terrorists have rights that they cannot be denied. A liberal society is committed to respect the rights of those who have shown no respect for rights at all, to show mercy to those who are merciless, to treat as human those who have behaved inhumanly. This commitment to observe obligations even when they are not reciprocated is a defining characteristic of any society under the rule of law. Why else do we believe that even the most odious criminal is entitled to a fair trial and proof of guilt beyond a reasonable doubt? We care about these standards, not simply for prudential reasons—to ensure that the correct person is convicted and taken off the streets—but also because we, the democratic we, believe we owe this to everyone. On this reading the rule of law is more than a procedure, treating like cases alike. It also seeks to serve a moral idea: that any human being is entitled to a basic equality of treatment. If this is what is owed common criminals in normal times, there is no convincing reason why it cannot be owed terrorist suspects in times of emergency.

This idea, however, is not shared by all. Of course, every democrat thinks that respect for dignity may be a *consequence* of a successful regime of laws. But not everyone thinks that this is the law's essential purpose and the test of its legitimacy. Such a view would be a "moral reading" of constitutional rights, to use Ronald Dworkin's phrase, and it is at odds with more pragmatic readings of constitutional rights—readings that would emphasize their procedural utility in arriving at judicial outcomes rather than the idea that they incarnate any particular moral commitments.[24] Rights, on a pragmatic reading, are side con-

straints on the public policy choices of legislatures and governments. As such, the rationale of rights is to protect public interests, not to instantiate dignity commitments. In times of
emergency, therefore, they can be properly abridged with no
negative consequences since they are, to begin with, a instrument of collective interests and nothing else.

Yet it is hard to see why anyone would care about the rule of
law if it is simply a piece of useful procedure or a public policy
side constraint. It is hard to understand how the rule of law
could generate allegiance unless it expressed a common moral
commitment to the dignity of individuals. At least some of the
reason why people obey the law has to do with the idea that it
is *theirs*, a product of democratic suffrage, but also that it expresses a commitment to accord them equal respect and equal
consideration.

Moreover, without some idea that dignity is at risk when
rights are abridged, there are few pragmatic grounds to care
when large numbers of people suffer harm from emergency
abridgments of rights. Richard Posner, a practicing judge and a
leading exponent of the pragmatic view, argues: "In hindsight,
we know that interning the Japanese American residents of the
West Coast did not shorten World War II. But was this known
at the time? If not, should not the government have erred on the
side of caution, as it did?"[25] This works well as an argument
against summary condemnation of Roosevelt's actions from the
safety of hindsight, but in saying the government was right "to
err on the side of caution," Posner passes over in silence the irrevocable harm that was done to a hundred thousand Japanese,
most of whom were citizens and none of whom turned out to
present a danger of subversion or sabotage. This example helps
to distinguish a lesser evil position from a pragmatic approach
to rights abridgment. Both seek to balance claims of liberty
against security, both deny trumping claims to either, but a
lesser evil position would put far more emphasis than a pragmatic one on the loss entailed in the abridgment of the rights of
the Japanese. This emphasis would be grounded in the idea that
rights-based commitments to individual dignity are intrinsic to

the definition of what a democracy is. By committing, in advance, to the idea of civil liberties' abridgment as an evil, to be avoided whenever possible, it weighs the internment of the Japanese by a less pragmatic standard than whether it would or would not shorten the war with Japan. A lesser evil approach would reason as follows. Shortening a war is a morally significant goal, but the loss of freedom that internment will entail is such a serious blow to the individuals involved, and the likelihood that internment will shorten the war is so uncertain, that the rights abridgments cannot be justified.

III

In retrospect, the Japanese internment seems like an obvious abuse. The real difficulty, as Richard Posner correctly says, is to get the balance right when emergencies are underway, and when no one knows what measures will turn out to have been necessary. Getting this balance right means taking a view on whether presidents and prime ministers are entitled to declare emergencies in the first place. Some civil libertarians believe that this exercise of prerogative power is dangerous in itself. But who else can decide when emergencies exist? A constitutional order that does not accord a leader the capacity to declare an emergency and take decisive action to meet it may perish through deliberative irresolution and paralysis.

Yet even if some exercise of prerogative power is inevitable, a civil libertarian might say, this leaves the determination of emergency in the hands of a single leader who is bound to manipulate a crisis to his or her own advantage. This may be true, but where is the remedy? Determination of whether an emergency exists is unavoidably political: there cannot be a science or a law of the matter. But this doesn't mean it has to be capricious or arbitrary. As constitutional scholar John P. Roche wrote more than fifty years ago, "when there is a consensus on the existence of an emergency; i.e., when public and congressional agreement on presidential action are apparent, an emergency exists."[26] While it is presidents and prime ministers who declare emergencies, their use of this power can be subjected to democratic regulation. There must be some consensus, among the public and their elected officials, that the executive is justified in declaring one. Where this consensus does not exist, the proclamation of an emergency will be regarded as an abuse of executive prerogative. If the institutions of adversarial review in a democracy are doing their job, they will resist and set limits to both the proclamation of emergency and the exercise of prerogative.

So the problem with emergency exercises of prerogative power is not, as civil libertarians imply, that they can never be justified, since they obviously can, nor even that their use is undemocratic in itself. For the recurrent rationale of the use of executive prerogative has been a threat to a vital majority interest. In 1861, Lincoln defended the measures he had taken—blockading the southern ports, suspending civil liberties, allocating funds to pay the army and navy without congressional approval—on the grounds that "these measures, whether strictly legal or not, were ventured upon, under what appeared to be a popular demand and a public necessity."[27] Emergencies become a challenge to democracy and to law when proclaimed on grounds that involve bad faith, manipulation of evidence, exaggeration of risk, or prospect of political advantage. Checks and balances cannot stop an executive from declaring an emergency, but Congress and the courts can step in, once emergencies are declared, to subject the exercise of prerogative to adversarial review. When President Truman nationalized the U.S. steel industry in April 1952, arguing that an impending strike threatened the national defense at a time when the nation was at war in Korea, the measure proved unpopular in Congress and the press, and the Supreme Court in June 1952 declared the measure unconstitutional.[28]

September 11, on the other hand, was an unquestioned emergency. The issue, then, is what measures such emergencies can justify.

A pragmatic view of rights, like the one adopted by Richard Posner, would hold that precommitment is unrealistic because it binds hands that need to be untied in time to cope with danger.

Adversarial review, likewise, could prevent a republic from taking swift and robust action in a time of invasion or emergency.

The Roman answer to this problem was temporary dictatorship. The fabled Cincinnatus left his plow and was given dictatorial powers by the Senate in order to lead the republican armies to victory against an invasion that had reached the gates of Rome. Roman thought thus saw dictatorship and republican authority as complementary opposites, not as enemies. This sounds strange to modern democrats, who are more likely to think of dictatorship as a permanent foe or as a potential nemesis. Modern democrats are also likely to think of democracy as being intrinsically self-sustaining, capable of reconciling presidential authority and rule of law at all times. Yet the historical record of the twentieth century suggests otherwise. In times of war, Roosevelt and Churchill were given dictatorial powers by their legislatures, with the approval of the courts, to save their countries.[29] The necessity of these powers suggests that democracies are not intrinsically self-sustaining; rather, as the Romans thought, their executives recurrently need dictatorial prerogative to cope with crisis.

Emergencies lay bare an enduring conflict in democracy between adversarial justification, which can make for indecision, and strong authority, which may lead to dictatorial abuse. Yet the wartime experience of democracies shows that these two tendencies can be reconciled. The dictatorial powers exercised by Roosevelt and Churchill remained subject to the supervision of the legislature and the courts and, once the emergency had passed, were quickly dismantled. Churchill was unceremoniously voted out of office within weeks of leading his country to victory. Democracy, therefore, can survive episodes of "constitutional dictatorship," provided that the dictatorship remains constitutional, and provided that it remains temporary.[30] This means that the executive's prerogative ought to be limited by the constitution: presidents should never have the power to prolong themselves in office, to suspend elections, to disband political competition, to alter the constitution itself, or to dissolve legislatures permanently.[31]

A war on terror sustained indefinitely, against a succession of rogue states or terrorist cells, poses unknown dangers, however, since no one knows how long the emergency will last. In a long twilight war, largely fought by secret means, the key issue is maintaining as much legal and legislative oversight as is compatible with the necessity for decisive action. Sunset clauses— setting time limits to extraordinary powers—seem an essential way to reconcile security and liberty. Thus in Great Britain, the original Prevention of Terrorism Act, which drastically increased police power in Northern Ireland, was not made permanent but was made subject to a periodic process of parliamentary renewal. The new Terrorism Act has no such provision, and this is its chief danger.[32]

In a war on terrorism, unlike the situation that Lincoln faced in the Civil War or the one that Roosevelt faced after Pearl Harbor, it is not obvious why the president's powers should be increased. He does not have to conscript labor or economic resources, as Roosevelt did, and he does not face a secession, as Lincoln did. There is no good reason, therefore, why his authority should not be kept under constant adversarial review by courts, Congress, and a free media.

The recurrent problem with keeping his authority under review is excessive deference on the part of both legislatures and the judiciary to an executive's power as commander in chief. In the United States, this deference to executive decision during emergencies has evolved into a legal convention, most recently on display in the U.S. federal court's refusal to grant habeas corpus petitions in the case of a U.S. citizen, Yaser Esam Hamdi, held incommunicado on a U.S. Navy brig as an enemy combatant. According to the court, "the federal courts have many strengths, but the conduct of combat operations has been left to others. The executive is best prepared to exercise the military judgment attending the capture of alleged combatants." The court held, in other words, that the deference accorded to an executive in wartime should also apply in the very different circumstance of a terrorist emergency. Even so, the court sounded troubled by the implication: "we ourselves would be summarily embracing a sweeping proposition—namely that with no judicial review, any American citizen alleged to be an enemy combatant could be detained indefinitely without charges or counsel on the government's say-so." Yet this is exactly the consequence of its decision, one that has been confirmed by a superior court. The best that can be said is that an extraordinary act of executive power—holding a citizen incommunicado—*has* been subjected to judicial review.[33] The worst that can be said is that courts have deferred to an executive at precisely the place where they should never defer, in a matter relating to the fundamental civil rights of an American citizen. As of this writing, Supreme Court review of this issue is pending. It remains to be seen whether the nation's highest court will accept the view of executive prerogative taken by the president, or whether it will insist that it is up to the judiciary to decide the due process standards that should apply to foreign nationals or U.S. citizens detained in a war on terror.[34] On the view of checks and balances taken in this book, the courts rather than the executive must remain control of due process standards for both civilian and military detainees. Failure by the courts to uphold their jurisdiction over this matter would weaken democracy itself.

IV

Emergencies bring into focus two radically different images of the law. In the image personified in Ulysses, law and human rights derive their legitimacy from their status as rules that should not bend to circumstance.[35] In the competing image, to use U.S. Supreme Court Justice Robert Jackson's phrase, the constitution cannot be a suicide pact.[36] When suicide threatens— that is, when democracy's own deliberative slowness threatens it with disaster, or when rights guarantees extended to the honest many frustrate the pursuit of the dangerous few—rulers must act decisively. But can they, as Locke implied, operate beyond the law, or should their prerogative be constrained by law?

In understanding what is at stake in the use of prerogative power in time of emergency, we need to come to grips with the thought of the Weimar legal theorist Carl Schmitt.[37] His jurisprudence was framed in the 1920s by Weimar Germany's struggle to preserve constitutional democracy in the face of terrorist violence from both sides of the political spectrum.[38] Schmitt understood our question to be this: does the exception save or destroy the rule? Schmitt was emphatic: without the power to declare exceptions, the rule of law cannot survive. "Sovereign is he," Schmitt famously wrote, "who decides the exception."[39] A state cannot remain sovereign, cannot reliably maintain an internal monopoly of the means of force together with the rule of law, if the president cannot exempt himself upon necessary occasions from constitutional rules that would prevent him from prevailing in a contest of force with the state's enemies. Schmitt notoriously said that politics was about punishing enemies and rewarding friends. Constitutional regimes, he went on, cannot save themselves from attack unless the friends of constitutionalism withdraw the law's protections from its enemies.

Schmitt also claimed that the question of whether exceptions destroy or save the rule was actually about what place to give political power and executive authority in the enforcement and defense of law. In his day, he was arguing against the legal positivism that dominated German constitutional thinking and sought to view law as a sphere autonomous from politics by virtue of its formal structure as a system of rules. Schmitt thought this image of law failed to represent the conditions of law's own creation, in the realm of politics. Since law was never the codification of an abstract set of absolutes but was, rather, the legal ratification, issue by issue, of political agreements between opposing social forces and interests, those who enforce the law were bound to make exceptions, as these forces and interests exerted their influence on the law's guardians.

In our own day, the defenders of legal invariance are not legal positivists but civil libertarians. They want to keep law as free as possible from political contamination and interference and believe that law's legitimacy derives from its capacity to resist political pressures. This might be a realistic expectation in times of peace. But in liberal democracies under attack, matters might stand differently.

Schmitt believed that this image of autonomous law was not merely unrealistic but foolish, since law was the creature of political power. Its enforcement depended entirely on the viability of a particular constitutional order. This seemed only too evident in Weimar, where law's survival depended on the capacity of a constitutionally elected president to defend an embattled regime by force. Hence, according to Schmitt, rights survive in emergencies to the degree that they enable the particular political regime that defends the constitutional order to survive. Rights that stand in the way of a regime's survival should be suspended in a time of crisis. The Ulysses metaphor would have made no sense to Schmitt. No regime can afford to tie its hands to the mast and stop its ears with beeswax if the ship of state is being boarded by pirates. Ulysses must untie himself, rally the crew, and fight back.

Confidence in Schmitt's judgment on these issues is not enhanced by the knowledge that he went on in the 1930s to become an apologist for Hitler. As Oren Gross has shown, in a close reading of Schmitt's theory, an intellectual project that began in the early 1920s as an attempt to save the Weimar constitution through the use of presidential power became, by the early 1930s, a project to justify extraconstitutional dictatorship.[40] From defending the president as guardian of the constitution, he ended up defending dictatorial power at any price. This later career suggests the weakness in his legal realism: yes, law is politics—the codification of often shabby compromises between competing groups in the political realm—but it is not just politics. Law ought to encapsulate right as well as might. Law's commitments to dignity and equal protection are supposed to enable right to prevail over might. The moral content of law that some legal pragmatists and positivists would see as dangerous because it provides a pretext for judicial moralizing and intrusion on legislative authority is, when seen against the catastrophe of Weimar, an essential element to rally moral and political support for constitutional order. Such ethical elements set limits precisely at the point where decisive use of executive authority could shade into extraconstitutional dictatorship. Schmitt's jurisprudence, in its worship of strong authority, lacked any conception of a constitution as a moral order of liberty. Of themselves, commitments to equal protection and dignity cannot save a society from tyranny during an emergency. But these values can operate as a moral depository to remind citizens, judges, and politicians of the limits that ought to guide a democracy in a time of trial.

In the tradition of liberal constitutionalism that descends from Locke, law's ultimate protection lay in morality, in the ability of citizens to rise to the defense of law when morality revealed law's exercise to be unjust. Citizens, judges, and politicians all have moral responsibilities to protect a constitution when it is under attack. Locke's argument for the necessity of executive prerogative was balanced by the people's right to take the government back into their own hands when liberty was usurped. In an argument which provided a key justification for the American Revolution, Locke wrote that when prerogative power threatened to "enslave or destroy" a people, they had the right to "appeal to Heaven," and by implication to take up arms to defend their freedom.[41] Locke's phrase "appeal to Heaven" implied clearly that the armed defense of liberty was a lesser evil, justified only to avert the greater evil of tyranny and enslavement. The Lockean view is more than a defense of revolution: it clearly prioritizes evils, preferring the risks of disorder to despotism. This moral ranking contrasts signally with Schmitt's, for whom the greater evil was disorder and civil war, and for whom dictatorship, in contrast, was the lesser evil.

In 1933, many, though not all, Germans made the same mental choice as Schmitt, believing that dictatorship was a lesser evil than either Communism or civil war. Yet once a constitutional order sacrifices its commitment to liberty, it quickly sacrifices everything else. The racialized jurisprudence of Nazism, by deliberately severing law from any commitment to equal protection and respect, deprived whole categories of German citizens of their rights, creating the nightmarish legal order in which they could ultimately be deprived of their lives. But this racialized jurisprudence found a willing accomplice in a tradition of German legal positivism and legal realism that sought to disinfest law of ethics.

Human rights emerged from the Holocaust as a rejection of legal positivism, as an attempt to provide citizens with an independent moral standard that would enable them, when the law of their country went mad, to say: this may be legal, but it is not right.[42] It is this belief in the existence of a higher law, to which statutes and constitutions are ultimately answerable, that was so absent in the fervent apologetics of those like Schmitt whose theory of prerogative power divorced law from ethics. The lesson seems clear: even in emergency, even if some liberties must be suspended, a constitutional state must remain answerable to the higher law, a set of standards that protect foundational commitments to the dignity of every person.

V

The question is: which higher law? In American constitutional doctrine there is no obvious answer. There is no higher law than the U.S. Constitution, though Supreme Court justices have recurrently resorted to claims of ethics, natural justice, and the higher law in crafting their interpretations of the Bill of Rights.[43] A lesser evil argument would make only a modest claim here, that precisely because emergencies appear to place the public interest so overwhelmingly on the side of the public safety, constitutional interpretation should give special weight to the rights claims of those who stand to be arrested, incarcerated, or deported in times of emergency. Human rights conventions, ratified by the U.S. Congress, provide a statutory form of this higher law, and precisely because they are international, they provide a vantage point outside the national jurisprudence of a state, which enables judges and politicians to stand back from the solipsism of threat and victimhood, that state of feeling embattled and attacked that often leads to excessive, arbitrary, and abusive measures.

In Europe, the higher law is more explicitly set out in the terms of the European Human Rights Convention. Yet here, too, the idea of a higher law is obscure because, according to the terms of the convention, many fundamental human rights can be suspended or derogated in times of emergency. Under Article 15 of the Convention, for example, states can suspend human rights guarantees when they are faced with "war or other public emergency threatening the life of the nation." The loose phrasing allows governments a wide latitude in deciding what constitutes a public emergency, but governments are required to justify to the court why a situation does constitute an emergency requiring the suspension of civil liberties.[44] In the United Kingdom, the legality of the government's suspension of civil liberties after September 11 has gone to the House of Lords for review and will probably go on to the European Court. The European human rights system thus attempts to balance the two principles of political necessity and adversarial justification. If a government must suspend civil liberties, it must justify its action to a court, and, moreover, one outside its own national boundaries. This is not an empty requirement. In a judgment against Turkey in 1997, the court found that the government was entitled to suspend certain rights, in order to suppress a Kurdish insurgency in the southeast of the country, but was not entitled to detain suspects beyond fourteen days without their being brought before a court for review of their detention.[45] The second restriction that the European Convention imposes is that states are not allowed to derogate from a few "absolute" rights, like the right to be free from torture, extrajudicial killing, slavery, forced labor, and punishment without due process of law.

Any regime to suspend rights is difficult to reconcile with human rights' supposed role as an unconditional, universal, and unchanging set of commitments. The distinction between rights that can be suspended and those that cannot clearly implies a hierarchy of rights. This, too, contradicts a fundamental premise of modern human rights doctrine. The Vienna Declaration of

1993, issued after a meeting of the state signatories to the major human rights conventions, rejected the idea of a hierarchy of rights and reaffirmed that all of them were both indivisible and universal.[46] Universality is usually defined as meaning that rights should be universal across *cultures*. But there is an equally important sense in which human rights should apply universally among all persons and at all times, whether normal times or states of emergency. Terrorist emergencies put these universalist commitments under strain. To say that some rights can be suspended, while others cannot be, is to suggest that some matter more than others, and that the whole is not an indivisible and interconnected package of entitlements.[47]

We can believe that human rights are indivisible, in the sense that having one right is a precondition for having another. So, to use Amartya Sen's famous example, having a right to free speech and free assembly makes it possible to defend a right to subsistence, since without political rights you will be unable to make your voice heard when food runs short.[48] But this sense of causal interdependence is distinct from the idea that all rights are equally important in a time of emergency. We can still argue that the rights are analytically indivisible, in Sen's sense, while admitting that in dangerous times some rights just turn out to be more fundamental than others. Derogation seeks to save what can be saved—an absolute prohibition on torture, cruel and unusual punishment, extrajudicial execution, and penal servitude—from the abridgments of liberty, chiefly habeas corpus, that political necessity may require.

No human rights advocate, let alone liberal democrat, can be happy, however, to discover that the rights which can be derogated in emergencies turn out to be the entire body of political rights essential to the preservation of democracy itself: freedom of thought and opinion, freedom of expression, freedom of assembly. The drafters of the European Convention crafted this derogation structure with the recent catastrophe of Weimar and the rise of fascism in mind, together with the rise of postwar Communist parties in Italy and France.[49] Apparently, the risk of a return of fascism or totalitarianism was sufficient, in their minds, to justify suspending democratic rights in order to prevent political parties' seizing power by force. States faced with such a crisis can suspend democratic rights, provided that the means of repression used to put down the challenge do not result in violations of the bodily integrity of detained suspects. Thus, according to the Convention, suspects can be held in indefinite detention as long as they are not tortured, killed, or subjected to penal servitude. This does protect them from the worst, but it sets up a hierarchy of rights, with "absolute" nonderogable protections applied only to infringements of bodily integrity, while all other rights are left in limbo, conditional upon the will of political authorities.[50]

But there are good reasons to insist on the indivisibility of rights. How are free citizens supposed to prevent their friends and neighbors, their union representatives, and journalists from being tortured, imprisoned without cause, subjected to penal servitude, or executed without trial, unless they can exercise undiminished rights of assembly and expression? Exercising the derogable rights is crucial to protecting the nonderogable ones. The survival of any rights depends on voice, on the capacity of citizens to protest, dissent, organize, and mobilize.[51] Once these rights are suspended, citizens would have no recourse other than to seize them back by force, especially since the European Court, which is supposed to protect the Convention, lacks the power to compel states that refuse to abide by its judgments.[52]

The danger of a radical overthrow by force of democratic governments in Europe seems remote. Much less remote, however, is the possibility that democratic governments might themselves misuse a supposed terrorist threat to justify abrogation of basic democratic rights. The European Convention, as it now stands, offers imperfect protection against that eventuality. To be sure, no court can save a democracy from self-destruction by judicial rulings alone. But courts also have a clear political function. If their rulings protect democratic rights in times of emergency, their clear signal can help rally domestic political support to the defense of civil liberties. The European Court thus has an important political role in signaling to European states that one of its members is tipping from democratic to authoritarian patterns of rule. It is up to strong democratic states to heed these judicial signals and use political leverage to pull states that may be lurching in an undemocratic direction back onto the democratic path. Thus while Turkey is not yet a member of the European Union, it ardently seeks membership, and this gives it a strong incentive to comply with decisions of the European Court, which does have jurisdiction in Turkey. Recently when a right-wing government was elected in Austria, other European governments threatened to suspend the Austrians from membership if they took actions against immigrants that would violate European human rights norms.[53] Here external human rights pressure played a role in preventing any recurrence of the 1930s.

But political will is a changeable thing. Austria is a small country. What would happen if Italy or Turkey or Russia were to fall under the sway of a genial demagogue with a popular touch and contempt for both democracy and the judiciary?[54] Terrorism would easily provide such a leader with a pretext for declaring a permanent suspension of the rule of law. In such a case, firm political action by other European states would be necessary, but to facilitate such action, European human rights norms—which have statutory authority in each of these countries—must be clear. The standard that defines when emergency powers can be introduced should be tightened up. It should refer only to a repeated and concerted campaign of violence whose purpose is not just political destabilization but the overthrow of the constitution by force. The European Convention should make it harder to suspend political rights, restricting suspensions exclusively to parties and persons explicitly advocating violence. While rights of assembly and free political participation for the population at large should never be suspended, it could be permissible to ban political parties when they engage in incitement, intimidation, or association with terrorist groups. Those who wish to express anticonstitutional views should remain free to vote for parties provided they have no part in violence. In emergencies, authorities should have the power to detain individuals on lower standards of probable cause than would suffice in a criminal matter, simply because, in conditions of uncertainty and possible threat, detaining them may be the only way to determine whether a plot is underway leading to further attacks. But those detained in this manner should always retain right of counsel and access to courts for expeditious judicial review of their detention.[55] Thus even if preventive or investigative detention can be justified as a lesser evil, it should not entail suspension of habeas corpus rights.[56] Anyone detained for longer than fourteen days, for example, must be brought before a civil magistrate with the power to confirm or terminate detention.

The case for suspension of rights also ought to require proving that you suspend some liberties in order to protect *other* equally important rights. If these suspensions cannot be shown to enhance the right of the majority to live in security, then they have no justification. You cannot suspend liberties simply to provide a public with a feeling that they are more secure or to gratify their anger at a terrorist outrage or to find some convenient scapegoat. You have to prove—to a legislature, a judiciary, and public opinion—that abridging a particular constitutional liberty will actually enhance the liberty and security of the law-abiding.

What the rule of law requires, as John Finn and other scholars have argued, is not invariance but public justification.[57] The question is not whether some restriction of civil liberties can be justified in times of emergency but whether these restrictions are undertaken secretly and arbitrarily or subjected to legislative scrutiny, justified with good reasons to an electorate, and, above all, subjected to full judicial review.

The same principle ought to apply to any derogation from international human rights. The International Covenant on Civil and Political Rights allows states to derogate or suspend rights.[58] "In times of public emergency which threaten the life of the nation," they can suspend rights provided that these measures do not discriminate "on the ground of race, colour, sex, language, religion or social origin."[59] With the Nazi concentration camps clearly in mind, the drafters of the Covenant precluded suspension of legal guarantees against cruel and unusual punishment, penal servitude, and torture, and, with the Nuremberg Laws in mind, they precluded any suspension of the right to remain a person under the law.

Nations that sign the covenant are required to publicly announce and justify their derogations to UN treaty bodies. The United Kingdom formally sought to suspend its obligations in 2001 after enacting legislation that empowered the government to continue detaining terrorist suspects from foreign countries who could not be returned to their home countries except at risk of persecution or torture there.[60]

This UK action seems a justifiable exercise in the lesser evil. The government did not act in secret. It engaged in public justification. Faced with two ways of jeopardizing the human rights of suspects, it chose the lesser form. Such a policy seeks to save what can be saved from the idea of precommitment, by focusing on preserving terrorist suspects from torture and by insisting on accountability and public review.[61]

There are two points here. One is that exceptions do not necessarily compromise the status of rules, provided that the exceptions are subjected to adversarial justification, and provided that the exceptions are highly specific, applied to named individuals, rather than blanket provisions applied to large bodies of citizens and noncitizens. The second is that the relevant institutions before which exceptions must be justified are not simply those of the constitutional state under attack. They include the institutions of international law. By going through a formal derogation procedure, the United Kingdom accepted this second point. The United States, by contrast, has not formally derogated from its obligations under the International Covenant on Civil and Political Rights.[62] In failing to do so, the United States clearly believes that the duty of justification it owes in a war on terror is restricted exclusively to U.S. institutions. In an international war, however, it is unconvincing to claim that national sovereignty should trump international obligations. The United States is de-

taining nonnationals, prosecuting its war across national boundaries. If this is so, international law should apply, and the duty of
adversarial justification, outlined in this book, extends beyond
national courts and legislatures to UN treaty bodies as well.

VI

An emergency is just that: a temporary state, not an indefinite
and open-ended revocation of the rule of law. The problem with
emergencies is that only the executive has sufficient information
to know whether they remain justified. Hence the speedy termi-
nation of emergencies remains a recurrent problem. Electorates
and legislators are invariably told by their leaders, "If you only
knew what we know . . . ," in justification of the continued suspension of civil liberties. But this is not good enough. It is the
very nature of democracy that we *should* know what they know.
It may not always be possible to know immediately: a government can be justified in withholding information on a sensitive
operation if disclosure would actually jeopardize lives. But the
justification for secrecy can be only temporary, not permanent.
Secrecy becomes a greater evil—a danger to democracy itself—
when it is used to prevent the process on which constitutional
liberty depends, the adversarial justification of lesser evils. That
is why sunset clauses, preset limitations on the duration of
emergency legislation, remain the legislature's chief weapon in
making sure that emergency exceptions do not become the rule.

Yet even when sunset clauses are in place, emergency legislation remains problematic. Legislators invariably respond to attack by giving police additional powers whether they need them
or not. A recent scholarly evaluation of Canada's Bill C-36, enacted after September 11 to tighten up Canada's antiterrorist legislation, questioned whether the legislation was actually necessary to meet the terrorist threat. The criminal law already on the
books may have been sufficient. The same point is often made
about the U.S. Patriot Act.[63]

The rule of law is not compromised by emergencies per se,
but by politicized construal of risk to justify emergency mea-

sures that are not actually necessary to meet the threat at hand. It is crucial to distinguish threat assessment from moral repulsion, to separate ethical judgment from the actuarial estimation of danger. The fact that terrorism is an attack on the political character of society does not mean that the society's identity or future is in question. As I shall demonstrate in the next chapter, the historical record shows that democracies are neither less ruthless nor more vulnerable than authoritarian states when faced with what they take to be an ultimate danger. The ruthlessness derives from the great strength of democracy, its capacity to mobilize the allegiance and self-sacrifice of its citizens. Controlling this potential for ruthlessness is partly the business of a good constitution. Checks and balances are there to prevent an executive from pandering to fear. But constitutions are never enough. Good institutions are never enough. Ultimately the protection of these rights devolves upon citizens themselves.

One of the strengths of the liberal tradition is its disabused realism, its belief that abuse of power is inevitable and no constitution can stop it. That is why, in Locke and Jefferson, for example, there remains an articulated right of revolution. Liberal theory places the final defense of constitutional liberty in ordinary citizens, in their willingness, when provoked by greater evil, to rise up and change their government, by peaceful means if possible, by force as a last resort. Civil disobedience has an honored place in the traditions of liberal democracy, precisely because it is the defense of last resort when the constitutional identity of liberal democracy is at risk.[64]

There is no reason to be complacent about the willingness of citizens to fight for their liberties or prevent their governments from abusing them. Less than half of the American electorate takes the trouble to vote, a sign that they may not care about their own rights, let alone the rights of minorities in their midst. As we have already seen, the number of people who value rights intrinsically will always be small. The capacity of a ruthless government, bent on abridging freedoms, must never be underestimated, especially not in an age in which government has such power to shape public perceptions and manufacture consent through the media. Yet is also dangerous to become cynical and to conclude that the defense of civil liberties is hopeless because of the manipulated apathy of the majority. The civil rights movement in the United States was one long struggle against manipulated apathy—and concerted racist resistance—by a handful of activists. Only in retrospect does their victory seem inevitable. At the time, it often seemed a hopeless cause. But it has always been true that the force which sustains the liberty of the many has been the intransigent courage of the few.

Sticking to the idea of rights as precommitments is hard when a liberal democracy is under threat. Rights express this recognition, this knowledge that we must precommit in times of calm to prevent ourselves, like Ulysses, from succumbing in times of danger. Precommitment is not a commitment to invariance, to never changing the law no matter what, but rather a commitment to adversarial justification, within a framework that maintains equality and dignity standards in times of safety and times of danger alike. To conduct a defense of liberal society in defiance of these precommitments is to betray the order that is being defended, as well as the citizens whose security depends on that order.

CHAPTER THREE

THE WEAKNESS OF
THE STRONG

I

One of the recurring difficulties in thinking clearly about terrorism is how to evaluate the threat it actually poses. In this chapter, I review the historical evidence about how seriously terrorism has threatened liberal democracy since the mid–nineteenth century, explain why liberal democracies have often exaggerated the threat, and suggest what we can do to get risk and reaction into a better balance.

When terrorist emergencies are proclaimed, abridgments of liberty are justified in terms which assert that "the life of a nation" is at risk.[1] When political leaders declare a "war on terror," they imply that terrorism poses a threat equivalent to war. Yet there is a world of difference between the threat posed by armed attack by another state and a terrorist incident. Even if the plane that came down in Pennsylvania had struck the White House or the Capitol, the attacks of September 11 did not endanger the social order of the United States or threaten its democracy with collapse.[2] Even if the president's office had been successfully struck, the functions of government would have continued, as they have done following the assassination of presidents from Lincoln to Kennedy. While September 11 is often compared to Pearl Harbor, Al Qaeda certainly has nothing like the resources of the Empire of Japan. In order to think clearly about terror, we must distinguish moral condemnation from threat assessment, to try to separate the anger we feel from the risk they actually pose. Terrorist attacks may be odious and they may demonstrate alarming shortcomings in the system of national defense, but they do not necessarily threaten us with defeat, collapse, or capitulation. Indeed, when public authorities exaggerate a terrorist threat, they risk instigating the panic that terrorists are seeking to achieve.[3] They also tend to take measures that democracy later regrets.

Yet getting risk and response into balance is easy only in hindsight. The challenge is doing so when a threat impends and, as is always the case, authorities lack adequate information about how serious it is going to prove. In American history, the episode that September 11 most clearly recalls is not Pearl Harbor but the Red Scare of 1919. In retrospect, the Red Scare is seen as a textbook example of unnecessary exaggeration and panic in response to a relatively trivial security threat.[4] But judging the response from the safety of hindsight misses the crucial fact that at the time, public authorities had good reason to be alarmed at the pattern they saw emerging. We need only view events as they unfolded to understand why U.S. state and federal authorities believed they were faced with a global terrorist conspiracy, akin to Al Qaeda. First, in 1917 a huge multinational empire—Russia—had been overthrown by a small band of revolutionary and terrorist agitators. Then, in short order, similar attempts were made to capitalize on the chaos at the end of World War I with a revolution in Germany. Revolution there was averted only by ruthless measures. Even after revolution in Germany had been beaten back, the Soviet revolutionaries urged workers of the world, particularly the millions of demobilized soldiers released from service in World War I, to join their cause. American authorities knew how many discontented unemployed soldiers in the United States might heed this call, and by 1919 they knew they no longer had the luxury of believing that revolutionary Communism was confined to Europe. By then, general strikes were taking place in Winnipeg, Canada, and Seattle, Washington. A wave of strikes in essential industries like coal and steel swept across the country in the summer of 1919; even the Boston police walked off the job. In some places, there was bloody conflict between strikers and police. Most seriously of all, bombs began going off at the homes and offices of mayors, judges, and other public officials across the country, one a suicide attack that damaged the house of the U.S. attorney general,

Mitchell Palmer. His department's intelligence operations, led by J. Edgar Hoover, uncovered evidence that substantial numbers of alien immigrants belonged to parties sympathetic to the revolutionary Communist cause, and that some of these parties supported terrorist methods.

This was the context which led Palmer to authorize the infamous raids of November 1919 and January 1920 that detained five thousand aliens and led to the deportation of many of them. The context brought together five unusual elements: (1) an international revolutionary movement, (2) domestic terrorist activity, (3) political organization of aliens, (4) high unemployment and substantial economic insecurity after a war, and (5) the wartime experience of civil liberties restriction. The last feature is important. By the time the Palmer Raids occurred, a duly elected congressman, Victor Berger, had been convicted under the Espionage Act for opposing the war and denied his seat in the House of Representatives; a presidential candidate, Eugene Victor Debs, had been imprisoned for voicing opposition to American participation in the war and for urging his audience to defy the draft; Oliver Wendell Holmes of the U.S. Supreme Court had ruled in the Schenck case that speech urging resistance to conscription constituted a "clear and present danger" and was not entitled to protection under the First Amendment. All of these wartime decisions, in retrospect so clearly in violation of fundamental civil liberties, created the permissive context for the violation of the rights of aliens in the peacetime conditions of 1919–20.

It turned out that Communist radicalism did not pose a clear and present danger to the United States. The political organizations that were smashed by the Palmer Raids proved to be innocuous. The terrorist attacks of 1919 and 1920 did claim close to a hundred lives, but they did not threaten the country's democratic institutions.

Despite the almost universal opprobrium that now surrounds the Palmer Raids, the problem of evaluating them honestly remains. At the height of his influence Attorney General Palmer's measures commanded almost universal assent: the democratic majority was clearly behind him. Even civil libertarians did not recover their voices until late in the crisis.[5] This does not make the majority right: hysteria does not cease to be irrational merely because it takes hold of everybody. But the fact that measures turn out to be excessive and unnecessary, while a terrorist emergency is underway, does not prove that they were unjustified at the time. Palmer and Hoover did not know what we know, and the claim that they did and went ahead anyway—because they wanted to smash radicalism, for their own political reasons—is a supposition about their real intentions that is impossible to prove. It is true that the raids and other forms of harassment of radical and Communist opinion exerted a decisive check on the development of a radical left movement in the United States. But these consequences prove nothing about the real intentions of those who were responding to a terrorist threat in 1919. Whatever other political agenda Palmer and Hoover may have had, terrorism was not just a pretext. This threat was genuine, if viewed from the standpoint of the time, and the measures taken look excessive and illiberal only when set against the later discovery that the threat was minimal. Time has judged Palmer harshly, as it may well judge the actions of other attorneys general. But decisions about risk are not made in the safe omniscience of hindsight.

If this is so, it raises doubts about whether risk and reaction are ever likely to be in adequate alignment. All reactions are likely to exaggerate, and as we shall see, the historical evidence from other societies seems to show that few countries have met the terrorist threat without taking measures in haste that they repented at leisure.

This is precisely why the strategies of precommitment, discussed in the previous chapter, and the conservative principle, outlined in chapter 1, are so important. In any situation of factual uncertainty about risk, we need to discipline our justified fears with commitments to respect equality and dignity standards and to make the fewest possible changes to our tried and tested standards of due process. We also need to learn from history. These standards may be tried and tested, but they have also been bent and twisted in emergencies past, and we need to reflect honestly on the price we have paid for unnecessary and unwise civil liberties restrictions in the past. If the Palmer Raids proved that indiscriminate roundups of aliens are unlikely to reduce a terrorist threat, then this lesson ought to have been applied to the roundups after September 11, which predictably yielded the same result.

One reason why we balance threat and response poorly is that the political costs of underreaction are always going to be higher than the costs of overreaction. Political leaders who fail to take adequate precautions after an initial attack will pay heavily after a second one, while those who pile on additional measures and still fail to deter the next attack may be able to survive by claiming that they did the best they could. Since no one can know in advance what strategy is best calibrated to deter an attack, the political leader who hits hard—with security roundups and preventive detentions—is making a safer bet, in relation to his own political future, than one who adopts the precautionary strategy of "first do no harm."

But there are other reasons why democracies overreact to terrorist threats. Democratic societies trust citizens as well as noncitizens with a great deal of freedom. Sleeper cells, like the ones that carried out the September 11 attacks, exploited the freedoms of American life and abused the trust of the country's citizens in order to pass undetected. Once the attacks took place, citizens felt that their trust had been abused and they rued their trust as a form of credulity. The institutional freedoms that underpin this trust—relatively open borders, relatively low levels of domestic police surveillance—were then reconceived as a foolish indulgence, permissible in times of peace but unsuited to a time of war. The welcoming face that societies built upon immigration turn toward aliens in times of prosperity and peace can be replaced, in the twinkling of an eye, with a hostile countenance and a feeling of trust betrayed. Abridging the civil liberties of the innocent majority of aliens capitalizes on anger at the perfidy of the tiny minority responsible for the attacks.

Doing so is relatively easy, moreover, because a majority of citizens is unlikely to bear any of the direct costs of abridgment, and also because only small numbers of citizens put an independent ethical value on the commitment to dignity that these rights represent. Civil libertarians make the way a society handles terror a test of its identity, while most citizens are interested simply in stopping terror in its tracks. Hence a majority of citizens is likely to believe that risk trumps rights, while only a civil libertarian minority is ever likely to believe that rights should trump risks.

When civil libertarians try to explain why their own governments adopt repressive measures, they often blame unscrupulous politicians exploiting terrorism to pursue their own agendas. This fails to explain why these politicians customarily get away with it.[6] Almost all liberal democracies have used September 11 to substantively expand the coercive powers of the criminal law and the police. What needs explaining is not that political figures exploit emergencies to suit their own ends, since they always will, but why they can usually count on substantial public support.[7] Unless we assume that the public are dupes, we need to consider the possibility that strong measures, harmful to civil liberties, actually appeal to majority opinion.

Public support, of course, doesn't make this position right, and the civil libertarian case against it is strong. Rights matter not just because they express ethical values, but also because respecting these values helps to guard against foolish excesses. The civil libertarian case is not merely that these rights abridgments are unjust, they are unnecessary too. A more devoted concern to avoid injustice might also avoid measures that turn out to be unnecessary.

Terrorism harms democracy, civil libertarians rightly argue, primarily by making a majority of citizens believe that their liberties are a source of weakness rather than strength. Preventing this damage in the future requires recommitting to the value of liberties both as guarantors of justice and as bulwarks against panic, anger, and misperception in public policy.

Historically, liberal democracies, faced with terrorist emergencies, have damaged themselves in two different ways, first by limiting political freedoms and second by limiting private rights. Democracies in Latin America have suspended elections, substituted rule by decree for rule by law, replaced democratically elected governments with military juntas, and suspended rights of assembly and free speech. Other democracies have banned political parties associated with armed struggle or terrorist campaigns. But a war against terror can also do permanent damage to private rights. Arbitrary search and seizure, detention without trial, confiscation of property, violations of privacy, expulsion of lawful aliens: all these may be part of the price a democracy pays to stamp out a terrorist cell in its midst.

The impact of a war on terror on political rights needs to be distinguished from the impact on private rights, since democracy might succeed in keeping its political system functioning while failing to preserve the full range of private rights.[8] No abridgments of democratic rights in the United States have followed September 11, and none appear to be in prospect. This is in marked contrast to World War I when, as we have just seen, the Espionage and Sedition Acts were used to convict elected politicians for the exercise of free speech, to deny them seats in Congress, and to convict other persons who opposed U.S. participation in the war. If this is a sign that constitutional protections of political utterance and free speech have grown stronger since World War I and now impose more stringent limits on government action in times of emergency, it would be a welcome development. Thus far, in the war on terror, the rights that guarantee the political system remain untouched, but there has been a price. While the free speech and political rights of American citizens remain unaffected, the rights of aliens, enemy combatants, and other terrorist suspects have been abridged.

The same trade-off is evident in other countries. The British government has kept the democratic system functioning in Northern Ireland, but only through abridgments of private rights such as internment and suspension of jury trial and of the right to keep silent during police questioning. In response to September 11, the British government has left democratic and free speech rights for the majority unaltered, while subjecting aliens to investigative detention and deportation.

This tacit trade-off—to maintain majority rights while restraining minority rights—has proven to be successful politically, since it has muted any criticism of the costs of the measures undertaken since September 11. But success has come at a price. The fact that the rights of the majority have not been harmed and democracy itself has continued to function through recent terrorist emergencies like September 11 does not mean that these emergencies do not do long-term institutional harm. Terrorism is one of the pressures that have led to more secretive government, more police powers, and increasing executive authority at the expense of the other branches of government. Terrorism is liberal democracy's nemesis, beleaguering it and deforming it even when terrorism goes down to defeat. In all these respects, it is the response to terrorism, rather than terrorism itself, that does democracy most harm.

These harms, it should be understood, are exactly what a certain kind of terrorism intends. The French have an excellent phrase—*la politique du pire*, literally the politics of the worst—that encapsulates the logic of terrorism. Its purpose is to make things worse so that they cannot become better. The first theoreticians of this strategy were the Marxist revolutionaries of the nineteenth century. Marxists always understood that where mass popular support for revolution was lacking, the pace of change could be accelerated by acts of indiscriminate violence designed to provoke the constitutional system to "throw off the mask of bourgeois legality" and reveal itself to the peasants and workers as a system of organized violence.

Marxist revolutionary theories of terrorism may now have little direct relevance, but the theoreticians of Al Qaeda have certainly thought deeply about *la politique du pire*.[9] They believe that by provoking the United States and its Arab allies into indiscriminate acts of oppression, they will turn them, as it were, into recruiting sergeants for their cause. They have understood that the impact of terrorism is dialectical. Success depends less on the initial attack than on instigating an escalatory spiral, controlled not by the forces of order but by the terrorists themselves. If terrorists can successfully draw democracies into this spiral and control its upward acceleration, they will begin to dictate the terms of the encounter. Success becomes a matter of inflicting losses, enduring harms, and gambling that the enemy has less endurance than they do. Since a state will always be too strong for a cell of individuals to defeat in open battle, it must defeat itself. If terrorists can provoke the state into atrocity, this will begin to erode the willingness of a democratic public to continue the fight. Democracies may have the stomach for the occasional atrocity, but over the long term a policy of atrocity is unsustainable. It is important for liberal democracies not to succumb to this provocation, not to allow attacks to become the pretext for abandoning law altogether. A civil libertarian case for restraint starts from foundational commitments to rights and then goes on to argue that restraint is the best political strategy to avoid playing into the terrorists' game. If a battle against terrorism is political, the best way to win is to remain on the higher ground. In a war on terror the only enemy that can defeat a democracy is itself.

Remaining on the higher ground depends on thinking clearly about risk. Sane public policy needs historical context: a clear sense of what the record tells us about the ability of liberal democracies to confront terror without jeopardizing their constitutions. The history matters. If there is no evidence that liberal democracy can be brought to its knees by a terrorist challenge, then we have additional reason to adhere to conservative principles and dignity and equality standards.

Of course history is not always a reliable guide, because the future may hold types of risk that have no historical precedent. If future terrorists were to acquire chemical, biological, or nuclear weapons, as well as the capacity to miniaturize, conceal, and transport them, many of the lessons of the past might cease to apply. This challenge has to be faced, and in chapter 6, "Liberty and Armageddon," I deal specifically with it. At least for now, the terrorism we face uses conventional weaponry, available for over a hundred years. At least for now, therefore, history remains a reliable guide.

II

The first society to face a sustained campaign of terror, designed to bring it to its knees, was czarist Russia.[10] Its example is instructive because it was a reforming autocracy, struggling to adapt a medieval political system to the demands of a modern economy and a multinational empire. Russian nihilists, as terrorists were then called, were the first to create the theory that animates insurrectionary terrorism to this day: using atrocities to provoke regimes into repression that will weaken their grip on citizens' allegiance and cause the discontented to embrace the terrorists as their spokesmen.[11] The tactic evolved out of disillusion with the alternative: going to the people and creating a popular political base for revolutionary change. When this failed, when the peasants and workers rejected revolution, some revolutionaries turned to terror. They struck against the regime not because it was immobilized in feudal reaction, but because it was reforming itself. The nihilists feared that reform would broaden the regime's base of support and make revolutionary change less popular. With this aim in view, the Russian nihilists succeeded in 1881 in assassinating Alexander II, the very czar who had freed the serfs in 1861, because destroying him was regarded as essential to dislodge the loyalty of peasants and workers. In killing a reformer rather than a reactionary, the nihilists sought to destroy faith in the possibility of peaceful political change.[12]

The assassination of Alexander did provoke repressive legislation against legitimate political expression and a tightening of penal legislation against the Jews, who were blamed for their role in the revolutionary upsurge. From then onward Marxist revolutionaries used terrorist attacks to push the regime from reform to reaction. After 1905, when Czar Nicholas II reluctantly conceded the election of Russia's first legislative assembly, the

Duma, terrorists tried to provoke the regime into undoing these reluctant reforms. The twilight years of the autocracy witnessed a race among reformers seeking to anchor the regime in constitutional liberty, terrorist revolutionaries seeking to provoke reaction, and reactionaries foolishly obliging. Prime Minister Stolypin's land reforms—an effort to create a capitalist peasant class in the countryside—were the high-water mark of reformist hopes. When Stolypin was assassinated in 1911, the regime lost its last chance to renew itself from within.[13]

Terrorism did enormous harm to the Russian ancien régime. It split the ruling class between reformers and reactionaries. It dug an ever deeper gulf between the state and the society. "The almost complete failure of the educated classes to support the government," as one report lamented, further isolated the czar from his elite.[14] Terrorism did harm to all progressive causes, from unionization of workers to the creation of the zemstvo (the rural council system), by making it easier for a reactionary government to associate such causes with subversion.[15] The insurrectionaries and terrorists did succeed in provoking it into ever more foolish measures of counterreaction, like Bloody Sunday in 1905, when troops fired on unarmed workers and peasants, killing several hundred in Winter Palace Square.

The Russian example teaches an obvious lesson for contemporary societies struggling with terror. Terrorists did succeed in gaining control of the czarist authorities' cycle of reaction and counterreaction, and constitutional monarchists and liberals were never able to gain and hold the political initiative. Contemporary ancien régimes, like Pakistan, Egypt, and Saudi Arabia, should take note: unless liberalization and reform get ahead of the terrorists, political momentum shifts back to the fatal dialectic between terrorist violence and government reaction, with the government risking loss of its remaining hold on its people.

None of this changes the fact that terror itself did not bring down the czarist regime. Despite all its institutional backwardness, Russian society underwent explosive economic, technical, and cultural growth until 1914. It was World War I and the institutional and military collapse that it engendered which caused the regime to fail, not terrorism. In the words of Theda Skocpol, "the revolutionary crises developed when the old regime states became unable to meet the challenges of evolving international situations."[16] Only then do regimes become truly vulnerable to terrorist threats.

III

A second example of a regime facing political violence and terrorism would be Weimar Germany.[17] Between 1918 and 1924, the fledgling democratic republic was assailed by putschs and uprisings from Rosa Luxemburg's Spartacists on the left to Adolf Hitler's fascists on the right. Even though Rosa Luxemburg was killed by rightist thugs in 1919 and Hitler's Beer Hall Putsch failed, the young republic barely survived.[18] Democratic politicians like Walter Rathenau met their death at the hands of assassins, and between 1919 and 1922 there were no fewer than 376 political murders.[19] Yet neither Communist nor fascist extremism prevailed in the 1920s, and the Weimar government was able to retain the loyalty of the police and army and go on to consolidate constitutional rule. Indeed from 1924 to 1929, under Gustav Stresemann, support declined for both the Nazis and the Communists, while attachment to constitutional democracy grew and the economy revived.

This is not to deny that the Weimar constitution suffered from weaknesses. It was both too democratic—allowing fringe parties with no commitment to constitutionalism—and too authoritarian. Article 48 of the constitution vested the president with dictatorial powers to repel terrorist political violence. By granting its president so much power, the constitution enabled an unscrupulous leader like Hitler to maneuver into a dictatorship by constitutional means. Yet without these executive powers Weimar would never have survived as long as it did. Stresemann used presidential decree to bring German hyperinflation under control, and his success paved the way for the political stability of the late 1920s. A more serious defect of the Weimar constitution was that it allowed political participation by parties, like the

Nazis, that made no secret of their desire to establish a dictatorship. Beyond the weaknesses in the constitution, as Richard J. Evans has shown, the civil service, the judiciary, and the army were all holdovers from the Wilhelmine regime and few gave the new regime their wholehearted support.[20]

By 1930, as Hitler began his rise to power, the Weimar state had lost both the will and the capability to challenge Nazi Brownshirts in the streets. Here the essential problem was not democratic constitutionalism itself, but rather the isolation and disunity of those charged with its defense. Faced with fascism on the right and totalitarianism on the left, the defenders of liberal constitutionalism splintered and collapsed. The Weimar example suggests that liberal democracy runs the greatest danger of digging its own grave when it faces a simultaneous extraconstitutional challenge from the extreme Left and the extreme Right. This leaves liberals in the middle isolated and exposed, unable to sustain the unity necessary to take firm measures against violence at both extremes.

Yet it would be a mistake to blame Hitler's rise to power exclusively on the weakness of German democracy or the irresolution of its defending elite. Without the world economic crisis of 1929 and its catastrophic effect on German political stability, it is unlikely that Hitler would have come to power, since his base of popular support eroded steadily before the Depression. Weimar tells us, just as czarist Russia did, that political terror is unlikely to crack a regime unless economic crisis simultaneously causes its material pillars to crumble.

IV

A third case of the impact of terrorism on constitutional regimes would be in twentieth-century Latin America.[21] In Argentina during the 1970s, Marxist terrorism succeeded in provoking the ruling elite into indiscriminate repression, which hastened the imposition of military dictatorship. Here, too, the persistent weakness of the Argentinian economy played a key part in weakening support for constitutional regimes. The military used the pretext of economic crisis and terrorist insurrection to institute a reign of terror in Argentina, based on torture and disappearances. Democratic rule was restored only in the 1980s when an ill-fated military adventure in the Falklands, growing resentment at illegal methods, and the failure of the military to solve the country's economic problems brought about the junta's downfall. The Argentinian case is indeed a case of terrorism as *la politique du pire*, but history did not unfold as the terrorists intended. They sought to make everything worse so that nothing could become better, but instead of bringing about a revolutionary transformation, they managed only to play into the hands of the military, with disastrous consequences for themselves and for Argentinian society.

A similar dynamic unfolded in Peru. A Marxist group, Sendero Luminoso (the Shining Path), killed villagers and government sympathizers to demonstrate that the government did not control the countryside, and to intimidate the populace into support for revolution. The tactic cost thousands of lives, but the strategy did not succeed. Instead, terrorism provided a democratically elected president, Alberto Fujimori, with the pretext to exploit a successful antiterror campaign and turn it into a mandate for an authoritarian type of rule.[22]

In Colombia, too, the insurrectionary group FARC has used terror to hold portions of the countryside, while the government licenses the counterterror of paramilitaries, all the while denying that it does so in order to hold its own territory.[23] Terrorism has neither brought the Colombian state down nor ushered in the revolution in the countryside under FARC control. All that it has achieved is enduring damage to the structure of constitutional politics, first by licensing authoritarian leadership and ruthless counterterror, and second by turning terrorist emergency into a permanent system of constitutional order.

Summing up at this point—*la politique du pire* often succeeds as a tactic, provoking regimes into unconstitutional measures, yet it has never succeeded as a strategy, bringing terrorists to power. More often than not, the result is strategic stalemate: terrorists and constitutional states locked in a struggle neither can win outright.

Where terror has succeeded, it has been as an ancillary tactic in a more general political strategy aimed at the revolutionary seizure of power. Lenin's Bolshevik putsch in 1917 and Hitler's accession to the chancellorship in 1933 represented a triumph for a decade of insurrectionary and antiparliamentary violence and terrorism, but even in this case, terrorist methods worked only where the constitutional state had already been weakened by other factors, such as major military defeat or economic crisis.

When such terrorist methods are used to win power, they become a staple of regular rule. Hitler's purge in 1934, during the Night of the Long Knives, represented the continuation of terrorism, now turned against the Nazi party leadership itself. Lenin's elimination of his Socialist Revolutionary rivals in 1918, after a failed attempt on his life, would be a second example of the institutionalization of terror. Regimes that use terror to win control of a state tend to hold power by the same method.

If we turn to South Asia and examine Sri Lanka, we find further evidence that terrorism may work as a tactic, while failing as a strategy. For twenty years, the Tamil Tigers used suicide bombings to crack the will of the Sinhalese majority government in Colombo and force it to concede a separate Tamil state. Moderate Tamils willing to negotiate with the government were a particular object of attack. These attacks were intended to coerce the Tamil minority into obeying the terrorist group, and to prevent the emergence of a negotiated settlement built around devolution. Yet the result was only a bloody stalemate. Tamil terrorism failed to break the Sinhalese leadership's will to resist. To be sure, terrorism inflicted a terrible price on Sri Lankan society: sixty thousand deaths, hundreds of thousands of people internally displaced, and economic paralysis in what should have been one of the most competitive economies of Asia. Yet terrorism did not succeed in its primary aim, which was to divide the island in two.[24]

Terrorism is the politics of the shortcut, a resort to force when peaceful means of political mobilization offer only a protracted and uncertain road to victory. Yet the shortcut rarely achieves its goal. The means tarnish the ends that are sought, and when directed at a robust and democratic opponent, they rarely succeed.

The Israeli-Palestinian conflict offers final confirmation of this. Suicide bombing purports to be a politics of desperation, undertaken only because peaceful negotiation with Israelis is hopeless. In reality, it is a politics of the shortcut, seeking to make peaceful dialogue on a two-state solution impossible. Its further purpose is to demoralize Israeli society to the point that it concedes defeat. Yet two years of attacks have not forced Israel into capitulation or appeasement or undone its democratic fabric.[25] Ordinary citizens in the military reserves, even those with profound doubts about the occupation, have done their constitutional duty to bear arms.[26] With the exception of some Arab Israeli politicians now in detention, most Arab Israelis, although profoundly opposed to Israeli policies and increasingly alienated by their second-class status, continue to give their allegiance to the Israeli state. Among the majority of the Israeli population, there is both a national consensus opposing negotiation with terrorists and an unstanched national debate as to how to reconcile security and survival. The secret services and the Israeli Defense Forces wage a relentless and brutal campaign against Hamas and Fatah terrorists. House demolitions, targeted assassinations, and the construction of a security wall that expropriates Palestinian land have all aroused incessant controversy, both inside and outside Israel. Inside the country, however, the campaign remains under democratic authorization and judicial review. Generals publicly question its effectiveness, pilots express moral and tactical qualms about certain operations, columnists insist these operations make Israel less, not more, secure, and so on, yet through it all Israeli democracy is surviving the ordeal. Terrorism has done terrible damage: grinding the economy down, forcing a society to divert resources to security and defense that should be spent on hospitals, roads, and schools, and strengthening the secret security and military elements of the society. Yet it has neither caused Israel to capitulate nor tipped its political system from democratic to authoritarian rule. National elections have been held, in the middle of the sustained emergency, and there have been peaceful changes of government.

V

A different story—but the same pattern of failure—is evident in terrorist attempts to destroy the political system of Western liberal democracies—Italy, Germany, Spain, and the United Kingdom.

During the 1970s in Italy and Germany, terrorists mounted a full-scale assault on liberal democracy, seeking to forestall the peaceful incorporation of Communist and socialist radicalism into normal parliamentary politics.[27] In Italy, the Communist Party was slowly making its way toward Eurocommunism and full participation in the democratic system. In Germany, post-1968 hopes of radical change had given way to the incorporation of German social democracy into the corporatist bargain struck between capital and labor. A tiny Marxist vanguard set out to sabotage the emergence of social democratic centrism and to force the coercive apparatus of the liberal democratic state to "throw off its mask of bourgeois legality" and engage in extra-legal repression.[28] In this sense, the Baader Meinhof gang were throwbacks to the nineteenth-century nihilists, but they brought to the "propaganda of the deed" a modern media sensibility, assuming—wrongly, it turned out—that terrorist spectaculars like the kidnapping and murder of a prominent German industrialist would succeed in mobilizing the marginalized and discontented where standard, nonviolent forms of political organizing had failed.

This strategy did not succeed. The terrorists who had hoped that ensuing violence would attract workers, intellectuals, and students into the streets to challenge liberal democracy ended up dead or recanting in prison. German and Italian democracy survived, and the terrorists are remembered not as martyrs but as criminals. More broadly, the decisive defeat of insurrectionary Marxism, plus the final defeat of Soviet Communism after 1989, ensured that the radical and Communist Left in Italy and Germany finally accepted that they belonged within peaceful parliamentary politics.

Both Germany and Italy developed effective antiterrorist teams and used amnesty legislation that offered immunity from prosecution to infiltrate and break up terrorist cells.[29] Yet while both had reason to congratulate themselves on the survival of their democracy, they had less reason to be complacent about what terrorism did to civil liberties and private rights. Both countries did expand the detention and search-and-seizure powers of the police. The harsh treatment of the German revolutionary detainees in prison, ending with their suicides, left many Germans who were otherwise not sympathetic to their goals convinced that the government had overstepped its bounds. The German example shows that democracies can defeat terror, but always at a price to their commitments to dignity and respect for rights.

While the Italians and Germans defeated insurrectionary Marxism, Britain and Spain have shown, over the same period, how to turn back terrorism in the name of a minority self-determination claim.[30] Basque terror did not arise because a peaceful avenue to promote constitutional change was denied, but because one was opened up. The bombing campaign actually accelerated as Spain left the Franco dictatorship and entered the era of constitutional democracy.[31] In the Basque country, terrorism was a strategy to forestall peaceful constitutional reform. The terrorists sought to intimidate the Basque electorate so that they would be forced to seek outright independence outside the Spanish constitutional regime. It was this challenge that Spanish democrats sought to defeat from the late 1970s onward. They have not eliminated the threat, but they have fought it to a standstill with military and police counterterror, combined with a package of devolutionary reforms and infusions of cash to win the hearts and minds of the law-abiding majority. The Basque region remains unstable, however, with covert intimidation of

Basques who refuse to support independence and continued government bans on separatist parties and their newspapers. This suggests that final victory in wars on terror is not always possible. While the threat of domestic terrorism in Germany and Italy seems to have been beaten back, in the Basque country it remains permanent.

The British in Northern Ireland faced a similar challenge from a small terrorist minority using violence to drive a nationalist community away from peaceful constitutional politics toward insurrection. Apart from Bloody Sunday, when British forces did kill innocent civilians engaged in peaceful protest, and apart from the detention without trial of nationalist sympathizers and terrorist suspects, the British managed to keep their antiterrorist campaign within the bounds of constitutional propriety. When terrorists intimidated juries, the British set up special courts where criminal trials were conducted in front of a judge. When nationalists argued that the British military presence amounted to an occupation, the British insisted that the troops were there merely "in aid of the civil power." This determination to preserve constitutional normality proved crucial to keeping political control of the province. Without careful control of military and police power, the British might well have lost the battle for moderate nationalist opinion in Ulster.[32] While the British have preserved their hold on the minds of a majority of both unionist and nationalist opinion in Ulster, it is important not to overstate this success or to assume it can continue forever. Nor are the security forces always under effective control. Recent judicial inquiries have confirmed that the Royal Ulster Constabulary, the chief security force in the province, colluded with Protestant paramilitary groups and had active knowledge of paramilitary murders of nationalist politicians and lawyers in the 1980s.[33] Maintaining effective political control, at all times, of police undercover activity is crucial to maintaining the political legitimacy of an antiterrorist campaign, and this has not proven easy.

Both the Spanish and the British have managed—just—to maintain nonviolent democratic politics in the two troubled regions, but the democratic process remains vulnerable to the threat of political violence by armed nationalist groups. Recently, the Spanish government moved to outlaw the Basque political party that functions as the political wing of the major Basque terrorist group.[34] Great Britain has suspended local self-rule in Northern Ireland because of its suspicions that the political wing of the IRA might have passed security-sensitive information to terrorists.[35]

Summing up so far, we can conclude that terrorism has damaged liberal democracies, but it has never succeeded in breaking their political systems. Liberal states turn out to be much less weak than they perceive themselves to be; indeed, their chief weakness is to underestimate their strengths.

VI

One further assumption of the terrorists has proven wrong: that democratic peoples lack the will to fight for democracy. It is a commonplace, of both Burkean conservatives and left-wing communitarians, to bemoan the dearth of civic spirit, the ennui and disenchantment, of elites and electorates alike in capitalist democracies.[36] These democracies, it is said, lack a common goal or a unifying civic purpose. Terrorist emergencies have shown, on the contrary, that democratic elites and publics alike can show a surprising tenacity when attacked. Even in Italy, with relatively weak coalition governments and a bureaucracy not known for its efficiency, the police and military forces proved energetic in fighting Red Brigade terrorism in the 1970s. Judges and juries did not hesitate to convict. The public strongly supported the defense of constitutional liberty.[37] Theorists who suppose that liberal democracy is enfeebled by capitalist individualism, incapable of mobilizing the civic will to stand together, should look at terrorist emergencies and think again. To take but one example, which I witnessed myself, in 1988 after a Basque group bombed a supermarket in Barcelona, killing several innocent shoppers, a huge demonstration took place in the streets, involving hundreds of thousands of citizens, trade unions, and professional organizations, all carrying their banners dipped to the ground, marching in perfect silence, to express their solidarity and their disgust. Such collective actions have a real political impact, cutting the ground from under the feet of those fellow travelers who are apt to say that they support the goals of terrorists but not their means. Here was an occasion where citizens en masse seemed to be saying, by their very silence, that some means irretrievably tarnish the goals themselves.

The American response to the catastrophe of September 11, 2001, fits into the same pattern. The courage of the police and firefighters who went up into the burning World Trade Center to help their fellow citizens revealed the true extent of the solidarity that democracies can call upon when attacked. This example inspired candlelight vigils, a flood of applications for public service work, and a host of other forms of civic activism and engagement. We had forgotten that democracies are also communities of sacrifice. September 11 proved that this capacity for sacrifice—as well as civic courage, ingenuity, and defiance—was as strong as ever.

We do not know exactly what image of liberal democracy Al Qaeda leaders have in their minds, but we can be reasonably certain that it includes an idea of decadence, a belief that Westerners are unable to match their technological superiority with a will to fight when attacked. This has surely been proven wrong. Certain virtues—specifically the capacity to improvise, to lead from the bottom, as in the heroic conduct of the passengers of American Flight 93—do seem to grow in democratic soils. They are less likely to be displayed in authoritarian societies. As Elaine Scarry has pointed out, the single most effective act of national defense during the September 11 attack was carried out, not by the armed forces, but by the ordinary citizens who rushed the cockpit of the aircraft heading toward Washington and managed to divert it so that it crashed in a field in Pennsylvania, killing all on board but possibly sparing the White House or the Capitol.[38]

Terrorists thus characteristically underestimate the will of democratic electorates to rally to the defense of their country and its political system. But the very strength of national feeling is not always a friend to the framework of individual rights protection. The same public spirit that rallies to the flag may also support measures to take away the rights of aliens and fellow citizens suspected of offenses. Politicians will wrap themselves in the mantle of national tragedy to justify coercive measures. In this way, the public-spiritedness that is the lifeblood of a democracy can become a menace to its liberty. A terrorist attack may stimulate civic sacrifice and chauvinism in almost equal measure.[39] As I have been arguing throughout, terrorist emergencies open up a fissure between democracy defined as majority rule and democracy defined as minority rights. When a national community is attacked, it naturally favors majority interests over minority rights, and its response to threat draws on everything—shared memory and common symbols as well as constitutional traditions that assert these majority interests. Scholars have distinguished between the "civic" and "ethnic" elements of national identity, between pride in constitutional rights and pride in culture, language, history, and common ethnic or racial feeling.[40] September 11 showed how deeply fused these elements become when a nation is attacked.

How the resulting patriotism influences a war on terror depends critically on the use made of it by political leaders, and the uses they can make of it depend on how the national community is defined. What has prevented leaders from turning the majority against ethnic or religious minorities in our midst is that the definition of the American national community—and of most liberal democracies—has become steadily more inclusive. This imposes practical political limits on the stigmatization of groups in times of crisis. In 1919 and again in 1942, American leaders were able to get away with discriminatory measures against aliens and immigrants, but also against bona fide citizens—the Japanese Americans, for example—because the national community under attack could be defined in such a way as to exclude them.[41] Nowadays this is more difficult. Mass migration has changed the rules of political appeal, and a political leader cannot easily focus paranoia and fear upon immigrants, aliens, or recently minted citizens. In the case of citizens or aliens of Islamic origin, a further crucial factor is their growing political influence at home and their membership in an immensely powerful global religion. Anyone tempted to turn a war on terrorism into an anti-Islamic crusade has to reckon with the political consequences of taking on a global community of more than a billion believers. As a result, with some exceptions, political leaders after September 11 have taken care to avoid anti-Islamic slurs and to dwell on common allegiance to constitutional and national values, irrespective of origins. Whether or not the messages of civic and political inclusiveness voiced by presidents and prime ministers are sincerely intended, it must be true that none of them has any interest in turning a war on terror into a war between religions. This is not to deny that there have been abuses and miscarriages of justice. Hundreds of illegal aliens, mostly of Islamic or Arabic origin, have been targeted for detention and deportation, and while these measures were as unjust as they were unnecessary, they were less severe than the measures taken in 1919 and 1942. This is not a matter for congratulation or an invitation to complacency, but an indication that the parameters of permissible injustice are not what they were.

VII

Even if a case can be made that the pluralism of modern societies makes it more difficult to stigmatize Arab and Islamic groups than it was to stigmatize Italian and Slavic anarchists after 1919 and Japanese Americans after 1942, a war on terror can still do serious harm to democracy. Most antiterrorist campaigns require the creation of secret, highly trained units, either in the police or in the armed forces, whose function is to handle hijackings and hostage takings, and to take the war to the enemy, with targeted assassinations, roundups, and arrests. A central political challenge in a war on terror is to keep such units under control.

In the Basque terror campaign, the Spanish police were recurrently targeted. Stung by their losses, infuriated by what they perceived to be insufficiently robust support from the politicians, the Spanish police created an elite assassination squad, the GAL, which then eliminated a number of Basque activists and operatives in hiding in France. These illegal actions received the tacit support of the minister of the interior. The assassinations did not stop Basque terrorism: they served only to call into question in the eyes of Basque people the competence and honesty of the democratic government of Spain. Fortunately, the extent of the dirty war was brought to light by the Spanish press and investigating magistrates, and some of the guilty politicians and police operatives were jailed.[42]

Democracies should have nothing to do with licensed hit squads. The British sent an army antiterrorist squad to Gibraltar to arrest an active service unit of the IRA. Because the squad and the local police failed to cooperate fully, the operation was botched and the squad executed the three IRA operatives in a public street. The resulting scandal—Death on the Rock—alienated Irish republican opinion and earned the British condemnation at the European Court of Human Rights.[43] More recently, a British inquiry found that security forces colluded with Protestant paramilitaries to execute a prominent nationalist politician. These examples show how difficult it is to keep counterterror forces from taking the law into their own hands. What loosens accountability is a malign confluence of anger and fear in the public at large, which sends the message to the political elites and their secret agencies that anything is permitted as long as it gets results, and an increasingly unconstrained executive branch, which—because it no longer fears effective scrutiny and control from the legislature or the courts—believes it can get away with taking the gloves off.

The Italian, British, and German experience shows that improving the command and control of counterterrorist operations is more effective than giving these units more search-and-seizure and arrest powers or further abridging the liberties of citizens. The crucial instruments of an effective counterterror operation are elite units that combine intelligence capability and strike capacity and are unified under one command and made as accountable to courts and legislatures as is consistent with operational efficiency.

Loyalty oaths for government employees or bans on trade union organization in the security services are often advanced as necessary to prevent infiltration by terrorists. The German experience of the *Berufsverbot*, banning radicals from public service employment, turned out to be counterproductive, violating both academic and political freedom and needlessly alienating groups who, while critical of German democracy, were in no sense its enemies. Analogous measures to ban trade union membership and activity in the U.S. Department of Homeland Security have been defended on grounds of operational efficiency, but they seem calculated to violate the rights such an organization exists to defend.[44] Loyalty oaths and restriction on trade union rights, moreover, seem unnecessary if scrupulous background checks are a part of recruitment to government service, provided that the data used for these checks is publicly available through the Freedom of Information Act.

Identity cards, and identity systems using biometric identifiers, are rapidly becoming mandatory for citizens in liberal democracies, and while civil libertarians have objected, it seems inevitable that their use will spread.[45] The United Kingdom has recently announced that it will gradually introduce a national identity card system making use of the latest biometric technology. Carrying these cards will become mandatory, first for all registered aliens, and then for all citizens.[46] The public interest grounds for such measures are clear. Law-abiding citizens want foolproof ways to ensure that their bona fides are accepted at security points.[47] They will want such systems because more accurate identification allows authorities to target searches more accurately. Greater accuracy enhances liberty because it reduces the likelihood of detention based on mistaken identity.

The problems with identity cards are serious, however. Any centralized data collection system is open to penetration by terrorists themselves, and to abuse by overzealous government departments. The critical challenge appears to be to set up digital fire walls between discrete sets of data, so that access is limited to those who have legal authority to view them. The major administrative problem is to guarantee the security, integrity, and inviolability of national identity registers. Already, however, it is possible to keep data systems clearly demarcated. Credit card companies should not have access to criminal record data or driver's license data banks and so on. Governments should have strictly limited access to the credit and banking records of citizens. While U.S. civil liberties groups object to national identity card schemes on the grounds that they violate privacy rights and authorize government intrusion, there does seem to be a lesser evil justification for a regulated form of national scheme. The right way to think about these problems is not to object to an identity card system in principle, but to devise legislation which restricts the kinds of data that can be retrieved through a national identity card, and to ensure that it can be accessed exclusively by law enforcement officials. A court with jurisdiction over national data registers could evaluate requests for information as well as complaints of privacy and rights violation. As things already stand, most citizens know that their personal data is available to a host of prying eyes, from the spammers who follow the trail of their Internet transactions to the credit agencies that deny them credit. The problem is that all of these systems appear unregulated or unlicensed by public authority. A national identity card system might provide the legislative point of entry for a regulation of all digital data banks and the creation of a framework of redress for privacy violation.

These measures are not necessarily harmful to the liberty of citizens. Nor is it unreasonable, if terrorism crosses national boundaries, to allow domestic crime fighting agencies to cooperate with international intelligence agencies. It may also be justified to allow antiterrorist squads the same powers of wiretapping and electronic surveillance the police already employ in the war against drugs and organized crimes. But these increases in police power have been hastily enacted, in the U.S. Patriot Act and Canada's Bill C-36, for example, and they do not appear to keep search-and-seizure, arrest, and surveillance powers under sufficiently close judicial control.[48]

If terrorism has never succeeded in breaking apart a liberal democracy, then it is not obvious that these measures can be justified on grounds of necessity alone. But this does not end the matter, for as I said at the outset, it is an illusion to suppose that legislative response will ever be in a fully adequate relation to the size of a terrorist risk. "Better safe than sorry" is likely to drive most reactions to threats, whether real or imaginary. The best that can be hoped for is that if more laws are passed than are needed, civil liberties groups and public interest lobbies will see to it that legislatures are put under sustained pressure to rescind unnecessary legislation as soon as it is seen to be so. If we cannot preempt exaggeration, we can at least correct it afterward. For the historical record shows that while no democracy has ever been brought down by terror, all democracies have been damaged by it, chiefly by their own overreactions. The slow accretion of unnecessary powers on the statute books is one way that the damage done by terrorist attacks endures long after the danger has passed. Pruning the laws of unnecessary power is one way, even if after the fact, to undo the damage that terrorism has done to the balance between liberty and order in democratic societies.

When terrorists strike against constitutional democracies, one of their intentions is to persuade electorates and elites that the strengths of these societies—public debate, mutual trust, open borders, and constitutional restraints on executive power—are weaknesses.[49] When strengths are seen as weaknesses, it is easy to abandon them. If this is the logic of terror, then democratic societies must find a way to continue to see their apparent vulnerabilities as a form of strength. This does not require anything special. It simply means that those who have charge of democratic institutions need to do their jobs. We need judges who understand that national security is not a carte blanche for the abrogation of individual rights; a free press that ferrets out the information an executive may wish to alter or withhold in pursuit of national security; a legislature that will not allow national security to prevent it from fulfilling its function of checking executive power. If a system of constitutional checks and balances continues to function effectively, that is, if power continues to be subjected to the test of adversarial justification, there is no reason to fear that a war on terror will lead us to betray the values we are fighting for.

CHAPTER FOUR

THE STRENGTH OF
THE WEAK

Prudence, indeed, will dictate that Governments long established should not be changed for light and transient Causes; and accordingly all Experience hath shewn, that Mankind are more disposed to suffer, while Evils are sufferable, than to right themselves by abolishing the Forms to which they are accustomed. But when a long Train of Abuses and Usurpations, pursuing invariably the same Object, evinces a Design to reduce them under absolute Despotism, it is their Right, it is their Duty, to throw off such Government, and to provide new Guards for their future Security.

—*The Declaration of Independence, 1776*

I

Terrorism is a violent form of politics, and it is because terrorism is political that it is dangerous. Terrorists represent causes and grievances and claim to speak in the name of millions.[1] If terrorism is a form of politics, it needs to be fought with the force of argument and not just with the force of arms. A war on terror that is not guided by a clear political strategy, to win support for democratic government and drain support from terror, is bound to fail. Indeed, it is a mistake to evaluate the effectiveness of military or police actions apart from their political impact. An operation that crushes a cell but alienates an entire population of innocent bystanders is not a success. It is a failure.

It's obvious that the tactics of a war on terror need to be focused by a long-term political strategy. But what strategy exactly? The answer depends on the kind of terrorism a state is facing and the types of demands that terrorists make. In this chapter, I want to distinguish among forms of terrorism, identify the political claims terrorists use to justify violence against civilians, and propose political strategies to defeat them.

Six types of terrorism—each requiring its own political response—need to be identified:

- insurrectionary terrorism aimed at revolutionary overthrow of a state
- loner or issue terrorism, aimed at promotion of a single cause
- liberation terrorism, aimed at the overthrow of a colonial regime
- separatist terrorism, aiming at independence for a subordinate ethnic or religious group within a state
- occupation terrorism, aimed at driving an occupying force from territory acquired through war or conquest
- global terrorism, aimed not at the liberation of a particular group, but at inflicting damage and humiliation on a global power

The previous chapter examined the first type—revolutionary terrorism seeking the overthrow of the state. Liberal democracies have seen off this challenge with a combination of political concessions to excluded groups and relentless counterterror measures. The second type of terrorism—loner terrorism, pursued by a single individual or a small group as a protest over a particular issue—requires a different response. Timothy McVeigh's attack on the federal building in Oklahoma City would fit into this pattern, as would the bombing of abortion clinics by antiabortion campaigners. A subvariety of loner terrorism would be the Aum Shinrikyo attack on the Tokyo subway system, initiated by a small group enthralled by a cult leader.[2]

Anyone wishing to challenge a liberal democracy, but lacking the political support to do so peacefully, is bound to at least consider breaking democracy's taboo against political violence. Thus a person who believes that abortion is murder may feel, in the face of the steady refusal of the American electorate to criminalize abortion, that the firebombing of clinics or the killing of abortion providers is a justified last resort. Since a majority of their fellow citizens cannot be persuaded to follow them, the only remaining choice is to acquiesce in majority rule or engage in terror. Once the taboo is broken, weakness can be turned into strength.

Given the number of minority positions that have no chance of political success in modern states, the risk of political violence, therefore, is never absent from democratic politics, especially if the fringes of its political culture encourage the belief, in the words of Barry Goldwater, that "extremism in the defense of liberty is no vice."[3] Verbal absolutism of this sort is dangerous in any political order, especially one that takes freedom seriously, for some marginal figures are bound to take their freedom of belief and opinion and turn it into an obligation to kill. In his extremism, McVeigh may have been a lone madman, but he also spoke in a deeply American vein—"the paranoid style in American politics"—and actually believed in American liberty, or at least his version of it, with chilling seriousness.[4] Terrorism, therefore, is not merely an external threat to democratic politics but is intrinsic to it.

There are no easy solutions for loner or issue terrorism. Using the law to restrict incendiary, extreme, or hate-filled opinion may encroach on guarantees of free speech. At the same time, hate-filled speech is often a prelude to hate-filled acts. Waiting for the acts may expose innocent parties to serious risk. European and Canadian states prohibit and punish these forms of speech more readily than does the United States.[5] A political strategy on terrorism needs to distinguish between defense of order and defense of values. Those who challenge majority values are not necessarily or even usually a threat to public order. On balance, unless political argument actively incites a group to commit acts of violence, it seems wise, especially in societies with a plurality of competing religious and secular opinions, not to allow public order considerations to override freedom of speech and freedom of religion. Public order grounds, moreover, are often a masquerade for censorship, as when a French general was convicted of incitement to hatred for publishing a book on his experiences in French Algeria that amounted to a justification of torture.[6] Justifying torture in a specific historical context seems altogether different from active incitement. Only when agitators pass from hateful speech to active endorsement of terrorist acts or crimes of hate should they be subjected to the penalties of the law.

Even more important, however, is how public opinion reacts to loner or issue terrorism. The Oklahoma bombing did not win adherents to McVeigh's cause. It had the effect of disgracing the militia movements who fomented it. Where terrorist outrages evoke support or passive complicity, they become dangerous. As Dostoevsky observed in Russia in the 1870s, what was more disturbing than the occasional bomb outrages of isolated nihilist revolutionaries was the almost universal failure of the elites to rally around the czarist regime.[7] The only defense against loner terror is for a society to rally around and convince other potential recruits that it is a cause fit only for loners. This can be done so long as a democratic society succeeds in persuading a majority of its people that peaceful constitutional mechanisms exist for the resolution of grievances and that those who use violence in a democracy are doing so illegitimately.

II

But what are we to say when peaceful constitutional remedies do not exist? Many liberal democratic states have denied such remedies to colonial populations; other democracies have held ethnic groups within their territories against their will; and some have subjected populations to permanent occupation. What I have called liberation, occupation, and separatist types of terrorism have all been directed at the attempt to rule others without their consent: colonial regimes, ethnic majority tyranny, or military occupation. The beginning of wisdom in any political strategy against terror is that democracies should not attempt to rule others against their consent. Doing so puts a democracy on the wrong side of its own core premise: the right of self-determination. This right was first elaborated on the international scene by Woodrow Wilson as the principle to guide the liquidation of the ruined empires of Europe at the Versailles Conference in 1919.[8] It has guided the liberation of colonial peoples ever since.

The entire anticolonial resistance to imperial rule after 1945—
in India, Indonesia, Algeria, and Vietnam—was justified in
terms of democracy. The anticolonial resistance prevailed in part
because the colonial democracies did not have the stomach to
resist democracy itself or the nerve to protect their settler minorities at any cost. In all these struggles, terror directed chiefly at
the settler minority was the tactic of choice because the groups
committed to armed struggle never had sufficient capability to
directly challenge the military forces of the colonial powers. In
the Algerian war of independence, the FLN (Front for National
Liberation) used terror bombings to radicalize the Algerian population and drive it into the arms of the liberation struggle, to
demoralize the French civilian inhabitants, the *pieds noirs*, and
to force the French government to recognize that their military
superiority could not prevail. The FLN terrorists portrayed
themselves as the authentic representatives of the Algerian people, but their resort to terror proved the reverse: that they did
not command, at least at the beginning, sufficient popular support to overcome the colonial authorities by nonviolent means.
Equally, the French colonial authorities portrayed themselves as
the legitimate government of all the Algerian people, French and
Arab alike, but their early resort to state terror proved the reverse: that they could maintain colonial rule only through force
and violence. Terror, by both the insurgents and the state, was a
confession of strategic weakness.[9]

The French were driven to engage in terror "pour encourager
les autres," to control those whom they were no longer able to
persuade. Any political strategy against terror has to draw the
lesson that force is bound to fail as a mechanism of control when
consent has been lost. Worse, force in the absence of consent
tends to get out of hand. When populations resent and hate you,
the temptation to dehumanize them becomes irresistible, and
what begins as coercion can end as terror.

In the end, the French conceded independence, not because
they were militarily defeated, but because the French republic
could no longer sustain the political costs of an indefinite war

for control. De Gaulle saved the French republic from disaster, but at the price of sacrificing the settler minority and their Algerian allies. Ending terrorist threats there required an especially painful choice, between trying to rule a colonial population against their consent and sacrificing the interests of settler minorities, even though they were members of his own political community. By choosing clearly, de Gaulle saved France from the horror of terrorist war.

This same logic of lesser evils applies only too obviously in Israel, where granting the self-determination claims of Palestinians—obviously the right political strategy to reduce terror attacks on Israel—simultaneously requires the Israeli state to forcibly withdraw settlers who believe they have an equal right to the land. Sacrificing the interests of a minority of your own people is justifiable only on the condition that it guarantees an increase in security to the majority. Thus far, an effective political strategy against terror has foundered because Israelis do not believe that the sacrifice of the settler minority will actually gain them enough security for the majority.

Where the self-determination in question is an ethnic claim to secession from the territory of a state, the dominant state must find a way to appease the claim without sacrificing its own sovereignty or territorial integrity. Where a state regards its territory as indivisible, and where the ethnic group claims that the territory they seek is essential to their own survival, violence is inevitable.[10] In Sri Lanka, the Tamil Tigers have resorted to terror, believing that civilian casualties will compel the government to grant secession. In a situation like this, the terrorists cannot prevail against the military, and neither can the military prevail against the terrorists. In this stalemate, only civilians suffer and die. The only way out is a political dialogue, sponsored by outside governments, that results in a compromise: meeting the legitimate claims of Tamils to federal self-rule without sacrificing the unity of the Sri Lankan state, and without exposing the Tamils in the south or the Sinhalese in the north to ethnic cleansing. It is not enough, in other words, to stop terrorist violence.

It is also essential to find a political solution to the security dilemmas of the minorities that are bound to be left behind when each side gets what it wants politically.

In these three cases—Algeria, Israel, Sri Lanka—where terrorism arises as a tactic to end colonial rule, occupation, or a denial of ethnic rights, it is possible to lay out what a political strategy against terror might look like, and to see why such strategies are so difficult. They require politically painful sacrifices of the rights and claims of your own people in order to secure peace with the enemy. But once the political sacrifices are made, terrorism can be ended. The French withdrawal from Algeria ended terrorism. A meaningful form of democratic self-government in Tamil areas might end terrorism in Sri Lanka. Statehood for the Palestinians might end terrorism against Israel, at least for a time.

A democracy's political concessions, however, cannot succeed unless terrorists and the communities who support them are willing to accept the basic legitimacy of the democratic state's right to survival. In the case of Israel, their enemies do not concede this. Hamas, Hezbollah, and other terrorist groups are fighting not for a two-state solution but for a single state in Palestine to be built on the ruins of the Israeli nation.[11] This presents Israel with a dilemma: concessions granted to groups that refuse to accept a state's right to exist will only produce further terror. Ending the occupation of Palestinian lands is the obvious prerequisite for Israeli peace and security, but only if Palestinian groups accept half a loaf as better than none, and as all they will ever have.

Political strategies have a chance of working only when both sides recognize each other politically. The democratic state has to acknowledge that the terrorist group represents a valid claim even though its means are unacceptable, and the terrorists have to accept that half a loaf is an honorable compromise.

The difficulty, however, is that the language of justice and human rights is commonly used as a moral trump, as a game-winning claim to entitlement that denies the rights of those who oppose it. Oppressed groups frequently argue as if the facts of their situation obviated any further negotiation. In fact there is nothing intrinsically just about any self-determination claim. Indeed, one usually competes with another, as the Palestinian claim competes with the Israeli, as nationalist claims compete with unionist ones in Northern Ireland. Instead of providing the grounds for mutual recognition, human rights have often reinforced belief that one's own moral claims are trumps and hence deserve to prevail over the other. Rights talk actually hinders the search for compromise and consensus,[12] when compromise may be the only way to obtain any political objective at all.

Despite the fact that self-determination occupies pride of place as the first right in both major international rights covenants, not all claims to self-determination are valid.[13] In 1965, white Rhodesians declared independence in order to prevent the British from granting independence under majority rule to the black population of Rhodesia. The white claim was unjust because it sought to prevent the majority of the country from running their own affairs. While whites could claim a right to stay in the land of their origins, and to retain their property and full democratic rights, they could not deny the right of the majority to rule themselves. A claim to self-determination is voided, therefore, if it denies another people a claim to freedom too.

By the same reasoning, Israel has a claim—grounded in a history of continuous settlement, in its religious traditions, and in the history of the Holocaust—to a right to statehood on enough land in Palestine to guarantee its people freedom and security from attack. But its claim to that land is conditional on its allowing the Palestinians, who have an equal history of continuous occupation and an equal claim in religious tradition, the same right over enough of the land to guarantee them freedom and security. Lands seized by the Israeli forces in the 1967 war cannot be held in perpetuity, as a part of an Israeli self-determination claim, since they were acquired through conquest and have been held through coercive military occupation. In other words, there is nothing about the Palestinian or the Israeli claim that gives one a moral privilege over the other. Both are equal claims to the same piece of territory, and if any justice is to be done to either, neither can have it all.

Human rights as a language of equality mandates respect and mutual recognition of competing moral claims. If this is so, human rights specify two ethical rules about the way a struggle for self-determination must be waged. The right to life condemns violence, and the equality commitments of human rights enjoin respect for the reasonable self-determination claims of others. The pursuit of self-determination, therefore, is substantially constrained by human rights principles themselves.

Fine counsels, I hear you say, but unlikely to have any purchase in the real world. Telling Palestinians to return to nonviolence and to recognize Israeli rights assumes that the other side is willing to negotiate in good faith. The history of the last fifty years does not encourage such a gamble. The historical record gives both sides reason to believe that violence pays, indeed that violence is the only tactic that pays. Calling on Palestinians to return to the path of deliberative nonviolence might be to condemn them to a Palestine reduced to the size of a Bantustan. Calling on Israelis to grant a self-determination claim backed by terrorism is to ask them to make concessions with no guarantee that their right to exist will finally be conceded.

Moral perfectionism—in this case well-meant condemnations of violence and injunctions to resume negotiation—will often be received as a strategy to keep the weak in submission and confirm the privileges of the strong. Certainly that is how my arguments would be heard were I to go to a Palestinian refugee camp in the occupied territories or Gaza.

I might argue that had these two principles—of nonviolence and deliberation—been observed by the Palestinians in their struggle, they might now be in possession of a viable state of their own, rather than locked in the nightmare of a war without end under permanent military occupation. Even if this is true, it is a hypothetical truth. We do not know what would have happened if the Palestinians had been led by nonviolent leaders or if Zionism had understood the folly and injustice of denying Palestinian rights. The fact that one's ancestors in a struggle did not behave with justice or prudence does not invalidate the legiti-macy of one's current political claim. History is no excuse. It merely forecloses possibilities, and if it has foreclosed nonvio-lent means of prosecuting a struggle, then it may be necessary for a people to embark on the path of violence. We must consider seriously the claim that to require the weak to observe human rights is to deliver them up, defenseless, to the ruthlessness of the strong.

This argument from weakness is the fundamental ethical justi-fication of acts of terror. Where a state or occupying power pos-sesses overwhelming military force, people fighting for freedom claim they will go down to defeat if they confine their struggle to nonviolent protest. Alternatively, if they take the path of armed resistance and challenge the military might of the other side, they will also be crushed. The only tactic that converts weakness into strength is terrorism, hitting the enemy at its most vulnera-ble point, its civilian population.

This is more than a tactical argument in favor of asymmetrical warfare. It also has a moral justification. The weak must have the right to fight dirty; otherwise the strong will always win. If you oblige the weak to fight clean, injustice will always triumph. Here the ethical justification is in the form of a lesser evil argu-ment. In order to overcome the greater evil of injustice and op-pression, the weak must be entitled to resort to the lesser evil of terrorist violence. If they don't have this ultimate right as a last resort, they will be condemned to an eternity of subjugation.

We can't counsel the oppressed with the piety that the weak are best served by not surrendering the moral high ground. This is sometimes true historically, but it is a counsel of perfection that the weak have reason to reject when it is argued by the strong.

Moreover, human rights principles themselves are not an ethics of resignation but a call to struggle. The European liberal political tradition which nurtured the idea of natural—that is, human—rights explicitly reserved a right for the weak to rise up in revolt against intolerable oppression by the strong. What is the chapter on the dissolution of government in John Locke's

Second Treatise but a justification of revolution when essential freedoms are usurped?[14] What is the U.S. Declaration of Independence but a reasoned defense of the necessity of political violence to overthrow imperial oppression?[15] To be sure, the Declaration of Independence was not a justification for terroristic targeting of civilians, but it did justify acts of political violence directed at British military forces and government installations.

Part of the difficulty democracies encounter in crafting a political response to terrorism, in other words, lies in the fact that their own political traditions do not condemn political violence in all circumstances. If the American revolutionaries had not taken up arms and drawn blood, they would not have won their freedom. The idea of rights as a codified set of ultimate commitments can justify the resort to violence to preserve, restore, or establish them in the face of tyranny or usurpation.[16] Rights would not be ultimate claims were they not worth defending, if necessary, at the price of one's life.

But the right of revolution is not a human right. It is contained within the liberal tradition, but revolution itself is not justified within the human rights lexicon. The Universal Declaration of Human Rights of 1948 confines revolution to its preamble: "Whereas it is essential, if man is not to be compelled to have recourse, as a last resource, to rebellion against tyranny and oppression, that human rights should be protected by the rule of law." This statement does not endorse a right to rebellion but asserts that rebellion becomes inevitable when essential rights are denied. General Assembly resolutions of the 1960s and 1970s justify the right of people suffering racist or colonial rule or alien occupation to take all necessary means to win their freedom.[17] But these same resolutions also take care to endorse the sovereignty of those states that have already achieved their national independence, thus seeking to close the door on the right of revolution for peoples suffering inside the newly minted states of the postcolonial era.[18] While international law clearly privileges state sovereignty, it does not deny the legitimacy of violence against occupation or colonial rule.

If alien occupation or colonial rule is a greater evil, what lesser evils can the right to self-determination justify? When considering this question, we need to move out from under the rubric of human rights altogether and guide ourselves according to the laws of war. The two systems of ethics are linked.[19] When a state has declared war on its own citizens and they take up arms to resist, the laws of war seek to save what can be saved of the humanitarian impulse of human rights once violence has begun. They do not, generally, seek to define when the resort to violence is justified. But in one instance, the Optional Protocol of 1977 to the Geneva Conventions implicitly accepts that armed struggle may be justified against "colonial domination and alien occupation" as well as "racist regimes." Not surprisingly, Israel and the United States have refused to ratify this protocol, maintaining that the Conventions are supposed to provide not justifications *ad bellum* but rather rules for conduct *in bello*. Even though the protocol does legitimize these armed struggles as a just cause, it insists that even a just cause must observe the same rules of proportionality and civilian immunity that govern the conduct of regular soldiers and regular armed conflict.[20] In other words, even when armed struggle against oppression is justified, attacks against civilians remain violations.

The very idea of civilian immunity illustrates the difference between the universalistic framework of human rights and the particularistic framework of the laws of war. Laws of war distinguish minutely among the moral statuses of various combatants, noncombatants, civilians, military, prisoners, and medical staff—while human rights principles explicitly reject moral discriminations based on status. From a human rights perspective, civilian immunity is an incoherent moral principle, inconsistent with the equal respect due all human beings. From a laws of war perspective, civilian immunity is the principle that preserves some measure of ethical discrimination in the midst of the savagery of combat.[21]

The rationale for civilian immunity is to restrict combat to the fewest possible combatants, to confine it to those with the capacity to defend themselves with arms. As Michael Walzer has argued, the rationale for affording protection to civilians but not to armed combatants lies in their very different capacities for self-defense.[22] An additional rationale is that in societies where enlistment is voluntary, those who wear a uniform do so of their own free will and thus can be expected to pay the price of this choice. Civilians will not have made this choice and should therefore be spared deliberate targeting.

Terrorists commonly justify the targeting of civilians by denying their moral innocence, by insisting that civilian settlers who profit from an unjust colonial occupation are not entitled to immunity from attack, since they are either beneficiaries or accomplices of injustice. If a settler goes armed, if he assists in military operations against the other side, there may be some justification for the claim that he becomes a legitimate target. But since terrorists rarely if ever limit their operations to these types of settlers, their justifications will not cover the majority of their actions, which target those without arms, as well as those—infants and the aged—without the capacity to assist a military power. Moreover, most terrorist attacks start from a racially, ethnically, or religiously motivated conviction that certain categories of human beings are not worthy of moral standing or consideration. To violate civilian immunity, therefore, is to assume that noble political ends, like the struggle against injustice, can justify treating any human being as a means. This way nihilism lies. If the civilians on the other side are legitimate targets, there is nothing to prevent your targeting your own side if they begin to inform on your struggle or resist your exactions. Once the principle of discriminating carefully in the use of violence is abandoned, it can be corrosive of the principles that supposedly guided the struggle for freedom in the first place.

If we view national liberation struggles through the lens of human rights, they must discipline themselves according to the two rules of nonviolence and deliberation. This may condemn them to political failure. If we believe that their oppression is such that it justifies turning to violence as a last resort, then the ethics of their struggle passes from the domain of human rights into that of the laws of war. Either way, the basic moral rules of international politics expressly forbid the targeting of civilians.

Thus there are relatively clear ethical rules for the use of violence in support of a struggle against oppression, injustice, or occupation: as a last resort, when nonviolent, deliberative means have been exhausted, and when armed force obeys the rules of war. To be sure, this limits the struggle for freedom. You can't fight dirty, you must take on military targets, not civilian ones, but at least you are not required to turn the other cheek when you are faced with assault and oppression. Those who observe such rules deserve the name of freedom fighters. Those who do not are terrorists.

It is a relativist canard to suppose that there is no real distinction between the two, or that the distinction is simply dependent on one's political point of view. The problem with the distinction is not whether it is clear in theory, but whether it is meaningful in practice. Has any freedom fighter actually succeeded in avoiding becoming a terrorist? Has any armed struggle successfully resisted the temptation of deliberately targeting civilians?

Many liberation movements themselves—from the Cuban revolutionaries to the Vietnamese insurgents—have taken care to distinguish themselves from terrorists. Such movements were battling to secure international support and domestic allegiance, and the avoidance of indiscriminate violence is critical to securing both. Achieving recognition under the Geneva Conventions as a regular belligerent is a first step toward securing international recognition for the cause itself.

Moreover, ethical regulation of violence is critical to the maintenance of the legitimacy of a people's war among the people for whom the war is fought. Thus Che Guevara: "We are sincerely convinced that terrorism is a negative weapon which never produces the desired effects and which can alienate the people from revolutionary movements while causing among those who use it human losses out of all proportion to the results achieved."[23]

Winning power, as was clear to Guevara and leaders of liberation movements in Angola, Mozambique, Vietnam, and else-

where, requires taking the people with you. Terrorizing informers and fifth columnists, destroying villages that reject your
cause or lend support to the government may arouse moral disgust among your own supporters and weaken political allegiance to the cause.[24]

Yet only some armed insurgents reason as Che Guevara
urged. Other insurgent groups—the FARC in Colombia and the
RUF in Sierra Leone—regularly use terrorist means to control
territory and ensure compliance among the civilian population.
Killing informers, taking hostages among the locals, or engaging
in summary executions may serve just as well as restraint in securing the obedience of the population one fights among, and
presumably fights for. While Che Guevara's words are what
supporters of liberation movements would like to believe—
namely, that they swim among the people, like fish in water—
liberation movements have often found, just as have the counterterror forces opposing them, that when they are faced with
civilian resistance in their zones of operation, it is more efficient
to drain the water and kill the fish.

This is especially the case when an insurgent group is numeri-
cally small and does not enjoy mass support. Atrocity creates
awe and dread and compensates for small numbers. In Sierra
Leone, the RUF were a nondescript band of predatory maraud-
ers, but they clearly grasped that amputating hands and legs
and disfiguring faces leveraged their military and political impact.[25] Terroristic methods are best understood as an attempt to
use atrocity as a tactic to offset military and political weakness.

On the other hand, once liberation movements become sizable
and are fighting on terms of relative equality with an opponent,
a different set of calculations may set in. They may decide that
compliance with the laws of war may gain them more than
would continuing terrorism, especially if their goal is international recognition and the acquisition of state power. A case in
point would be the Umkhonto we Sizwe, the military arm of the
African National Congress. In November 1980, the ANC declared its adherence to the Geneva Conventions, some eighteen

years after beginning armed struggle against the South African apartheid regime. It did so to consolidate support among UN member states and to outflank its South African opponent. As ANC leader Oliver Tambo said, in explaining why he was willing to adhere to the Geneva Conventions, "we do so in the consciousness that we do not take our standards from those of the enemy."[26]

While there is little doubt that the ANC's declarations of high ethical intent contributed to the apartheid regime's increasing isolation, the ANC's military wing did not always adhere to the distinction between lawful combat and terrorism. Bombings of civilian bars and churches were carried out, while summary execution of suspected collaborators and spies tarnished the ANC's reputation. Once it took power, it was forced into an extensive exercise in self-justification.[27] In its submissions to the Truth and Reconciliation Commission accounting for these abuses, the ANC, now in government, made prominent use of lesser evil arguments. Apartheid was a crime against humanity, the ANC maintained, and the military campaign against the ANC was ferocious. Mistakes and misjudgments occurred, but these needed to be understood in the context of a struggle against a greater evil. Moreover, the ANC pointed out, a guerrilla movement cannot exert the same degree of control over its operatives as can a regular military force.[28] This argument, while probably true in fact, runs close to the claim that the standards applied to the weak should differ from those applied to the strong. Such an argument is inconsistent with a signature to the Geneva Conventions, whose language does not admit of one standard for states and one for guerrillas.

As the ANC example shows, armed struggles for freedom avoid terrorism when they have incentives to differentiate their moral identity from that of their oppressors and when they calculate that targeting civilians would alienate valuable foreign support, as well as the local population.[29] In Sri Lanka, the Tamil Tigers, by contrast, placed little emphasis on winning international support, at least outside their own ethnic diaspora, believing that international opinion was indifferent to the outcome in their faraway country. As a result, Tamil terrorism was certainly more unconstrained and vicious than the ANC.[30]

Where insurgents know that the opposing state is protected from international opprobrium by another strong state, they will have little incentive to restrain their conduct. For example, the international community has allowed the Russians a free hand in Chechnya. As a result the Chechens have lost all incentive to restrain their own conduct, and the struggle goes on in a twilight limbo, safe from international condemnation.[31] Where no one cares either way, barbarism rules. The rebels in eastern Congo have no incentive to behave better, because no one is watching.[32] This suggests that the world's attention matters. Condemnation of terror, wherever it happens, concerted international action to penalize the funding of terror, action to deny territory to those who commit terrorist acts in a neighboring state, extradition of terrorists who seek refuge next door, and military intervention to protect civilians terrorized by rebel groups would all do something to keep self-determination struggles from descending into carnage. Most of all, states need to become more consistent in their condemnation of terrorist methods, whether committed by their friends or by their enemies. Judging friends by one standard and enemies by another is a dangerous game, since a friend today may well turn out to be an enemy tomorrow. State complicity or collusion in terrorist methods is the single most important reason why terrorism continues, and therefore the single most important policy that states can adopt is to refuse to lend tacit or overt support to any group that uses terrorism even in pursuit of goals that the state supports.

III

In the examples considered so far, it has become clear that where armed groups have a real prospect of obtaining recognition and statehood, they may be persuaded to abstain from terrorism. Where their success in this struggle depends on retaining the support of local populations, they may also conclude that restraint pays better than atrocity. But these incentives and re-straining factors do not apply to all terrorist groups. No such factors discipline the conduct of Al Qaeda. They have no aspira-tions to statehood and therefore no incentive to play by any known rules. They do not serve a determinate population and are therefore unconstrained either by their supporters' moral code or by their vulnerability to reprisal. They even appear in-different to casualties inflicted on Muslim populations who live or work in proximity to their targets. This is what makes them so dangerous. This is also why they cannot be engaged politi-cally and must instead be defeated militarily.

Al Qaeda is therefore a distinctive kind of terrorism, no longer in the service of a people's freedom or in the name of the over-throw of a given state. The apocalyptic nihilists who attacked the United States on September 11 did not leave behind justifi-cations, noble or otherwise, for their actions. They directed their propaganda and their justifications not at a specific state deny-ing a claim to self-determination, but at the United States as the hated imperial capital of a materialistic, secular, and alien civili-zation. The so-called martyrs defended their actions in the lan-guage of Islamic eschatology, not in the language of rights.[33] Moreover, their intentions were apocalyptic, not political: to hu-miliate the archenemy of Islam and secure martyrdom in the process. It is difficult to see, in principle, how acts unaccompa-nied by demands can be accommodated politically. If the goal of terrorism is neither territory nor freedom, if its purpose is to strike a blow that asserts the dignity of Muslim believers while inflicting horror and death upon their enemies, then it is difficult to envisage a political response of any kind. Such an attack can-not be met by politics but only by war.

But this is not all there is to say. The 9/11 attackers may not have left demands, but this has not prevented their supporters throughout the Muslim world from claiming that they acted in the name of the Palestinians and in support of the just demands of believers to worship in the Holy Places free of foreign—that is, American—occupation. It is this echo of justification that lends the attack its enduring impact. These are not rights claims, exactly, since Muslim extremists disdain the language of rights. But they are a demand for justice, and it is when terrorism appropriates justice that it is at its most dangerous. As a recent study by Robert Pape shows, most suicide attackers have chosen suicide as a tactic in service of a political and ethical purpose.[34] A claim of justice and a chance of success are critical for finding suicide recruits. Improving homeland security, building walls to keep terrorists out, may reduce their chances of success, but unless the basic motivation for terrorism—the perception of injustice—is addressed, no strategy against terror can succeed by purely military means.

In responding to this perception of injustice, the United States faces the dilemma that it has been allied since 1945 with Arab regimes, like Saudi Arabia and Egypt, which have failed their people and now confront radical Islamist movements that are capitalizing on disillusion with secular and nationalist modernization. A political response to Al Qaeda has to encourage these embattled elites to allow political competition and give way to new social forces that are capable of addressing the failures of these societies across the Arab world. There is no shortage of Arab thinkers and social scientists who see the failures of their societies and want to confront them, without outside help or interference.[35] But real reform—to improve literacy and female education, to open up the economy to competition, and to widen political participation—requires consistent international support and, at times, U.S. pressure on reluctant elites. Recent speeches by the U.S. president appear to commit the United States to just such a strategy.[36] Yet painful experience with Iran under the shah suggests that pressuring authoritarian regimes to reform may help trigger Islamic revolution. Fear of such a prospect, however, should not guide policy in the direction of shoring up the Arab ancien régime. There are versions of Islamic revolution that would only result in tyranny, and there are versions that would serve the people's pent-up longing for social and economic justice and political participation. Which version prevails depends on the type of Islamic leadership available in each society and not primarily on American influence. A political strategy to compete with Al Qaeda in the Arab world cannot work if Islam and democracy are assumed to be incompatible.[37]

Yet while Al Qaeda claims that it is entitled to represent the demand of the Muslim masses for justice, it is a mistake to suppose that it seeks the reforms that would relieve this injustice. Al Qaeda terrorism is intended not to hasten reform in the Arab world but to prevent it, to drive these embattled regimes into ever more authoritarian forms of reaction, unleashing a popular Islamic revolution that would take the whole region back to 700 C.E. and the time of the caliphate.

It would be an elementary mistake to consider the September 11 hijackers as authentic representatives of the Muslim masses. It remains essential, however, to distinguish between conceding the legitimacy of terrorism and conceding the legitimacy of grievances. One can refuse the first premise while accepting the second. It is inevitable that, in response to the attacks of September 11, leaders in liberal democracies should pronounce a moral anathema on those who resorted to them. Yet the consequence of an anathema is to declare an end to the political processes of engagement that a liberal democracy stands for. To declare a war on terrorism risks, in itself, compromising the political values that should guide relations even with a liberal state's enemies. If terrorism is actually a politics of grievance and if liberal democracy is committed to political solutions to these problems, it must remain engaged in practical efforts to assist Muslim societies to reform and develop.

IV

A political response to terror requires a painful admission that injustice prevails in the Arab states where terrorists find their recruits. But this is not to say that violent struggle against such injustice is justified. A critical question in assessing the morality of political violence is whether it genuinely meets the test of last resort. Time and again, terrorists resort to violence not as a last resort, turned to reluctantly after peaceful means of political action have been exhausted, but as a first resort. The weak conclude it best to go the fast way. The fast way is to kill as many civilians as possible to get the world to take notice, or to provoke the other side into a downward spiral of repression that will brand them as unjust oppressors in the eyes of the world at large.

This is what, as I have already said, the French call *la politique du pire*. The purpose of terror is to make properly political solutions impossible. Modern Basque terrorism reached its peak, not during the years of Franco's repression, but in the early years of Spanish democracy, when Madrid granted the Basque country substantial autonomy, entrenched Basque language rights, and poured money into Basque economic development.[38] Terrorism was an attempt to defeat a reasonable constitutional settlement of Basque claims. The further purpose was to intimidate the constitutional parties in the Basque region, to silence support for devolutionist, federal, and nonviolent political demands. Violent groups, in other words, with no reasonable prospect of electoral success within a constitutional order used violence to leverage their influence and intimidate their rivals, and thus to expropriate political representation by use of force.

The same pattern is apparent in Irish terrorism. The worst of the Troubles date, not to the period of Protestant ascendancy in Northern Ireland, but to the 1970s when the British government finally made a concerted attempt to redress the civil, political, and social disabilities of the Catholic population and to engage both Protestants and Catholics in power sharing.[39] Terrorist violence, by both sides, has been an attempt to silence reasonable voices in the two communities, to prevent them from giving their support to peaceful constitutional solutions.

In Sri Lanka, terrorism was also timed to wreck the chances of peaceful reform. Tamil Elam's attacks on the government in Colombo were designed to make any devolutionist, federal compromise impossible and thus to force their solution of choice—statehood for Tamils—upon Tamils and Sinhalese alike. Female suicide bombers were dispatched to strike down such moderate Tamil politicians as Neelan Tiruchelvam, whose only offense was a willingness to engage in dialogue and to propose federal alternatives to secession.[40]

In Palestine, the liberation movement was committed to violence from the very beginning of its struggle against "the Zionist entity" in the early 1950s. It scored its first spectacular success at the Munich Olympics of 1972, during the early period of Israeli occupation when many voices inside Israel, including the state's founding prime minister, David Ben-Gurion, were questioning whether occupation was compatible with a Jewish state and when Israel might have responded to a Palestinian campaign of peaceful civil disobedience. Because these roads were not even tried, the legitimacy of Palestinian violence, even against strictly military targets, is doubtful. In a similar vein, the upsurge of Palestinian terrorism in the 1990s coincided with the Oslo peace process, which sought to create a Palestinian state.[41] The terror campaign of Hamas and other insurrectionary groups was designed to destroy the Oslo process, discredit the Israeli and Palestinian leadership who had committed themselves to it, and radicalize the Palestinian population in favor of a rejectionist platform, based on denial of Israel's right to exist. No campaign of violence can be justified in the name of self-determination if its essential premise is to foreclose peaceful negotiation and to deny the right of another people to exist.

Thus while it is possible to justify armed struggle in defense of self-determination, it is possible to do so only under four conditions: the group's just claims must have been met by violence; the failure to accommodate these claims must be systematic, enduring, and unlikely to change; the claims must be fundamental to the survival of the group; the struggle must observe the laws of war and the rule of civilian immunity. In none of the above cases—Palestine, Northern Ireland, the Basque country, or the Tamils—have these conditions been met.

Besides last resort, a further ethical test of political violence is whether it actually serves the interests of those in whose name it is conducted. Terrorists may purport to speak for the weak and defenseless, but once terrorist acts begin in the name of liberation, they are quickly directed not just at the oppressor but at all those within the oppressed group who oppose terrorist means, or who have collaborated or worked with forces on the opposing side. A war against traitors, informers, fellow travelers, fifth columnists, and spies—a war against your own people, in other words—is a necessary feature of any terrorist campaign. Terrorists argue that their acts express the will of the people: in reality, violence silences them. In the Basque country, in Catholic areas of Northern Ireland, in Tamil areas of Sri Lanka, and finally in Palestine, terrorist groups rule their populations with the same violence they deploy against the oppressor. In a properly political world, those who are represented freely grant the right of representation to those they elect. In the antipolitical world of terror, such representation as exists is a facade maintained by intimidation and violence. In all of these communities, it can be a death sentence to defy the rule of the armed minority who purport to speak in their name.

Seen in this way, terrorist violence is usually a preemptive strike by the terrorist group against free political expression within their own population. Terrorist campaigns seek to take hostage the population in whose name they purport to act. Instead of using properly political means to achieve hegemony within their own population, terrorists use violence to do so. This ruthless suppression becomes all the more essential since this population, and not just the terrorists alone, have to pay the price of the reprisals and counterrepression. Thus the civilian population of Palestine, of the Sri Lankan Tamil area, of the Basque country find themselves taken hostage twice, first by the terrorists and then by the state seeking to repress them. In the process, terrorism does not merely expose them to the horror of violent reprisal, but worse, it confiscates and silences their political capacity to articulate their own demands.

Terrorist struggles also damage the political system a liberation campaign hopes to create when freedom is finally won. The use of terrorist violence by the Algerian freedom fighters in the 1950s burned political killing into the culture of postliberation Algeria, so that in 1992 when the ruling elite disallowed an election which would have brought the Islamists to power, both the state and the insurgents had no threshold of repugnance to overcome in resorting to terrorism. In the ensuing struggle, sixty thousand lives were lost.[42] In Palestine, terrorism—and the counterterrorist campaigns by Israel—have all but destroyed the governing institutions of the Palestinian Authority and have set back the Palestinian claim to statehood. Even when they finally secure statehood, it will remain a central task of liberation for Palestinians to drive violence out of the practice of politics in a free Palestine.

It is also the case that when a people use terror to win freedom, and then seek to keep people under occupation, the oppressed group is bound to copy the political example of their oppressors. The Zionist struggle for statehood in 1947 and 1948 engaged in acts of terrorism directed at targets like the King David Hotel, which housed British military personnel and civilians alike.[43] Terror attacks were also directed at Arab villages, like Dir Yassein, in order to force Palestinians to flee.[44] Jewish terrorism does not justify Palestinian terrorism, and Jewish terrorism did not teach Palestinians terrorism: they had models and inspirations all their own. But there is little doubt that it makes it easier for Palestinians to claim legitimacy for their own acts of atrocity. Political struggles that use terror to achieve freedom—Zionism is no exception—leave themselves open to terrorist campaigns that seek revenge for the terror used against them.[45] The conclusion is inescapable: the use of terror to secure freedom can poison freedom itself.

V

A political response to a war on terror means facing up to the dilemma of negotiating with armed groups and deciding whether groups associated with violence can play any part in legitimate politics. To negotiate is an act of recognition. It is impossible to negotiate with violent groups without according them this recognition, and without running the risk that they will use this recognition to lure a democratic state into damaging concessions. Hence there are good reasons never to negotiate with terrorist groups. But most liberal democratic states, while refusing direct negotiation with men of violence, open channels of political dialogue with any group committed to nonviolence who can drain away the terrorists' constituency of support.

The weak and oppressed must be given a peaceful political alternative that enables them to rise up against the violence exercised in their name. They must be given the chance to refuse to allow their sons and daughters to be recruited. They must have the option of refusing to vote for parties with any connection to violence. They must be given the opportunity to refuse to shelter or keep silent about the gunmen in their midst. This revolt can occur only when democratic states encourage political competitors to the men of violence. The peace process in Northern Ireland was pursued not just in Dublin and in London but in the streets of Belfast, Omagh, and Derry, where ordinary members of both the Protestant and Catholic communities decided, not that they necessarily wanted to be reconciled, but that they wanted to regain control of their own politics, that is, to free their communities of the intimidation and violence inflicted by groups purporting to speak in their name.

Communities cannot do this while they simultaneously face the violence of the state and terrorist groups. The state and the terrorist often conspire, unwittingly, to keep the hostages captive. In this malign alliance terror and counterterror become mutually dependent, and the only possible exit—the politics of reconciliation and compromise—is sealed off.

Once terrorists have been beaten back, even if not destroyed, it becomes possible for peaceful political groups to begin competing for votes. Inevitably, however, terrorist groups form political fronts of their own in order to fight off the competition. In Northern Ireland, Sinn Fein seeks to present itself as a legitimate representative of the nationalist cause, even though its leadership maintains links with men of violence. In the Basque country, political parties with terrorist affiliations competed for power throughout the terrorist campaign, profiting from the violence of their secret allies to intimidate voters. Similar shadowy linkages exist between terrorist groups and ostensibly nonviolent political parties elsewhere. A political strategy to keep electoral preferences safe from intimidation is difficult to fulfill when terrorist groups exploit a free political sphere to masquerade as properly political organizations.[46]

All liberal democracies proscribe parties that promote violence, but it can be difficult to define what connections count as complicity with terrorism. Even when such complicity can be established, banning such organizations is always a lesser evil. It exposes liberal democracies to the charge that they are rigging the political process and driving people into the arms of the terrorists. Spain has recently banned a Basque political party associated with terrorism, while in Britain the government has resisted repeated calls by Ulster Unionists to ban Sinn Fein.[47] While each case needs to be assessed on its own merits, the general bias of a liberal democratic state should always be against the banning of political parties, either on the basis of their platforms, or on the basis of their association with other groups. Restrictions on the basis of content violate freedom of expression, and restrictions on the basis of association can be tendentious and impossible to prove. The test of a party's legitimacy as a political actor should be its actual conduct in democratic politics. If it seeks allegiance by holding peaceful rallies and meetings, if its members and leaders forswear any conduct or speech that amounts to intimidation, if it abides by electoral results, then it should be allowed to compete for votes. If it beats up opponents or calls on supporters to commit acts of violence, it should be dissolved, if necessary by force.

It is more questionable whether groups that remain nonviolent can be banned merely because they do not support the constitutional terms of democratic debate—for example, the legitimacy of Spanish claims over the Basque country or British claims over Northern Ireland.[48] U.S. constitutional doctrine supports proscription of political parties where they pose a clear and present danger to the Constitution, as when they advocate overthrow of government by force, but banning parties simply because they advocate revolutionary goals, while conforming to constitutional norms of behavior, risks endangering basic democratic freedoms.

The Canadian example—where a party committed to independence for Quebec has peacefully competed for votes in both federal and provincial elections—provides a competing model. In Canada, Quebecois separatist parties compete for power, even though their election might actually mean the dissolution of the constitutional system in which they seek office. No one has ever challenged their right to do so, because their political conduct has been entirely peaceful. On the one occasion in which Quebec separatism turned to violence, Canadian liberal democracy reacted swiftly. In October 1970, when a small separatist group kidnapped and murdered a provincial politician, the federal government invoked the War Measures Act and arrested and detained without trial more than five hundred individuals suspected of association with the group. All were released without charge. The justification for the use of the War Measures Act in 1970 was that it was necessary to protect the Quebec political system from intimidation and, more generally, to send a message that the federal government would defend itself robustly. The War Measures Act did put an end to political violence, but it did not stop separatism. Within six years, the first government committed to an independent and sovereign Quebec was elected, and one reason for this may have been widespread revulsion at excessive use of federal power in the October crisis six years earlier.[49] In the end, what turned the tide against separatism in Quebec was the successful functioning of the federal system itself, which has allowed Quebec sufficient political autonomy to protect its language, culture, and economy. Effective self-government in these domains, together with the robust performance of the Quebec economy within a federal union, has weakened the appeal of separatist politics, at least for the present. The implication of the Quebec case for states facing separatist challenges to their authority would be that while a state must take robust measures to prevent separatist violence from going unchallenged, it must also take care to allow peaceful and constitutional opposition to its political system, and it must ensure that this system responds substantively to legitimate claims for self-government in realms like culture, language, and education, vital to the survival of a minority group identity. On balance, allowing peaceful advocacy of constitutional change, up to and including the dissolution of the constitutional order itself, is essential to preserving the legitimacy of constitutional politics, since without peaceful avenues for political expression, demands for separation, autonomy, or independence are bound to turn violent.

VI

If force must be the ultimate response to violence against a constitutional state, what is to keep state violence from becoming as unconstrained as the enemy it is seeking to destroy? The only answer is democracy and the obligation of justification that it imposes on those who use force in its name. The liberal state and its terrorist enemy stand under very different obligations to justify their actions. The agents of a constitutional state are aware that they may be called to defend and explain their actions in adversarial proceedings, possibly even in court. Terrorists do not stand in any institutional setting that holds them accountable. They may have an informal moral contract with their base of support, a tacit set of understandings of what types of violence are acceptable, and, in particular, which kinds will expose their base of support to reprisal. But this is not the same as an institutional obligation to render an account of your actions. This absence of any institutional obligation to justify helps explain why terrorism so often escalates into extremism for its own sake. Yes, states can be guilty of acts of terror, but it is false to equate these with the acts of terrorists. Punishment shootings by the IRA in Northern Ireland occur without censure. The republican community whom the IRA purports to protect by kneecapping informants, shooting drug dealers, and so on has no institutional capacity to regulate the popular justice meted out in its name. Any punishment shooting by a British soldier is subject to disciplinary hearings. The IRA commonly tortures and executes informers. If allegations of torture are made against British forces, they end up under investigation in the European Court of Human Rights.[50] Recent assertions that UK security forces colluded in political assassinations by Protestant terror groups have been made the subject of judicial inquiry.[51]

Those who equate the violence inflicted by Israel with that inflicted by Palestinian suicide bombers ignore real differences in institutional accountability in the two cases. In Israel allegations of torture, house demolition, illegal detention, and unjustified force have all ended up before the Israeli Supreme Court, and in a significant number of instances the conduct has been censured and stopped.[52] This is not to claim that legal oversight is always effective, or to acquit Israeli forces of blame when crimes are committed. But it is to argue that all agents of force in a democratic state, like Israel, lie under a burden of justification, and the possibility of review and censure, that are entirely absent on the other side. Indeed, one of the strongest justifications for a Palestinian state is that it will provide a structure of law and accountability to constrain future encounters between its security forces and the Israelis.

The preceding discussion makes it possible, at last, to define precisely why terrorism constitutes a greater evil, justifying the lesser evils of a liberal democracy's response. The evil does not consist in the resort to violence itself, since violence can be justified, as a last resort, in the face of oppression, occupation, or injustice. The evil consists in resorting to violence as a first resort, in order to make peaceful politics impossible, and, second, in targeting unarmed civilians and punishing them for their allegiance or their ethnicity. This is to condemn them to death not for what they do, but for who they are and what they believe. Finally, terrorism is an offense not only against the lives and liberties of its specific victims, but against politics itself, against the practice of deliberation, compromise, and the search for nonviolent and reasonable solutions. Terrorism is a form of politics that aims at the death of politics itself. For this reason, it must be combated by all societies that wish to remain political: otherwise both we and the people terrorists purport to represent are condemned to live, not in a political world of deliberation, but in a prepolitical state of combat, a state of war.

CHAPTER FIVE

THE TEMPTATIONS OF
NIHILISM

"They cannot be otherwise. Their character is built upon conventional morality. It leans on the social order. Mine stands free from everything artificial. They are bound by all sorts of conventions. They depend on life, which, in this connection, is a historical fact, surrounded by all sorts of restraints and considerations, a complex organized fact open to attack at every point; whereas I depend on death, which knows no restraint and cannot be attacked. My superiority is evident."
—*Joseph Conrad*, The Secret Agent *(1907)*

I

In Joseph Conrad's *The Secret Agent*, written under the impact of anarchist terrorist incidents in London and Paris in the 1890s, there is a character called the Professor who walks about the streets of London, one hand clutching a detonating switch attached to a supply of explosive in his coat.[1] He can blow himself up at any moment if the police try to arrest him. Conrad imagined the Professor as having been an assistant demonstrator at a technical institute and then a lab technician for a dye manufacturer, who after being dismissed, conceives a grudge against the world. As Conrad remarks, "The Professor had genius but lacked the great social virtue of resignation." Living in extreme poverty in rented rooms in one of London's poorest neighborhoods, the Professor devotes himself day and night to perfecting detonating systems. He is prepared to sell them to anyone who wishes "to break up the superstition and worship of legality" in the society around him. He frequents the edges of the revolutionary socialist underground but actually regards the revolutionists with the same contempt as he does the police. "The terrorist and the policeman both come from the same basket. Revolution, legality—counter moves in the same game; forms of idleness at bottom identical." They cling to life, he says bitterly, whereas he only wants death and is therefore invulnerable. Revolutionary dreams, bourgeois legality, all these ideals were indifferent, the Professor thought, compared to the goal to which he had devoted his life: making "the perfect detonator."[2]

The Professor is the first great portrayal of a suicide bomber in modern literature. What Conrad wants us to see in this demonic portrait of terrorist motivation is that political goals as such—revolution, justice, and freedom—have little to do with what really drives the Professor. The core of his motivation is much darker: contempt for a society that refuses to acknowledge his genius; fascination with the invulnerability that his own willingness to die confers upon him; and an obsession to master the means of death. The Professor's Holy Grail—the perfect detonator—is only a symbol of the true promise of terrorism: a moment of violence that will transform a penniless nonentity into an avenging angel.

This portrait of the terrorist poses a particular challenge to the analysis I have been pursuing so far. What happens to a war on terror when violence gets out of control, when both sides begin to behave like the Professor, obsessed with the means of their struggle and indifferent to the ends these means are supposed to serve? Thus far I have argued as if terrorists and the states that fight them discipline the means they employ by the ends they seek. Those who resort to political violence do so in the name of freedom and self-determination on behalf of the oppressed. Counterterrorists, for their part, fight to defend the principles of their state. On the basis of these assumptions, it becomes possible to imagine that both of them might wish not to tarnish the ends they seek by the means they employ. An interrogator working for a liberal democratic state could be persuaded—by the values he is charged to defend—that the use of torture betrayed that state's very essence. Terrorists who might justify killing civilians as the lesser evil could be persuaded to turn away from terror if they could be shown that the same goals could be achieved by peaceful means. On the assumption that both terror and counterterror are political phenomena, driven by political goals and ideals, it might be possible to imagine that these goals could prevent both sides from sliding down a spiral of mutually reinforcing violence.

What if these assumptions aren't true? What happens when political violence ceases to be motivated by political ideals and comes to be motivated by the emotional forces that Conrad understood so well: *ressentiment* and envy, greed and blood lust, violence for its own sake? What happens when counterterrorism, likewise, ceases to be motivated by principle and comes to be driven by the same complex of emotional drives?

It is one thing to argue that terrorism must be understood politically, another to pretend that political goals always determine the actions of terrorists. It may be that much lower motives, those animating the Professor, are the ones we need to understand if we are to grasp why it is that noble goals are so often betrayed by those who think they are serving them. The same may be true of the agents sent to apprehend people like the Professor. They may be guided by codes and values that have nothing to do with those of the society they are representing: the warrior codes of loyalty to their own, values of revenge, and the pure excitement of instilling fear in others.

In this chapter, I want to look at violence as nihilism and seek to explain why both terror and counterterror can become ends in themselves, and why so many wars on terror degenerate into a downward spiral of violence. I have already suggested one reason why this should be so: terrorists deliberately seek to provoke it, in order to get inside the decision cycle of the state they are opposing and drive it toward ever more brutal oppression. The goal of terrorists is to erode the moral identity of the state, together with its will to resist, and pry a subject population away from obedience to its rule. If this is an explicit political goal of most terror strategies, it is vital for leaders in democratic states to avoid falling into this trap.

But this is easier said than done. What needs explaining is why counterterror wars slip beyond political control, why they fall into the trap set by terrorists, but also why terrorists themselves lose control of their campaigns and impose horrible losses on their own side before acknowledging defeat. In order to explain these dark features, we need to move from politics and law to the psychology of nihilism.

First a word of explanation about nihilism. It literally means belief in nothing, loss of any restraining or inspiring set of goals. I do not want to use it literally or to imply that counterterrorists or terrorists believe in nothing. They may both start with high ideals and lose them in the carnage of the struggle. I am using the word, first of all, to capture a form of alienation, in which both sides in a war on terror lose proper sight of their own objectives. Coercive means cease to serve determinate political ends and become ends in themselves. Terrorists and counterterrorists alike end up trapped in a downward spiral of mutually reinforcing brutality. This is the most serious ethical trap lying in wait in the long war on terror that stretches before us.

The word *nihilism* was first paired with terrorism in the 1860s in czarist Russia. Dostoevsky and others used it to describe the worldview of the terrorists led by Sergei Nechaev, whose *Catechism of a Revolutionary* set out a program for the seizure of power.[3] Nechaev deliberately promoted acts of savagery designed to provoke the czarist regime into a bloody showdown. Nihilism originally meant an aggressive hatred for suffocating and hypocritical bourgeois convention. The program of the nihilists was not literally nihilistic, however, since destruction was supposed to prepare the way for the building of a just society on the ruins of the old. But opponents of these groups seized on the epithet, arguing that their destructive methods vitiated their redemptive social ideals. Groups who accepted nihilism as a designation did so because it captured their utter rejection of the existing social order. One such group eventually assassinated the Liberator Czar, Alexander II, in 1881.

The greatest literary portrait of terrorism as nihilism is not coincidentally Russian: Fyodor Dostoevsky's *The Possessed*, published in 1871. It tells the story of a small terrorist cell led by the charismatic Stavrogin and the malicious trickster Verkovensky, who take over a small Russian town, enlist the support of gullible and self-hating liberals, and then set off on a fire-raising rampage that leaves buildings burned, innocents dead, and one recanting member of the terrorist group murdered. This last murder is the moral clue to the meaning of the tale, since he alone believed in the political ideals for which the violence was carried out. Because of this, Dostoevsky seems to say, he is the only one to realize that the ends had been hijacked by the means. For his moral recognition and for his attempt to denounce the group and leave, he pays with his life.

Dostoevsky, who had been in a conspiratorial group himself, was, like Conrad after him, a master of terrorist psychology. But his portrait of terrorism depended on an elaborate metaphysical criticism of modernity in which the terrorist became the pathological expression of a society that had lost shared faith in God and surrendered to a cruel and narrow individualism.[4] Terrorism, in Dostoevsky's analysis, is the mirror image of the nihilistic society the terrorists want to destroy.

We don't have to accept Dostoevsky's apocalyptic musings about modernity or believe, as he seemed to imply, that when modern societies were struck by terror, they were getting what they deserved. We can set these thoughts aside and concentrate instead on the unparalleled acuity of the Russian author's portrait of nihilism as a state of mind. In the novel, the terrorists spout the rhetoric of revolutionary politics, but their rhetoric is as empty as their souls. Evil fills their spiritual void. What appeals to them is extremism for its own sake. This is nihilism, in a second sense, as cynical disbelief in the goals one outwardly professes. By setting the action in a small town, rather than in Moscow or Petersburg, Dostoevsky wants to emphasize the political futility of the exercise: burning down a remote Russian town is hardly likely to start a revolution across the Russian Empire. But this doesn't seem to matter to the conspirators. They are in love with conspiracy itself. Dostoevsky's portrait of the terrorists is both comic and ruthless, capturing the po-faced babble of the conspirators, their ludicrous incapacity to attend to what they are saying. Of one character, Dostoevsky writes, "he rejects morality as such and is in favor of the latest principle of general destruction for the sake of the ultimate good. He already demands more than a hundred million heads for the establishment of common sense in Europe."[5] The ringleader Verkovensky deliberately cultivates the rhetorical extremism in the circle in order to create a demented world in which no one is capable of seeing the true insanity of the destruction they propose. Verkovensky is Dostoevsky's portrait of the terrorist as trickster, reveling in his own capacity to exploit the emptiness and gullibility of his fellow conspirators. Politics, for Verkovensky, is a cynical game, sustained by the delights of duplicity. He mouths platitudes about justice because they enable him to capture adherents, make sexual conquests, and secure power, money, and influence along the way. In this portrait of evil as a monstrous inversion, high principles become the means and violence the true end of political action.

Dostoevsky perfectly captures this second sense of nihilism as cynicism. In this sense, the term denotes the commission of violence for the sake of personal aggrandizement, immortality, fame, or power rather than as a means to a genuinely political end, like revolution or the liberation of a people. This inversion may be what has happened to the suicide bombers attacking cafés, bars, and bus stops in Israel. It may also have occurred among the suicide bombers who hijacked the planes on September 11. Since they have paid for their acts with their lives, we have no way of knowing what their motivations were.[6] The fact that some suicide bombers taped declarations of high political intent does not prove that these intentions actually drove their actions. Suicide bombing may be a death cult, in which the stated political goals—freedom for oppressed or occupied peoples—are less important than objectives of the kind Conrad's Professor so obviously craved, such as fame, immortality, an instant of significance. While suicide bombing does take courage, it might be a mistake to assume that courage is necessarily motivated by a noble goal. Courage may be inverted in the service of cult-like goals: death, immortality, self-vindication as a martyr. Moreover, in a process of inversion, estimable goals like freedom and justice are perverted into justifications for inhuman crimes and atrocities. This matters because political concessions to the causes represented by suicide bombers might not have any effect on the motivations of the bombers themselves, for these have moved beyond politics into an eschatology of personal redemption through death.

Neither side in a war on terror is immune from this temptation of coming to see violence as an end in itself. Agents of a democratic state may find themselves driven by the horror of terror to torture, to assassinate, to kill innocent civilians, all in the name of rights and democracy. Succumbing to this inversion is the principal way that both groups slip from the lesser evil to the greater.

If, however, this temptation is strong, a strategy of combating it with lesser evils may not be plausible at all. A lesser evil morality may be too rational. It makes the assumption that violence by a liberal democratic state faced with terror can be controlled in the name of ethically appropriate ends like rights and dignity. A lesser evil approach to a war on terror would assume, for example, that agents of a liberal democratic state should be able to hold the line that divides intensive interrogation from torture, or the line that separates targeted assassination of enemy combatants from assassinations that entail the death of innocent civilians. Current U.S. policy does not allow assassination of civilians in peacetime but does permit killing of enemy combatants in wartime, with the proviso that such assassinations must be discriminate and avoid collateral damage.[7] This policy—a lesser evil approach if there ever was one—implies that the agents charged with defending a state have the strength of character, together with a clear enough sense of the values of the society they are defending, to be trusted with morally ambiguous means. But a perfectionist case against such an approach would argue that morally equivocal means are hard to control and thus liable to end in betrayal of the values that a liberal democracy should stand for. Hence liberal states should not allow those who defend them to have any of the moral discretion implied in lesser evil approaches. States should absolutely ban extreme interrogations, targeted assassinations, and other uses of violence, because once you start with means like these, it becomes next to impossible to prevent the lesser from shading into the greater evil.

Another problem with the lesser evil would be that liberal democratic regimes encourage a kind of moral narcissism, a blinding belief that because *this* kind of society authorizes such means, they must be acceptable. Thus democratic values, instead of preventing the lesser from shading into the greater evil, may actually blind democratic agents to the moral reality of their actions. The nobility of ends is no guarantee against resort to evil means; indeed, the more noble they are, the more ruthlessness they can endorse. This is why democracy depends on distrust, why freedom's defense requires submitting even noble intentions to the test of adversarial review.

I can see three distinct ways—the tragic, the cynical, and the fanatical—in which nihilism can come to dominate both a terrorist campaign and a war on terror. The first might be called tragic because it occurs despite the political intentions of all concerned, when terrorists and counterterrorists become trapped in a downward spiral of reprisal and counterreprisal. One side kills to avenge its last victim; the other side replies to avenge its last victim. Both sides start with an ethic of restraint and end up in a struggle without end.

Here shedding of blood creates two communities—the terrorists and the counterterrorists—in which loyalty to the group prevails over institutional accountability or individual principle. Both sides are bonded to their own because both have blood on their hands or blood to avenge. Their bonds to the group are stronger than any they have to the institutions that could possibly restrain their behavior. Violence creates belonging and belonging produces closure. Terrorists listen only to themselves and no longer to restraining messages from the communities their violence is supposed to serve. Counterterrorist agencies, having suffered losses, bond with each other, view their civilian superiors as spineless libertarians, chafe under operational restrictions on their use of force, seek to evade these wherever possible, covering up as they do so, and seek to fight the terrorists on their own terms. At the bottom of this downward spiral, constitutional police forces and counterterror units can end up behaving no better than the terrorist cells they are trying to extirpate. Their moral conduct becomes dependent on the increasingly repellent conduct of the other side. This is the unintentional path to nihilism, taken by constitutional forces to defend the fallen and to revenge their losses. In the process, torture and extrajudicial killing may become routine.

Gillo Pontecorvo's masterful film *The Battle of Algiers* (1965) portrays the Algerian war for independence, between 1955 and 1962, as a tragic duel in which two sides, conscientiously believing in the rightness of their course, become trapped in just such a downward spiral as we have been considering. The film may be fictional, but it is drawn from extensive documentary research into the actual history of the Algerian struggle. While clearly siding with the Algerian revolution, Pontecorvo takes care to avoid any moral caricature of the French, and shows why torture could be seen as a rational and effective way to break up the terrorist cells working in the Algiers Casbah. Nor does the filmmaker conceal the bloody reality of the liberation struggle, showing the full horror of an attack on a café that leaves the street strewn with mangled bodies and traumatized survivors. The film maintains an extraordinarily subtle moral balance, supporting the Algerian struggle for freedom without mitigating the crimes committed in its name; condemning the French use of torture without failing to do justice to the reality that it was committed not by brutes but by people with dedicated convictions. *The Battle of Algiers* thus becomes a testament to the tragedy of terrorist war.

Calling this path tragic is not to excuse it, merely to distinguish it from a second path, which is altogether more cynical. In the tragic path, violence, once used as a means, becomes an end in itself, to the horror of those who are trapped by the conduct of the other side. In the second path, violence doesn't begin as a means to noble ends. It is used, from the beginning, in the service of cynical or self-serving ones. On both the terrorist and counterterrorist sides, there are bound to be individuals who actually enjoy violence for its own sake. Violence and weapons exert a fascination all their own, and their possession and use satisfy deep psychological needs. It isn't necessary to delve into the question of why human beings love violence and seek to use weapons as instruments of power and even of sexual gratification. The fact that violence attracts as well as repels is a recurring challenge to the ethics of a lesser evil, since it explains why the appetite for violence can become insatiable, seeking ever more spectacular effects even though these fail to produce any discernible political result. Many terrorist groups use political language to mask the absence of any genuine commitment to the cause they defend. In their cynicism, they can become uncontrollable, because once violence is severed from the pursuit of determinate political ends, violence will not cease even if these goals are achieved.

What is true of terrorists can also characterize counterterrorists. The type of personnel attracted to police and antiterrorist squads may be recruited because they are drawn to violent means. These means confer power, boost sexual confidence, and enable them to swagger and intimidate others. The type of personality attracted into a counterterror campaign may not have any intrinsic or reflective commitment to democratic values of restraint. Rules of engagement for the use of deadly force need be obeyed only when superiors are watching and can be disregarded at any other time.

There may always be a gap, therefore, between the values of a liberal democracy when it is under attack and the conduct of the counterterrorist forces who have to take the war to the enemy. There is no necessary reason to suppose that those who defend a democracy do so out of any convinced belief in its values. Their chief motivation may be only the thrill of the chase and the glamour of licensed violence. Liberal states cannot be protected by herbivores. But if we need carnivores to defend us, keeping them in check, keeping them aware of what it is they are defending, is a recurrent challenge.

On the terrorist side, there will always be a gap between those who take the political goals of a terrorist campaign seriously and those who are drawn to the cause because it offers glamour, violence, money, and power. It is anyone's guess how many actual believers in the dream of a united Ireland there are in the ranks of the IRA. But it is a fair bet to suppose that many recruits join up because they want to benefit from the IRA's profitable protection rackets.[8] The IRA bears as much relation to the Mafia as it does to an insurrectionary cell or a radical political party, and the motivations that draw young people into the movement are often as criminal as they are political. When criminal goals predominate over political ones, it becomes difficult for leaders to prevent their followers from turning violence into an end in itself.

The criminal allure of terrorist groups and the cynicism of those who join them are additional reasons why it is a mistake to conciliate or appease a group like the IRA with political concessions. Their political goals may be subsidiary to their criminal interests, and like any criminal enterprise they can be driven out of business only by the force of the law. Equally, to express surprise that they tarnish political ideals with squalid tactics, or that they seem to be indifferent to the costs that their violence imposes on the communities they purport to represent, would be to misunderstand their real nature and purpose.

Not all terrorists, however, are moral cynics. Not all terrorist groups use politics as an excuse for other straightforwardly violent ends. There are other groups whose political purposes are genuine, but who nonetheless end up turning violence into a way of life. These are the groups that have the characteristics, not of criminal gangs, but of fanatic sects. Here nihilism takes the form, not of believing in nothing, but of believing in too much. What I mean is a form of conviction so intense, a devotion so blind, that it becomes impossible to see that violence necessarily betrays the ends that conviction seeks to achieve. Here the delusion is not tragic, as in the first case, because believers are not trapped into violence by the conduct of the other side. Nor is it cynical: for these are true believers. They initiate violence as a sacred and redemptive duty. This is the third path to nihilism, the fanatical use of high principle to justify atrocity.

What is nihilistic is the belief that such goals license all possible means, indeed obviate any consideration of the human costs. Nihilism here is willed indifference to the human agents sacrificed on the altar of principle. Here nihilism is not a belief in nothing at all; it is, rather, the belief that nothing about particular groups of human beings matters enough to require minimizing harm to them.

The high principles commonly used to justify terrorism were once predominantly secular—varieties of conspiratorial Marxism—but today most of the justifying ideologies are religious.[9] To call religious justifications of violence nihilistic is, of course, to make a certain kind of value judgment, to assert that there cannot be, in principle, any metaphysical or God-commanded justification for the slaughter of civilians. From a human rights standpoint, the claim that such inhumanity *can* be divinely inspired is a piece of nihilism, an inhuman devaluation of the respect owed to all persons, and moreover a piece of hubris, since, by definition, human beings have no access to divine intentions, whatever they may be.

The hubris is not confined to vocalizing divine intention. It also consists in hijacking scriptural tradition. The devil can always quote scripture to his use, and there is never a shortage in any faith of texts justifying the use of force. Equally, all religions contain sacred texts urging believers to treat human beings decently. Some may be more universalistic in these claims than others. Some may confine the duties of benevolence to fellow believers, while others may extend these duties to the whole of humankind. But whatever the ambit of their moral concern, all religious teaching offers some resistance to the idea that it is justifiable to kill or abuse other human beings. This resistance may range from outright condemnation to qualified justification as a last resort. A nihilist use of religious doctrine is one that perverts the doctrine into a justification for inhuman deeds and ignores any part of the doctrine which is resistant to its violent purposes. The nihilism here engages in a characteristic inversion: adjusting religious doctrine to rationalize the terrorist goal, rather than subjecting it to the genuine interrogation of true faith.

It is unnecessary here to document the extent to which Al Qaeda has exploited and distorted the true faith of Islam. To take but one example, the tradition of jihad, which refers to the obligation of the believer to struggle against inner weakness and corruption, has been distorted into an obligation to wage war against Jews and Americans. In the hands of Osama bin Laden, the specifically religious and inner-directed content of jihad has been emptied out and replaced by a doctrine justifying acts of terror.[10] This type of religious justification dramatically amplifies the political impact of terrorist actions. When Al Qaeda strikes, it can claim that it acts on behalf of a billion Muslims. This may be a lie, but it is an influential one nonetheless.

Appropriating religious doctrine in this way also enables the group to offer potential recruits the promise of martyrdom.[11] Immortality complicates the relationship between violent means and political ends, for the promise of eternal life has the effect of making it a secondary matter to the suicide bomber whether or not the act achieves anything political at all. What matters most is securing entry into Paradise. Here political violence becomes subservient not to a political end but to a personal one.

Once violent means cease to serve determinate political ends, they take on a life of their own. When personal immortality becomes the goal, the terrorists cease to think like political actors, susceptible to rational calculation of effect, and begin to act like fanatics.

It is not easy to turn human beings into fanatics. In order to do so, terrorist groups that use suicide bombers have to create a cult of death and sacrifice, anchored in powerful languages of belief. Osama bin Laden used an interview with an American journalist in May 1998 in Afghanistan to justify terrorism in the language of faith:

> The terrorism we practice is of the commendable kind for it is directed at the tyrants and the aggressors and the enemies of Allah, the tyrants, the traitors who commit acts of treason against their own countries and their own faith and their own prophet and their own nation.[12]

What is noticeable here is the use of religion not just to justify killing the infidel but to override the much more serious taboo against killing fellow believers. The function of nihilism here is to recast real, living members of the Islamic faith as traitors deserving death. Nihilism takes the form of nullifying the human reality of people and turning them into targets.

Hijacking the jihad traditions of the faith is essential to creating the conditions for nihilist violence. The cult needs the mysteries of faith and the promise of the afterlife in order to prevent individual terrorists from asking whether their act contributes usefully to a discernible political end. Once the capacity to ask this question is lost, death becomes an end in itself, the doorway to Paradise. Repeated political failure becomes an irrelevant distraction. What matters is not achieving anything political but earning eternal life.

To the degree that any political goal remains, it ceases to be the attainment of a real objective—such as self-determination— and is deformed into a desire to humiliate, shame, degrade, and kill. It is enough to destroy lives; enough to humiliate the other side, enough to cause panic and fear, and as long as these gratifications are evident, it need not matter that your cause has not been advanced at all.

The promise of eternal life, therefore, can be seen as an ingenious solution to the problem of sustaining the motivation of a terrorist cell in the face of failure. As we have already seen, terrorist actions rarely secure the weak the victory they are seeking, and while violence offers reliable satisfactions, a career of violence is likely to be nasty, brutish, and short. Once immortality is on offer, political failure in the here and now ceases to matter. Once it no longer matters, a terror campaign is not easily defeated, since recurrent failure will not discourage or deter it. This is how, as means come to be severed from realistic ends, terrorism becomes a way of life.

This should also explain why it is a mistake to view Al Qaeda's assassins as warriors in the cause of freedom for the Palestinians and humiliated Muslims around the world. The reality is otherwise: their goals are less political than apocalyptic, securing immortality for themselves while calling down a mighty malediction on the Great Satan. Goals that are political can be engaged politically. Apocalyptic goals, on the other hand, are impossible to negotiate with. They can only be fought by force of arms.

Terrorist movements like Al Qaeda or Hamas are death cults, organized by their leaders to invert the normal psychological priorities of adherents, to make them think their own love of life and their scruple about taking the lives of others are forms of weakness to be overcome in favor of a worship of death as a deliverance from sin, oppression, and shame.[13] If your own life is worth sacrificing, then by the logic of the cult the lives of others come to be worth sacrificing too.

Death cults go to some lengths to deaden and desensitize the scruples that might otherwise stay the hand of a suicide bomber. The Tamil Tiger suicide bombers, mostly female, were indoctrinated to offer their sacrifice as an act of love for the Tamil leader.[14] Dying was reconceived as an orgasmic reunion with the leader in death. Channeling sexual desire away from life is an important process in the creation of the death cult. It harnesses erotic energies so that the martyr thinks of death as a form of erotic release. At the same time, the cult mobilizes sexual phobias in order to dehumanize potential victims. The September 11 hijackers shaved their body hair and sought to avoid all polluting contact with infidels, especially women. If we are to judge from the note left behind by one of the September 11 hijackers, Mohamed Atta, fear and loathing of women mixed with anxiety about his own sexuality formed one of the psychological sources of his hatred for what he saw as a threateningly eroticized and decadent Western culture. I am not implying that terrorism, in Atta's case, was simply an acting out of private sexual insecurities. A man like Atta might have had rational grounds for being repelled by the overt sexuality of Western culture, at least as compared to the reserve of most Islamic societies. Sexual propriety is central to any culture's ideas of human dignity. Even if they were mistaken about Western society, their loathing of Western sexuality helped to drive them to terrorist acts.[15] The point here is not psychological but ethical: if you can find erotically charged grounds to loathe Western society—and this man did—it becomes a great deal easier to be indifferent to the fate of the innocent civilians you condemn to death.

Sexual phobias and hatreds are a powerful source of nihilism, particularly of the idea that victims are unworthy of moral concern. This phobic sense of pollution, in the case of Mohamed Atta, was reinforced by a particular reading of the Qur'an, emphasizing that moral duties are owed only to fellow believers, not to infidels. The Qur'an, of course, admits of many readings, some endorsing a universalistic conception of moral duty, others restricting full moral concern to the faithful alone. It is true that the terrorists hijacked Islam, but any religious doctrine can be hijacked in the same way. Religious traditions are always polyvalent: they can be interpreted in a wide variety of ways. No doctrine has any power in itself to withstand moral mutilation by wicked people. All that can ever stand in the way are the living convictions of fellow believers and the institutions that guard the faith, and in this particular case they were silent. Authoritative voices in the Islamic world who might have condemned the deformation of the idea of jihad into a justification for terror did not do so in time. In the absence of such condemnations, the perpetrators of September 11 saw no morally problematic aspects to their acts.

A key feature of nihilism, therefore, is the redescription of intended victims as inferior creatures to be brushed aside on the path to a higher goal. Phobic sexual dislikes, religious fanaticism, and, finally, political ideology can all contribute to a nihilistic deadening of moral scruple. In the twentieth century, the language of the class enemy in Stalin's Russia, like the fascist language of the Jew as vermin, served as a powerful justification for exterminatory violence. In the twenty-first century, it is religion that has been made the unwilling accomplice of nihilism.

II

If terrorism is armed nihilism, its adherents require, not just a general theory of why human beings who stand in the way do not matter, but a specific theory about why killing civilians is justified. All terrorist campaigns have to discredit the idea of civilian innocence. Bin Laden's statements take explicit aim at such ideas:

> Our mothers and daughters and sons are slaughtered every day with the approval of America and its support. And, while America blocks the entry of weapons into Islamic countries, it provides the Israelis with a continuous supply of arms allowing them thus to kill and massacre more Muslims. Your religion does not forbid you from committing such acts, so you have no right to object to any response or retaliation that reciprocates your actions.[16]

Likewise, the Palestinian suicide bombers are taught to view Israeli passengers on a municipal bus not as innocent bystanders but as accomplices in the crime of occupation. If this is not enough, then standard varieties of anti-Semitism, which have semiofficial standing in the politics of the Arab world, are enlisted to further dehumanize the intended victims.[17]

In Algeria, the FLN (Front for National Liberation) maintained that French civilians were legitimate targets because they were beneficiaries of French colonial oppression. In South Africa, white civilians were gunned down in churches and public squares on the grounds that they were complicit in the evil of apartheid.[18]

Preventing a war on terror from becoming nihilistic means, first of all, insisting that counterterror forces observe the distinction that terrorists sweep away, namely, between innocent civilians and legitimate military targets. A war on terror that does not struggle to hold the line against the temptation to become as indiscriminate as the terrorists will surely lose both its political and its moral legitimacy.

But let us admit just how difficult it is to maintain discrimination. Civilian complicity makes civilian immunity a complex affair. In South Africa, all whites were complicit beneficiaries of apartheid, but there is a material difference between working for the police and military forces and merely voting for the regime, or between being white and actively giving apartheid your sup-

port. Many whites, after all, opposed apartheid, and it is doubtful that the system would have fallen when it did had the regime
not lost its own basis of support. In moral terms, it seems wrong
to accuse someone of complicity on the basis of attributes rather
than conduct, to condemn whole categories of people—white
South Africans, Israelis, or any other group—on the basis that
they derive benefit from some injustice, rather than on their particular actions as individuals.

On the other hand, where civilians take a direct personal part
in counterterror actions—as, for example, when the *pieds noirs*
in French Algeria armed themselves and carried out preemptive
or revenge attacks against Algerian fedayeen, or when Israeli
settlers do the same in the occupied territories, passing from defense of their settlements to active combat operations against
Palestinian fighters or their civilian supporters—they deserve to
lose their immunity from military attack.[19] They become legitimate military targets, but their families do not.

Where terrorists hide in refugee camps, conceal their weapons
in civilian areas, and attempt to pass themselves off at check-
points as civilians, a counterterror operation may be tempted
to ignore civilian immunity altogether. It may seem necessary to
penalize the population, to indefinitely detain young males, to
demolish the houses of those who lend support or refuge to terrorist groups, or to lock down women and children and prevent
normal movement and economic activity. The use of Israeli military bulldozers to destroy civilian housing in the Jenin refugee
camp was a response to the use of civilian dwellings as ambush
points.[20] Civilian complicity may also lead military authorities
to relax fire discipline among soldiers charged with controlling
civilian populations or to relax targeting discrimination when
striking terrorist leaders hiding among civilians. Selective assassination of terrorist leaders has been a feature of the Israeli war
against Palestinian terror, and while it is justified as a lesser evil,
there is evidence that civilians with no direct connection to terrorist groups have been killed when these leaders are struck. Israeli authorities have expressed regret for these mistakes and
have argued that under the laws of armed conflict they are not

liable, ethically, for unintended collateral damage effects of a targeted assassination policy. But assassination can be justified only if civilian immunity can be observed.

The risk of such tactics is that instead of isolating the terrorists, you increase their support. As you escalate repressive measures, and they fail, exposing your forces to more resistance, your troops will come to view the population with hatred, thus increasing the chances of abuse and atrocity. Gradually, they come to view the entire population as the enemy and the civilian-combatant distinction is entirely obliterated. This is an especial danger when the two peoples at war come from different religions and races. Then it becomes all too easy for the counterterror agents of a democratic state to live inside a schizophrenic moral duality: treating their own fellow citizens and their own families as equals, while treating the occupied population as things. This duality in fact shelters counterterrorists from the nihilism that is gradually taking them over in their professional life. Faced with the evidence of their own inhumanity on the job, they take refuge in their humanity as parents, neighbors, friends, and citizens. On the job, however, the counterterrorist will gravitate toward the same nihilistic pole as does his terrorist opponent: everyone is an enemy, everyone a legitimate target. When both sides reach this abyss, a terror and counterterror campaign can easily become a free-fire zone.

But free fire is unlikely to produce victory for either side. The terrorists, even if they become indiscriminate, will not have the force to prevail against an armed state, and free fire by counterterrorist forces, unless it proceeds to the extermination of the entire resistant population, cannot hold them under control. Taking the gloves off may appear to promise victory; it usually delivers only a bloody stalemate.

Nihilism—which is the blunt name for taking the gloves off— holds real dangers for both sides. When a democratic state licenses all means to repress a terrorist group, it may only play into the hands of its enemy. Some terrorist groups deliberately seek to draw reprisals upon themselves in order to radicalize their own population. As the state's repression increases, the ter-

rorists respond by tightening their screws on their base of support, replacing a political relation to their own side with one of
unvarnished tyranny, killing or intimidating anyone who questions whether the costs of the campaign are outweighing the
gains. Populations that once supported armed struggle for reasons of conviction become trapped either in fanaticism or in
complicit silence. In the process, political regulation of terrorist
groups by their community at large becomes impossible. Moderate voices who might persuade a community to withdraw their
support from terror are silenced. In place of a properly political
culture, in which groups and interests compete for leadership, a
people represented by suicide bombers ceases to be a political
community at all and becomes a cult, with all the attendant hysteria, intimidation, and fear. This is the process by which nihilism leads to a war without end.

In such a terrorist cult, many praiseworthy moral virtues are
inverted, so that they serve not life but death. Terrorist groups
typically expropriate the virtues of the young—their courage,
their headstrong disregard for consequences, their burning desire to establish their own significance—and use these to create
an army of the doomed. In this way, violence becomes a career,
a way of life that leads only to death.

Once violence becomes part of a community death cult, the
only rational response by a state under attack must be to eliminate the enemy one by one, either by capture and lifelong im-
prisonment or by execution. Those for whom violence has become the driving rationale of conduct cannot be convinced to
desist. They are in a deathly embrace with what they do, and
argument cannot reach them. Nor can failure. It counts for nothing that violence fails to achieve their political objective because
such achievement has long since ceased to be the test of their
effectiveness. It is redemption they are after, and they seek death
sure that they have attained it. They have nothing to negotiate
for, and we have nothing to gain by negotiating with them. They
will take gestures of conciliation as weakness and our desire to
replace violence with dialogue as contemptible naïveté. To say
we are at war with Al Qaeda and suicide bombers in general is

to say that political dialogue is at an end. We have nothing to say to them nor they to us. Either we prevail or they do, and force must be the arbiter.

This may be so, but it does not invalidate the necessity of balancing purely military responses to terror with a political strategy that redresses the injustices that terrorists exploit. Not all of those who support terrorist acts are in love with violence or deaf to conciliation. Some Palestinians may support suicide bombers, not because they endorse human sacrifice, but because they sincerely believe that such sacrifice, however horrific, is the only way to make the injustice of the Palestinian situation plain to the world. Such persons might indeed abjure violence if their political demands for statehood and dignity were met. A war on terror that fails to make political gestures to this community will fail. The political gestures required need to be more than tokens: they have to offer moderates a political horizon, a possible political alternative to a community captured by the logic of terror.

The need to respond politically—and not just militarily—is more than a matter of pragmatics. It relates to the very identity of liberal democracy. Liberal democracy proclaims justice as its rule of life, and because it does so, it cannot remain true to itself if it indefinitely denies a claim to justice—in this case, statehood for the Palestinians. Yet recognizing a claim is not possible when a gun is held to your head. Palestinian terrorism has set back the cause it serves precisely because true recognition of a moral claim is possible only when antagonists meet in a condition of freedom, and people under attack are not free. Israel will never negotiate under duress, but it cannot survive without negotiation, without withdrawal from the occupied territories and the emergence of a viable, contiguous Palestinian state. When suicide bombing has been beaten, when the other side runs out of martyrs, when Palestinians themselves recognize the political futility of violence, then politics—negotiation and compromise—will have to resume. A liberal democracy cannot maintain its own identity in freedom if it rules others without their consent.

III

The larger question is how liberal democracies elsewhere, faced with nihilistic violence, can prevent their own security agents from descending into the very nihilistic trap that ensnares the terrorists. One example will make clear how difficult this can be. During the Vietnam War, the CIA engaged in Operation Phoenix, a counterinsurgency program whose purpose was to convert, neutralize, or kill the political cadres infiltrated into South Vietnam by the northern forces. The program resulted in the deaths of thousands of these cadres, who were often labeled as terrorists. The program did not stop the North Vietnamese from gaining control of the South, but it did leave many Americans, and many congressmen, disgusted that their government could authorize covert assassination of foreign nationals. Revelations about Operation Phoenix, together with disclosures of attempts by the CIA to assassinate foreign leaders including Salvador Allende, Fidel Castro, and Rafael Trujillo, led to a congressional investigation, under Senator Frank Church, that recommended a ban on assassination. President Ford responded with an executive order banning the practice.[21] The ban endures where the United States is at peace, but where it is at war, as with Al Qaeda, the ban has been lifted. Targeted assassinations of enemy combatants have occurred, most notably in the missile strike on a car carrying alleged enemy combatants in Yemen.

Assassination can be a justified lesser evil, but only against bona fide terrorist targets actively engaged in hostilities against a democratic state, and even then only under certain conditions: (a) where less violent alternatives, like arrest and capture, endanger U.S. personnel or civilians; (b) where information exists that the targets in question are planning imminent attacks that cannot be stopped in any other way; and (c) where all reasonable precautions are taken to minimize collateral damage and civilian harms.

Assassination may be a justified lesser evil, but regulating it is not easy. Previous attempts to do so illustrate the unintended ironies that accompany sincerely intended attempts to control the conduct of a counterterror campaign. The original ban, instituted in the 1970s, formed part of a larger attempt to bring the CIA back under congressional and executive control. Some former agents have argued that the new systems of regulation and oversight led, inadvertently, to an institutional culture of risk avoidance which, over time, began to damage the effectiveness of the institution as an intelligence gatherer. Because infiltrating terrorist organizations, especially in the Middle East, is a dangerous business, the CIA chose to rely instead on signals intelligence and failed to develop the human intelligence that might have provided early warning of the September 11 catastrophe.[22] This account of the unintended consequences of regulations needs to be taken with a grain of salt, since it is obvious that agents who relish extralegal methods would have an interest in promoting their resumption. Still, in a consideration of the lesser evils of a counterterror war, the possibility that overregulating intelligence agencies may make them overcautious needs to be taken into account. A balance needs to be struck between holding agents accountable to their superiors and to elected officials and tying them down so that they cannot take the calculated risks necessary for the public safety. These risks should not include assassination of civilian leaders in peacetime, but they might include targeted killing of terrorist combatants, where no feasible alternative existed. Intelligence agents might also be authorized to make payments to dubious characters and to use deception and entrapment to secure intelligence, all under the cover of official denial. There is no alternative to secrecy in intelligence operations, but this need not preclude administrative and legislative review in camera. The U.S. Foreign Intelligence Surveillance Court, a secret court composed of federal judges who hear applications for wiretaps on foreign sources in the United States, provides an example of the ways in which covert activity with risks of rights violations can be made subject to judicial review.[23]

The larger concern, when political leaders are regulating their own warriors in a war against terror, is to guard against so alienating them that they come to have greater loyalty to each other than to the institutions they are charged to protect. This conflict of loyalties arises because a liberal democratic society will, by its nature, impose some limitations on what intelligence and counterterror squads can do: restrictions on search and seizure, on clandestine operations, on torture and the use of deadly force. These restrictions are problematic because they increase risk to our own side while not applying to the enemy. So counterterror forces will come to believe that they are being asked to fight with one hand tied behind their back.

This in turn presents civilian leaders with a dilemma: either they give way to their police and allow them to take the gloves off, risking acts of violence that will disgrace the political order they are seeking to defend, or they stand up to the police, refuse them the extra powers they want, and then watch the police taking the law into their own hands or losing the war to the terrorists.

Since the latter is unthinkable, democratic politicians have incentives to take the gloves off too. They need results from their security services, and in the pressure of the moment, they may not care overmuch about how these results are obtained. A culture of silent complicity may develop between civilian political leaders and their security chiefs, in which both sides know that extralegal means are being used but each has an interest in keeping quiet about it. In this way, the clear constitutional duty of civilian leaders to maintain executive control over security services can be subverted and replaced by a complicit bargain in which politicians keep silent for the security forces and the security forces keep silent for the politicians.

Something like this seems to have happened in French Algeria in the 1950s. The democratic government in Paris publicly denied that it was using torture to defeat the FLN, while privately ministers were perfectly aware that it was going on. This set up a perverse relationship with the security forces who, because the politicians had not been truthful with the public, were in a position to blackmail them with threatened disclosure of the facts. Both sides, the political elite and the security forces, were then locked together, not in an appropriately constitutional relation of supervision, but in a blackmailer's pact of silence. The silence was about the existence of torture, but also about its purpose, which was to cow and break the political will of the Algerian population as a whole.[24] This is the way with torture: it is originally justified as a lesser evil, as a regrettable necessity in the struggle to extract timely information to prevent greater harms, and slowly but surely it becomes a standard technique, explicitly used to humiliate, terrify, degrade, and subdue entire populations.

I V

Torture, by which I mean the deliberate infliction of physical cruelty and pain in order to extract information, brings together all of the dilemmas that a liberal society has to face in a war on terror. For here is the problem of nihilism in a form different from the ones we have been discussing so far: where believing that majoritarian interest—in this case the survival of democratic society itself—could legitimize committing an ultimate violation to human dignity. Nobody denies that the physical torture of individuals amounts to an ultimate violation. There is no doubt about the moral facts. The question is whether democratic survival or national security could override the overwhelming claim that these facts usually make upon the allegiance of a liberal democracy. Those who defend torture would insist that their choice is not in fact nihilistic—denying the ultimate value of human beings—but rather motivated by a value-filled concern to save innocent human life. Those who insist that torture is an ultimate form of nihilism believe that a majoritarian justification for torture amounts to a failure to understand what is special, inviolable, and worthy of ultimate respect in a human being.

There is not much doubt that liberal democracy's very history and identity is tied up in an absolute prohibition of torture. The elimination of torture from the penal process, beginning with Voltaire's campaign on behalf of Calas and Beccaria's great Enlightenment *Essay on Crimes and Punishments*, has always been seen as an intrinsic feature of the story of European liberty it-self.[25] In this story, constitutional freedoms matter positively be-cause they enable men and women to choose the lives they want to live, and matter negatively because they help eliminate need-less and unjustifiable cruelty from the exercise of government.[26] Liberal democracy stands against torture because it stands against any unlimited use of public authority against human be-ings, and torture is the most unlimited, the most unbridled form of power that one person can exercise against another. Certainly the United Nations Convention on Torture—to which all liberal democracies, including the United States, are signatories—for-bids it under any circumstances and does not allow the prohibi-tion to be derogated even in conditions of national emergency.[27]

Yet the matter does not end here. There are those who find it peculiar that liberal democracy proscribes torture and cruel and unusual punishment, but not lawful killing in war. How can one object to the torture of persons to secure valuable information for reasons of state, and not object to killing them? Both could simply be regarded as acceptable lesser evils, forced on unwill-ing liberal democracies by the exigencies of their own survival. But the cases are not the same. A liberal society that would not defend itself by force of arms might perish, while a liberal soci-ety that refused to torture is less likely to jeopardize its collective survival. Besides, there is a moral difference between killing a fellow combatant, in conformity to the laws of war, and tortur-ing a person. The first takes a life; the second abuses one. It seems more legitimate to ask a citizen to defend a state by force of arms and, if necessary, to kill in self-defense or to secure a military objective, than it does to ask him to inflict degrading pain face-to-face. On this reading of a democratic moral identity, it may be legitimate to kill in self-defense, but not to engage in cruelty. Another way to seize the distinction between torture and killing in combat would be to observe that in combat pain or death is inflicted on those whose job it is to do the same. In the act of torture, pain and possible death are inflicted on a per-son who is disarmed and helpless.

This is a relevant distinction, but it fails to capture the potential dangerousness of disarmed and helpless subjects. The knowledge they possess may pose a mortal danger, if not to the survival of democratic society itself, then at least to large numbers of its citizens. Because this is so, many democracies nominally committed against torture have felt themselves compelled to torture in the name of necessity and national security. The French in Algeria, the Israelis in the occupied territories, and now American CIA and Special Forces interrogators in the war on terror have all been accused of torture. As for the last of these cases, there are denials that the methods involved actually constitute torture. The interrogation methods of which the Americans have been accused since 9/11 are held to include nothing worse than sleep deprivation, permanent light or permanent darkness, disorienting noise, and isolation.[28] If this were true, if interrogation remained free of physical duress or cruelty, it would amount to coercion, rather than torture, and there might be a lesser evil justification for it.[29] The grounds would be that isolation and disorientation that stopped short of physical or psychological abuse might gain the authorities vital information about ongoing terrorist operations. Yet there have been unexplained deaths in captivity in interrogation centers, and because the authorities are not disclosing anything, we simply do not know what is happening to the numberless captives taken either in Afghanistan, in antiterrorist sweeps in Pakistan, or in the postconflict operations in Iraq. In addition, there are allegations of rendition, the handing over of terrorist suspects to intelligence officials in Egypt, Jordan, Morocco, and other countries where both media and judicial oversight of interrogation methods is likely to be cursory.[30] Rendition, it need hardly be said, is a violation of the Convention on Torture, which outlaws extradition to any country where torture is suspected to be a state practice.[31] Given the uncertainty about the facts, it would seem essential for Congress to insist on the right to tour detention facilities, to hold interviews with detainees in camera, and to disclose the information they get in closed session, so as to keep interrogation techniques under democratic scrutiny. As I have already argued, persons detained by a democracy ought not to forgo all due process rights, whatever their nationality, their conduct, or the circumstances of their capture, either on the field of battle or in a noncombatant setting. If a democracy wishes to keep actual physical torture out of its interrogation rooms, it has to grant detainees access to counsel and the possibility of judicial review. While it may compromise interrogations if detainees secure access to counsel immediately, they must have access within a short period of time. At all times, the identities and whereabouts of detainees must be available to judges and legislators, in camera if need be.

Subjecting detention to every possible form of legislative and judicial scrutiny is one way to prevent legitimate interrogation, involving isolation and some nonphysical stress, from turning into outright torture. But it has been argued that keeping to this line is bound to be futile in so-called ticking bomb cases, where physical torture might seem to be the only way to extract information necessary to save innocent civilians from imminent attack. In these cases, majoritarian interest would seem to trump rights and dignity claims. The temptation to use torture in such a case might be so strong, Alan Dershowitz has argued, that, whatever we might think about torture in the abstract, the pressure to use it in cases of urgent necessity might be overwhelming. The issue then becomes not whether torture can be prevented, but whether it can be regulated. Dershowitz suggests that instead of trying to maintain an unrealistic ban on torture, the United States should regulate it through the judicial process. Police authorities needing to torture a suspect would apply to a judge for a "torture warrant" that would specify the individual being tortured and would set limits to the type and duration of pain allowed. Limitations on the admissibility of evidence extracted under duress would continue to apply, but the information could be used to prevent impending attacks.[32] Anyone found torturing outside the terms and conditions of the warrant would be guilty of a criminal offense.

The legalization of torture, under the formula suggested by Dershowitz, seeks to prevent it from becoming a first resort of interrogators in terrorist and criminal cases as well. The proposal seeks to bring the rule of law into the interrogation room and keep it there. All this is well-intentioned, but as an exercise in the lesser evil it seems likely to lead to the greater. Legalization of physical force in interrogation will hasten the process by which it becomes routine. The problem with torture is not just that it gets out of control, not just that it becomes lawless. What is wrong with torture is that it inflicts irremediable harm on both the torturer and the prisoner. It violates basic commitments to human dignity, and this is the core value that a war on terror, waged by a democratic state, should not sacrifice, even under threat of imminent attack.

It might be argued that such dignity commitments are a luxury when a state is fighting for its life. But the Israeli case shows that a democratic state engaged in a war with terror can still maintain these commitments. The Israeli Supreme Court has ruled on the issue of torture, arguing that extreme shaking of suspects, and holding them in chairs, tipped forward, for long periods of time, are violations of dignity that cannot be allowed even in a state under threat.[33] The Israeli court also ruled that no regulation of the practice could make it acceptable. As for the defense of necessity, the court accepted that there might be cases where an interrogator was genuinely convinced that physical duress was the only way to secure information to save life. If an interrogator violated the rules and engaged in torture, however, the court was prepared to accept necessity as a plea in mitigation, not as a justification or an excuse. In this formulation, the court sought to reconcile an absolute prohibition against torture with an acknowledgment that, in rare and extreme cases, a reputable interrogator might find physical duress unavoidable. It accepted that there had been cases, in Israeli history, where physical methods of interrogation had actually saved lives.

Torture is probably the hardest case in the ethics of the lesser evil. A clear prohibition erected in the name of human dignity comes up against a utilitarian case also grounded in a dignity claim, namely, the protection of innocent lives. In adjudicating this conflict, we must stress, first, that while conscientious people may disagree as to whether torture might be admissible in cases of necessity, all will agree that torture can never be justified as a general practice. The problem lies in identifying the justifying exceptions and defining what forms of duress stop short of absolute degradation of an interrogation subject. Permissible duress might include forms of sleep deprivation that do not result in harm to mental or physical health, and disinformation that causes stress. Impermissible duress would include any physical coercion or abuse, any involuntary use of drugs or serums, and deprivation of basic food, water, medicine, and rest necessary for survival, together with permanent denial of access to counsel.

As with all attempts to distinguish lesser from greater evils, this definition of the line between permissible and impermissible interrogation, between coercion and torture, will strike some as permitting too little and others as allowing too much. Those who think it allows too much probably underestimate just how important accurate and timely information can be in a war on terror, and just how resistant terrorist suspects can be. Those who think this distinction between coercion and torture allows too little will want to know why the line should be drawn at physical abuse in cases where extreme physical duress might save lives. Here the case to be made would be both practical and ethical. On the practical side, there is some evidence that physical duress is unnecessary where interrogators are skilled and persistent. There is also the fact that those who are subjected to physical torture, when not actually broken psychologically, usually conceive undying hatred for their torturers. Members of the Muslim Brotherhood, tortured in the aftermath of the assassination of Anwar Sadat, conceived just such a hatred, both for the Egyptian regime and for its strategic ally, America. One such victim of torture was Osama bin Laden's second in command.[34] As a practical matter, torture may help, if not to create terrorists, then to harden them in their hostility to the state responsible for their suffering.

One way around this problem, obviously, is to dispose of the tortured, in order to prevent their returning as threats. Once torture was routinized in Chile and Argentina in the 1970s, it was soon followed by disappearances, as the military sought to dispose of the evidence of torture by killing their victims.[35] In Argentina, thousands of torture victims were thrown, sometimes dead, sometimes alive, from planes into the ocean. As a practical matter, therefore, once a state begins to torture, it soon finds itself required to murder, in order to eliminate the problem of releasing hardened and embittered enemies into the general population. Once torture becomes a state practice, it entrains further consequences that can poison the moral reputation and political legitimacy of a state.

A further problem with physical torture is that it inflicts damage on those who perpetrate it as well as those who are forced to endure it. Any liberal democratic citizen who supports the physical torture of terrorist suspects in ticking bomb cases is required to accept responsibility for the psychological damage done, not only to a foreign victim, but to a fellow citizen, the interrogator. Torture exposes agents of a democratic state to ultimate moral hazard. The most plausible case for an absolute ban on physical torture (as opposed to coercion) in every circumstance is related precisely to this issue of moral hazard. No one should have to decide when torture is or is not justified, and no one should be ordered to carry it out. An absolute prohibition is legitimate because in practice such a prohibition relieves a state's public servants from the burden of making intolerable choices, ones that inflict irremediable harm both on our enemies and on themselves, on those charged with our defense.

If we are to understand the moral hazard at stake for everyone involved, it is worth listening to the testimony of one of torture's victims. Jean Amery, a Belgian resistant, was arrested in Brussels in 1943 for distributing tracts in German urging soldiers of the German occupation to desert. He was tortured by the SS in a Belgian jail in 1943, before being shipped off to Auschwitz. Amery's hands were bound behind his back and he was suspended by a hook from the ceiling until his arms were pulled out of their sockets. While this was occurring, his captors beat him with a whip, seeking to extract information about his companions in

the Resistance. Amery survived this ordeal, but in his account
of it, written twenty years later, he said that a tortured man always stays tortured.[36] The experience leaves scars that no state
of necessity or social peril can justify. Indeed, Amery argued that
what was worse than the memory of the pain was the moral
shock of seeing other human beings reducing him to a carcass
of meat. The experience destroyed all his remaining social trust:
"someone who has been tortured is never capable of being at
home in the world again."[37] Amery was not able to write about
his experiences in the SS detention center or in Auschwitz until
twenty years later, and like his friend and fellow inmate at
Auschwitz, Primo Levi, he ended his life by suicide.[38] It would
be impertinent to attribute so private a decision to so public a
calamity as torture, but, equally, we cannot think of Amery's fate
without at least considering that he was right about the experience: torture destroyed, once and for all, the trust necessary for
living among fellow human beings.

Amery also insisted that torture should be viewed not in individual terms as the psychosexual aberration of particular torturers but as a key to the identity of the society responsible for it.
He argued that torture was not an incidental feature of the Third
Reich but the essence of its view of human beings. By extension,
the same premise is true of Saddam Hussein's Iraq or Burma or
North Korea. For these societies, the practice of torture is definitional of their very identity as forms of state power. This idea
helps us to see why torture should remain anathema to a liberal
democracy and should never be regulated, countenanced, or co-
vertly accepted in a war on terror. For torture, when committed
by a state, expresses the state's ultimate view that human beings
are expendable. This view is antithetical to the spirit of any constitutional society whose raison d'être is the control of violence
and coercion in the name of human dignity and freedom.

We should have faith in this constitutional identity. It is all
that we have to resist the temptations of nihilism, but it is not
nothing. It is the paramount duty of political leaders in a democracy under attack to keep the forces of order intently focused on
the political requirement of maintaining legitimacy. The only

cure for nihilism is for liberal democratic societies—their electorates, their judiciary, and their political leadership—to insist that force is legitimate only to the degree that it serves defensible political goals. This implies a constant exercise of due diligence: strict observance of rules of engagement regarding the use of deadly force and the avoidance of collateral damage. Democracies must enforce such rules by dismissing from service any of the carnivores who disgrace the society they are charged to protect.

We should remember, in fact, that liberal democracy has been crafted over centuries precisely in order to combat the temptations of nihilism, to prevent violence from becoming an end in itself. Thus terrorism does not present us with a distinctively new temptation. This is what our institutions were designed for, back in the seventeenth century: to regulate evil means and control evil people. The chief ethical challenge with relation to terrorism is relatively simple—to discharge duties to those who have violated their duties to us. We have to do this because we are fighting a war whose essential prize is preserving the identity of liberal society itself and preventing it from becoming what terrorists believe it to be. Terrorists seek to strip off the mask of law to reveal the nihilist heart of coercion within, and we have to show ourselves and the populations whose loyalty we seek that the rule of law is not a mask but the true image of our nature.

CHAPTER SIX

LIBERTY AND
ARMAGEDDON

The greatest danger to civil liberties and human rights emerging in the aftermath of September 11 is that leaders will think we are without courage; without concern for non-citizens within the United States; indifferent to the welfare of citizens repressed by despotic governments; prepared to accept without question unequal treatment based on ethnicity; and unable or unwilling to see that there will and must be trade-offs even among our own freedoms and to share in considering them carefully.

—*Philip Heymann*

I

Terrorism requires us to think carefully about who we are as free peoples and what we need to do in order to remain so. When we are confronted with terrorist violence, we cannot allow the claims of national security to trump the claims of liberty, since what we are trying to defend is our continued existence as a free people. Freedom must set a limit to the measures we employ to maintain it. But this is not the only limit that our political and moral identity imposes. We must preserve ourselves and our freedom, but we cannot do so by denying the moral claims of others who do not belong to our national community. If we are constitutionally committed to respect the rights of our fellow citizens, it is in part because they are members of a national community and in part because they are fellow human beings. If being a free people means respecting the claims that human beings make upon one another as human beings, then we are obliged to do so, not merely for our own people, but for our enemies as well. This means that while a war on terror is indeed a war, in which we must defend ourselves with the force of arms, it is a war for the sake of law, and not a war against law itself. Our constitutional commitments oblige us to respect the rights of enemies who do not respect us, to use lawful methods against those who observe no laws at all. Keeping faith with these commitments has never been easy, and our record against terrorism shows that we have not been immune from the temptations of nihilism, fear, and anger. Even when we succeed in resisting these emotions, necessity may require us to take measures that put constitutional commitments under real strain. Where lesser evils—preventive or investigative detention, targeted killing, intensive interrogation—become necessary in a war on terror, I have outlined principles to guide public policy so that they will not turn into greater ones.

If these are the constraints that our moral and political identity imposes on a war on terror, the question is whether we can continue to abide by them as the threats against us increase. So far in history, terrorists have made use only of conventional weaponry. While September 11 showed how devastating such conventional capabilities can be, they are by no means the worst that we can imagine.

What happens when terrorists acquire weapons of mass destruction? Although we have no direct evidence that this has actually occurred, it seems reasonable to suppose that it will. The director of U.S. Central Intelligence has told Congress that Al Qaeda is in the market for chemical, biological, and nuclear weapons.[1] Both the cost and the size of these technologies are declining, and the capacity of states to maintain control over information relating to weapons of mass destruction is also decreasing. Already, miniature nuclear weapons, transported in backpacks or suitcases, are technically feasible. The first attempts to place mass casualty poisons in subways and water supplies have occurred. Weaponized anthrax spores have been sent through the U.S. mail.[2] Inexorably, terrorism, like war itself, is moving beyond the conventional to the apocalyptic.

It is important to appreciate the historical departure this might represent. In the near future, if it has not happened already, the monopoly of the world's states on the ultimate means of violence will be broken. When this happens, a liberal democracy could then be attacked, not by another state, but by a small group consisting of only a few individuals equipped with lethal technologies.

A long historical parenthesis—the ascendancy of the modern state—might be closing. Since the Peace of Westphalia in 1648, ending the Thirty Years War, international order has depended on states' possessing a monopoly of the legitimate means of force within their own territory and having this monopoly recognized by other states.[3] Of course, states have been prodigal with violence, and the Westphalian system failed to stop the orgy of interstate war that nearly destroyed European civilization between 1914 and 1945. Despite these failures, such order as there is in international relations has depended on the fact that states alone possessed the capacity to make war, and that holders of state power could reliably assume that other holders of state power would desist from aggression if presented with a credible threat of force. Since 1945, this model of deterrence has achieved important victories for international stability. Nuclear weapons used twice in August 1945 have never been used since. Chemical weapons, used by major states in the First World War, have never been used thereafter. While Iraq did use them against its own population in 1987 and against opposing Iranian forces, the exception proves the rule: among modern states, the use of chemical weapons has remained beyond the pale. As for biological weapons, in 1969 the United States unilaterally forswore their use for "hostile purposes or in armed conflict." Other nations have followed suit, continuing to stockpile them, but not to deploy them for defensive or offensive purposes.

The success of deterrence has encouraged us all to believe that states could be presumed to be rational enough not to engage in surprise or preemptive use of these weapons on any occasion. These assumptions have depended, to a degree we did not realize, on the belief that the weapons themselves would always remain so expensive to produce, so difficult to store safely, that only states would possess the financial and coercive power to maintain them. This era may now be ending. While it remains true that only states have the resources to produce the key ingredients for nuclear weapons, components like highly enriched uranium have been stolen from ill-guarded nuclear plants in the former Soviet Union. We do not know whether they have reached terrorist networks, but it is possible that they will. Once these networks have the material, the necessary know-how is not difficult to assemble. These networks already have contact with nuclear weapons scientists and engineers, some of them trained in the Pakistani nuclear program.[4] As for biological weapons, already terrorist cells have been arrested in Britain attempting to produce mass casualty agents like ricin.[5] Relatively inexpensive, miniaturized weapons of mass destruction may soon be available for sale in the illegal international arms market.[6]

In order to think about how the acquisition of these weapons by terrorists might play out, we need to distinguish among three distinct types of terrorism:

- loner terrorism
- self-determination terrorism
- the terrorism of the global spectacular

Not all terrorists are equally dangerous, because not all terrorists are undeterrable. As we have already seen, most terrorism is conducted in the name of a determinate people seeking emancipation from occupation or alien rule. While these terrorists may not care about their own lives, they may be deterred by the penalty likely to be inflicted upon the populations who support their cause. Palestinian suicide bombers, for example, are unlikely to detonate weapons of mass destruction, because they would kill many of their own people and inevitable Israeli retaliation would kill still more. This might not prevent Palestinian terrorists from seeking to acquire weapons of mass destruction to wield as a threat. If Palestinians made such a threat, Israel might feel compelled to preempt with a conventional response. Such action, of course, would inflict losses on Palestinians and Israelis alike. As long as terrorists represent populations who can be harmed by reprisal or retaliation, and as long as the state fighting them has populations who could be harmed by its own reprisals, it seems safe, though by no means certain, to assume that the conflict between the two of them will remain conventional.

Matters stand differently with two other kinds of terrorism. The first type is what I have already called loner or issue terrorism, perpetrated by single individuals or small groups who do not have a constituency of support, and who therefore do not need to calculate the consequences for their own side when they contemplate the detonation of weapons of mass destruction. Loners who have nothing to lose but their own lives, and who are so isolated that they no longer care about the fate of anyone else, may be undeterrable in any circumstances. Before September 11, the worst terrorist attack on America was committed by American citizens, Timothy McVeigh and his right-wing coconspirators, who planted the bomb that destroyed the federal building in Oklahoma City. After September 11, the most serious security threat—the anthrax attacks claiming four lives—was probably mounted by a disgruntled American technician or scientist with access to the technologies necessary to weaponize the spores.[7]

While loners may be difficult to deter, not all of them have nothing to lose. Judging from the careers of loner political assassins, their motive is not to die for the sake of a cause but to survive and establish their place in history. The assassin of President Kennedy and the would-be assassin of President Reagan wanted notoriety at whatever price.[8] This distinguishes their motives from purely destructive nihilism. Their point is to *survive* in order to savor the attention, however hostile or tawdry. Were such publicity-seeking loners to acquire weapons of mass destruction, they might seek not annihilation in itself but rather the publicity that comes from an apocalyptic threat. The chief cost here would be the immense amount of investigative resources required to find and neutralize them.

This leaves the true nihilist—the loner who is indifferent to fame and posterity and who wishes to destroy everything and everyone, including himself—as the chief menace. The frequency of random killings by loners, as the Columbine murders and the Washington sniper case attest, suggests that there is no shortage of undeterrable nihilists. Nor are they confined to the United States. At the moment, their weapons of choice are high-powered sniper rifles. Acquiring weapons of mass destruction remains expensive and currently beyond the resources and abilities of such assassins, but sometime in the future they might not exceed the capacities of a superempowered, highly educated, and wealthy psychopath. If such weaponry comes within their grasp, liberal democracy will face a genuinely undeterrable threat. Western individualism is a great achievement, but it would be ironic indeed if its nemesis were to arrive in the form of a superempowered loner equipped with mass destruction weapons.

The third type of terrorist who might prove undeterrable were they to acquire these weapons is Al Qaeda itself. Unlike terrorists who serve the liberation claims of a particular group of people, Al Qaeda does not depend for its support on a particular population who could be subjected to revenge or retribution following an attack. Thus the attackers themselves cannot be restrained by fear that others they care about may suffer for their actions. The fact that Afghans were likely to suffer consequences after the terrorist spectacular of September 11 had no evident effect in restraining the terrorists who trained on Afghan soil. Once Afghanistan had served its function as a base, it was dispensable as far as Al Qaeda was concerned. Since their goal is not the acquisition of power itself but the punishment of the United States and its strategic allies, they cannot be stopped by political negotiation, concession, or appeasement. Nor are they susceptible to the incentives that make some armed groups conform to the laws of war in order to achieve international recognition or legitimacy.

This indifference to incentives and sanctions applies not merely to Al Qaeda but to any cult with charismatic psychopaths at its head. It is hard to see what political action a state could have taken to deter the Japanese cult group Aum Shinrikyo before it released toxic agents in the Tokyo subway system.[9] Unlike political groups seeking liberation or national territory, these cults cannot be engaged politically, and since they are closed and conspiratorial, they are difficult to infiltrate and neutralize. The logic of deterrence that once kept state violence in some kind of check has no traction with loners and the cult leaders of global terrorism. Since they promise their followers eternal life, they create a cadre of undeterrables.

This analysis, which warns of a breakdown in the state system of deterrence as weapons of mass destruction are privatized, might seem to neglect the extent to which terrorist individuals and their networks depend on the tacit support of states. If so, terrorists could be deterred by sanctioning the states that harbor them. It is true that terrorists need territorial sanctuary and the weapons that states provide. These states can be punished, and if they can be punished, they can be deterred. Libya was a sanctuary and base for terrorist activity until Western states decided to strike back with a concerted program of international sanctions and isolation. Now it is less obviously an instigator and paymaster of terror.[10] Libya, however, is a cohesive state with control throughout its territory. Many of the other sanctuaries for terror are to be found in failing or failed states—like Afghanistan or Somalia—that do not actually control their territories.

The terrorist challenge to liberal democracy coincides with a double crisis of state order: first, the failure of many postindependence states in central and southern Africa and, second, the failure of democratic transitions in the states that won their freedom with the breakup of the Soviet empire. A band of failed states, running from Somalia on the east coast of Africa through Congo to Liberia on the west, offer territorial sanctuary, money-laundering facilities, and access to the international arms trade for modern global terrorists. A second band of failing states on the southern edge of the former Soviet empire—from Moldova through Georgia, Abkhazia, Kirghizstan, and Tajikistan, ending in Afghanistan—also offer sanctuary for terrorist operations. Some of these states have pledged to assist liberal democracies by denying terrorists' sanctuary yet lack the capacity to do so. Of the 190-odd states in the international system, between 10 and 15 may lack the capacity to deny sanctuary to international terrorist groups because they are weak, poor, and corrupt, or because they are split apart by internal territorial conflicts that terrorists can exploit.[11] Westphalian deterrence cannot work when states do not have effective coercive control over their own territory. The walls of the state that once contained their monopoly of violence have broken down. Evil has escaped the prison house of deterrence.

This vision—collapsing states and cadres of undeterrables equipped with weapons of mass destruction—might seem a lurid exaggeration, and if so dangerous. Frightening scenarios of this kind might trigger the excessive reactions I have criticized earlier. It could be argued that the attack of September 11, terrible as it was, is unlikely to recur, since security has been tightened and Al Qaeda's recent attacks have all been on secondary rather than primary targets. September 11 might turn out to represent the worst that will ever happen, rather than the first stage of an escalating series of apocalyptic spectaculars.

Yet even if every one of bin Laden's followers is tracked down, the example of September 11 itself will remain as an inspiration to others. September 11 will have the same place in the history of Islamic terrorism as the assassination of Czar Alexander II had in the history of European terrorism. The nihilists of mid-nineteenth-century Russia were primitive amateurs by later standards, yet they created a template that inspired all antibourgeois insurrectionary politics from their day forward. September 11 is certain to have the same effect. In addition, the international grievances that fuel mass casualty terrorism—the power of America, the existence of Israel, the corruption and decay of the Arab and Islamic political order—are also likely to endure. Terrorism will remain a threat to liberal democracy, simply because liberal democracy cannot detach itself from a world that holds it responsible, rightly or wrongly, for its misery.

If weapons of mass destruction become available to terrorists, we may move from a pattern of high frequency–low casualty attacks to a low frequency–catastrophic casualty pattern. This second pattern will be even more difficult to defend against than the first. Terrorists will calculate—correctly—that no state, however vigilant and well-organized, can remain on guard forever and everywhere. Democracies, by their very nature, are less capable of vigilance than authoritarian regimes. The steady relentlessness necessary for vigilant security is not easily maintained in nations with four-year electoral cycles and constant turnover in their leadership elites. Terrorism is a waiting game and victory goes to the patient. Future terrorists may have the financial resources to let sleepers sleep for years at a time. Sooner or later, someone's guard will slip—a container inspector will miss a container, an airport screener will miss a passenger or a bag, a water filtration system will fail—and an attack will succeed.

Liberal democracies are thus faced with an enemy whose demands cannot be appeased, who cannot be deterred, and who does not have to win in order for us to lose. The police, military, and intelligence agencies may succeed in detecting, stopping, or preempting ninety-nine potential attacks. But if the enemy possesses chemical, radiological, bacteriological, or nuclear weapons, they need succeed only once.

It is a commonplace of presidential and prime ministerial rhetoric to insist that their democracies cannot lose in a war on terror. My own analysis thus far has confirmed that no democracy has ever been toppled by a terrorist campaign, unless other factors, like economic collapse or military defeat, were present too. But faced with terrorism that deploys weapons of mass destruction, we cannot be as certain that the historical pattern, argued for in this book, would prevail in the future.

In other words, we *could* lose.

What would defeat look like? It would not be like invasion, conquest, or occupation, of course, but rather would entail the disintegration of our institutions and way of life. A succession of mass casualty attacks, using weapons of mass destruction, would leave behind zones of devastation sealed off for years and a pall of mourning, anger, and fear hanging over our public and private lives. Such attacks would destroy the existential security on which democracy depends. Recurrent attacks with weapons of mass destruction might not just kill hundreds of thousands of people. We might find ourselves living within a national security state on permanent alert, with sealed borders, constant identity checks, and permanent detention camps for suspicious aliens and recalcitrant citizens. A successful attack would poison the wellsprings of trust among strangers that make the relative liberty of liberal democracy possible. Our police forces might descend to torturing suspects in order to prevent future attacks, and our secret security forces might engage in direct assassination of perpetrators or mere suspects as well. Our military might itself use weapons of mass destruction against terrorist enemies. If our institutions were unable to stop the attacks, the state's monopoly of force might even break down, as citizens took the law into their own hands seeking to defend themselves against would-be perpetrators. Vigilantes would patrol blighted and deserted streets.

This is what the face of defeat might look like. We would survive, but we would no longer recognize ourselves or our institutions. We would exist but lose our identity as free peoples.

So what can be done? What resources do we possess?

As the threat of terrorism targets our political identity as free peoples, our essential resource has to be that identity itself. We cannot fight and prevail against an enemy unless we know who we are and what we wish to defend at all costs. If the automatic response to mass casualty terrorism is to strengthen secret government, it is the wrong response. The right one is to strengthen open government. Democratic peoples will not lend assistance to authorities unless they believe in the system they are defending. No strategy against terror is sustainable without public assistance and cooperation, without eyes that detect risks, ears that hear threats, and the willingness to report them to authorities. As two world wars have shown, a democratic people mobilized by fear and led by hope can prove a formidable foe. Despite their checks and balances, democratic systems do not have to be less decisive than authoritarian ones, and democratic institutions have the advantage of marshaling the wisdom, experience, and talent of the citizens as a whole rather than relying on the shallow pool of a closed elite.

Faith in democracy need not make us blind to its faults. Indeed, our democracies are not doing as well as they could in dealing with conventional threats, and it is to be feared that they will do still worse with weapons of mass destruction. So far, information about risk has been doctored for public consumption. Media, with more concern for market share than for the public interest, have colluded in disinforming the public. Judges have accorded excessive deference to government actions. Legislatures have lacked the courage to subject the facts of risk to clear-eyed scrutiny. Government departments have abridged the liberties of aliens and minorities, safe in the knowledge that the victims lack the voice to make injustice heard. The public has gone along, unable or unwilling to force their elected officials to serve them better. When democratic institutions malfunction in this way, bad public policy is the result. Legislatures have crafted legislation that provides the police with powers they do not need; the public lends its support to measures that do not increase its security; the secret services, observing a deceived public and a deceiving leadership, may take the law into their own hands. A war on terror thus waged by secret and unaccountable agents, working on or beyond the margins of the law, on behalf of depoliticized and demobilized citizens who remain in the dark about what is being done in their name, may end up damaging democracy forever.

We do not want a war on terror fought on behalf of free peoples who are free only in name. What we need is a reinvigoration of the institutions of freedom—government by checks and balances, by open forms of adversarial justification in courts, legislatures, and the press. Reinvigoration means simply that our institutions need to do the job that they were designed to do. We need to understand what they are there for, trust in them, and make them work.

II

In addition to requiring a renewal of democracy at home, a war on terror cannot be successful unless states engage in a renewal of democracy abroad.[12] Global terrorism, using weapons of mass destruction, challenges the stability of the state order itself, and no single state, not even the United States, has the capability to defeat the challenge on its own.

Before September 11, state collapse and state failure were seen chiefly as humanitarian tragedies. Mass casualty terrorism helps liberal democracies to see them as potential national security threats. Strengthening honest government in burdened societies, helping them to deny sanctuary to terrorist groups, has passed from a merely desirable goal to an essential one.[13] If apocalyptic nihilism feeds on political despair, it is in the rational self-interest of wealthy states to invest in assistance to help authoritarian societies in the Arab world—societies that have failed their people—to move toward democracy, even if the result is likely to bring Islamic parties to power.[14] For sixty years, Western states have been on the wrong side in a suppressed civil war between Arab peoples and their government. It is time to get on the right side, and to do what we can to channel popular discontent into democratic political forms. Obviously such a path is risky, but clinging to discredited regimes that have failed their people is even riskier.[15]

Where failing states possess nuclear weapons, we must prevent them from failing. Helping societies like Pakistan to secure their weapons program, to extend their control over the border regions with Afghanistan, and to pour resources into education and development is no longer one priority among many.[16] Given the degree to which Al Qaeda feeds off the failures of Pakistan as a state, strengthening Pakistan's state capacity without tipping it into outright authoritarianism has to be a central objective of any antiterrorism policy.

Terrorism also presents a very powerful argument for the reinvigoration of all forms of multinational and multilateral cooperation. September 11 did seem to herald a change in this regard. All member states of the United Nations condemned the attacks and passed resolutions pledging to impound the funding and weapons that make terrorism possible.[17] This newfound unanimity reflects an important sea change in attitude. For as long as international terrorism has existed, it has depended on the complicity of states. Palestinians went to Czechoslovakia to buy

Semtex explosives and to Yemen or Syria for training. Nicara-
guan contras and so-called Cuban freedom fighters looked to
Washington for funding and support. Libya sponsored terrorists
from Northern Ireland to Sierra Leone. Sudan provided refuge
for Islamic terrorists, including Osama bin Laden. When it was
under Taliban control, Afghanistan invited Al Qaeda to train its
cadres in its remote valleys. The Al Qaeda recruits arrived first
as guests of the Taliban government and then stayed on to become masters of the house. This pattern of state complicity depended on the calculation that "the enemy of my enemy must be
my friend." States supported terrorists because they destabilized
rival states. States with imperial interests—like the United States
or Soviet Russia—supported terrorist groups as proxies in their
war with each other. As long as terrorist weaponry remained
conventional, neighboring states were happy to support their fa-
vorite "freedom fighters," safe in the knowledge that this support would destabilize their rivals without endangering their
own interests.

As the threat of terrorism escalates from conventional to nuclear, states have begun to repent of their former promiscuity.
As the phenomenon of mass casualty terrorism emerges, it has
made nearly all states realize the danger of a complicity they
once engaged in. Just as Hiroshima convinced the world of
the unprecedented danger of nuclear weapons, September 11
awakened states to the reality that the terrorism they had once
willingly sponsored now risked getting entirely out of their
control.

The motives for reasserting control relate less to moral outrage
than to vital national interest. Whatever their differences of religion and ideology, all states share an interest in keeping weapons of mass destruction under their own lock and key. In the
case of nuclear weapons, the small club of nuclear states has an
interest in preventing proliferation, but as Pakistan and India reveal, states have only limited capacity to stop other states from
going nuclear. So the number of states with these capabilities
will grow. Indeed, it is not obvious how nuclear states can stop
other nations from going nuclear. Such weapons are the irresist-

ible coinage of power for states like North Korea that have failed to acquire power's true coinage, the wealth of its people.

While it is inevitable that more states will acquire weapons of mass destruction, allowing individuals or criminal or terrorist groups to do so is another matter entirely. This might happen in one of three ways. First, rogue states might sell or transfer weapons of mass destruction to terrorist groups, in the mistaken belief that they can direct their use against the state's enemies. Second, these capabilities might be stolen from reputable states and sold to terrorists on the black market. Finally, rogue scientists, working within either reputable or rogue states, might transfer weapons technologies or secrets to international groups. All three forms of proliferation—or civilianization—of weapons of mass destruction threaten the monopoly of states. All responsible states therefore have an interest in joining together to place these weapons and capabilities back in state hands.

Even a rogue state is not necessarily less rational than a reputable one, and rogue states can understand the dangers posed to them by terrorist groups possessing weapons of mass destruction. Moreover, rogue states can be made to pay a price. Libya, a notorious sponsor of terrorism, has been punished for its part in the Lockerbie bombing. Comprehensive international diplomatic isolation resulted in a change of heart, signaled by the reparation agreement between the Libyan government and the victims.[18] Three other rogues are extant. North Korea has a nuclear program that in the very near future will be capable of producing weapons.[19] Iran is also using a civilian nuclear program to develop weapons. Finally, Iraq, under Saddam Hussein, engaged in a twenty-year program of research into chemical, biological, and nuclear weapons, though there is controversy over what weapons these programs actually produced by the time of his overthrow in April 2003. There was also no hard evidence that he had transferred technologies or scientific information to terrorist groups. What was not in doubt was that he had used weapons of mass destruction twice, against his own Kurdish population and against Iranian forces.

Rogue states could be controlled if they could be prevented from trading in the international market in lethal technology. When the illicit market in weapons was confined to small arms and conventional weapons, states turned a blind eye to it and allowed the development of a complex, global weapons transfer system.[20] States did so because they had a strong economic interest in the trade or because it benefited powerful interests inside their own states. Now that we are on the threshold of a market in weapons of mass destruction, this long-standing complicity has ceased to be a minor embarrassment and threatens to become a danger to vital state interests.[21]

Liberal democracy depends upon the existence of capitalist markets, but a free market in everything—including plutonium, anthrax, and ricin—poses a direct threat to the survival of liberal democracy itself. Economic globalization could become the means of our own destruction, unless globalization is accompanied by a steady expansion of regulatory capacity on the part of states, companies, and international institutions. Otherwise, neither the free market nor the liberal state will survive. Yet no single state, not even the global superpower, has the resources to police a global market in lethality. Hence all states have an interest in devising effective regimes of multilateral regulation.

As the number of problems—from environmental harm to cross-border weapons trading—has grown, the capacity of states to cooperate in devising means to solve these problems has failed to keep up.[22] The reasons for this lie in the fact that liberal democracies have mostly benefited from globalization, while the costs—environmental, social, and economic—have been borne by less developed countries. Where transnational cooperation is most likely to develop is in those areas—crime, drugs, and terrorism—that do threaten the prosperity and order of liberal states. Global governance in these areas has ceased to be simply desirable. It has become a matter of mutual survival.

Such a global, multilateral effort against terrorism will entail some obvious lesser evils. One is more intrusive regulation of market transactions of all kinds. We will have to spend a great deal of money in order to regulate, inspect, control, and interdict the small portion of international trade that poses a danger to our survival. This regulatory burden will have to be shared between business and government. Governments will have to invest in more sophisticated systems to control the flow of money, goods, and people across their borders, and companies with substantial transborder trade will have to invest in delivery systems that guarantee the security of cargo from point of production to point of sale.[23]

This is the price that international business and the international traveling public will just have to pay if they want to be safe from terror. The second price will be increasingly stringent international regimes that interfere in a sovereign state's capacity to do what it likes with these technologies. For these regimes to be legitimate, *all* states, and not just the rogues, will have to submit to intrusive inspection of their lethal capabilities, and, where international agreement is possible, to get out of their production and stockpiling altogether.

The successful effort by the Americans and post-Soviet states like Ukraine and Kazakhstan to identify and render safe the errant nuclear capabilities left behind by the departing Soviet military is one example of what can be achieved.[24] The International Atomic Energy Agency, while underfunded and underresourced, has built up considerable expertise in regulating civilian nuclear programs and should be able to develop an authoritative international inventory of plutonium and other materials and enforce protocols for their transshipment, exchange, and deactivation.[25] Obviously, it is less easy to do this with chemical and biological agents. Yet it should be possible to require global corporations with chemical or biological capabilities to desist from selling their technologies to rogue states, and to prevent, as far as they can, their networks of distribution and sale from being infiltrated by terrorist groups. The success of the UN weapons inspectors in Iraq, between 1992 and 1996, in tracing the origins of Iraqi chemical agents back to their European commercial suppliers suggests that it should be possible to police the international traffic in agents and technologies that produce mass casualty weapons.[26] It should also be possible for states to increase security at all commercial, government, and military laboratories that make use of these agents. And it could be made a crime for a scientist to knowingly contribute to the manufacture of weapons for terrorists.[27]

One of the lesser evils that may become necessary is closer regulation of scientific research and free communication of its results. Already the U.S. Patriot Act requires any scientist working with certain biological agents to register with federal agencies and imposes penalties on anyone transporting agents or maintaining any scientific contact with a list of proscribed countries. U.S. university laboratories are prohibited, by presidential directive, from employing foreign students in research in biological fields with potential weapons applications. Editors of scientific journals have accepted that they should not publish scientific results where these might be used by terrorists, or even more broadly where the "potential harm of publication outweighs the potential societal benefits."[28]

Tightening up the security of labs, checking on the bona fides of all who work with sensitive agents, seems appropriate, provided that security remains in the hands of the free institutions—laboratories and university departments—that direct the research itself. The same principle should apply in determining what kinds of scientific research or publication do constitute a national security threat. This decision should also remain in the hands of scientists themselves, and the grounds for legitimate self-censorship should be precisely drawn so as to allow free publication of all but the most obviously dangerous papers. Dangerousness must be defined as an imminent, practical reality, not as a distant, speculative possibility, since it is impossible to accurately predict which forms of basic scientific research are likely to lead to dangerous applications. Maintaining free circulation of scientific ideas is a critical value, not just for science, but for democracy itself.

An era of mass casualty terrorism, in other words, forces us into a domain of lesser evils that did not arise when the threat was conventional: the regulation of the free market in technologies, technology transfer, and ideas themselves. Regulation cannot devolve on government alone; the task needs to be structured so as to allow maximum adversarial review. All of the parties—companies, universities, and government—must test proposals for regulation in open discussion and ensure that the regulators are themselves regulated. And regulation must seek a conscientious balance between the freedoms—of commerce and ideas—necessary for the survival of free peoples and the security that a new era of mass casualty terrorism requires.

In addition to regulation, there has to be leadership. This can come only from the United States, not simply because it is very powerful, but also because it is the principal terrorist target, as well as the chief site of weapons research and thus a possible source of rogue scientists. Even the United States, a nation with long-standing resistance to multilateral commitments that infringe on its sovereignty, can easily understand that it stands little chance of regulating the global market in lethal technologies on its own. International police cooperation between the United States and its European friends has proven crucial in apprehending active terrorist cells in cities from Hamburg to Madrid. Multilateralism in these matters has gone from being merely desirable to being a matter of life and death. States will either learn to cooperate or they will suffer the consequences separately. This will mean prohibition of the production, transshipment, and sale of weapons; the development of international regimes of coercive inspection for states that violate; and, as a last resort, the use of preemptive force to prevent the sale or distribution of such weapons to nonstate actors.

III

Preemptive military action, the last of the lesser evils to be considered in this book, poses three distinct problems: how to control the resort to preemption in a democracy, how to determine when it is justified, and who should authorize it internationally. Two obvious kinds of preemption come to mind: strikes against individuals or training camps in order to prevent them from executing imminent attacks; and military action against states that harbor terrorists or that produce weapons of mass destruction. Hitting terrorists before they can hit you, provided that less risky and costly means are unworkable, is less problematic than full-scale war against states.

The first type of difficulty, with wars of preemption, relates to democratic regulation of the war-making powers of presidents and prime ministers. Fighting foreign wars and confronting international terrorism have both increased executive power at the expense of legislative review in the twentieth century. The power to make war, vested in a president, is supposed to be balanced by the power to declare war, vested in a legislature. In the course of the last sixty years, this legislative regulation has weakened. Presidents have committed the country to combat without legislative authorization at all, or they have sought it only when combat was well underway.[29]

Preemptive war against terrorist threats would be still harder for legislatures and electors to subject to control. The case for such wars will always be speculative, based on uncertain intelligence gathered by means that require the concealment of sources and methods, and therefore extremely difficult for an electorate, let alone a legislature, to judge for credibility. Instead of claiming in the run-up to the Iraq war, as they had good reason to do, that the Iraqi regime possessed both the intentions and the resources to *eventually* acquire weapons of mass destruction, the president and the British prime minister asserted that the regime had actually developed and deployed these weapons.[30] In stretching the evidence, they sought to manipulate democratic consent for war, and even those who supported them cannot feel that a desirable end justified such means. As it happened, the war does not appear to have had a preemptive justification at all, since no actual weapons or advanced programs have been found in the year since the regime's fall.

It will not be enough for our leaders to escort us down the path toward the lesser evil of preemption in the future by simply reassuring us, over and over, "If you only knew what we know . . ." The facts may not be entirely uncertain, and the truth may not be as clear *ex ante* as it is likely to be *ex post*, but we can and should be told what we need to know. We are entitled to some unvarnished facts about a state's real capabilities and indications about whether these could be made available to global terrorists. Our leaders are under the strictest obligation, inherent in democratic government itself, to provide these facts and to consult our representatives before putting us all in harm's way. Preemptive war can be a justified lesser evil only when the case for it is sustained by evidence that would convince free peoples.

Since the risks of action are inherently more knowable than the risks of inaction, and since the facts concerning the threat are never going to be clear, the bias of any citizen's mind will be against preventive war. Such a bias helps to restrain political leaders from intemperate and unwise action, but a bias is not the same as a reason, still less a good one. We need to be open to the possibility that preventing the transfer of weapons of mass destruction from states to terrorist groups is a lesser evil necessary to forestall a still greater one.

Unless rogue regimes with a history of internal repression and external aggression can be prevented from acquiring and transferring lethal technologies, they become undeterrable. They can proceed to destroy dissident elements in their own populations, while making incursions into the territory of neighbors. Once they have weapons of mass destruction, they can transfer these with impunity to terrorist groups.

Although there is a case for preemption, where there is a feasible military strategy to prevent rogue states from transferring lethal technologies or terrorist groups from acquiring them, the threat must be imminent and demonstrable. Otherwise, preemption shades into aggression. Aggression is banned under the UN Charter, while actions in self-defense are not. Preemption is usually justified as a form of anticipatory self-defense, where the threat is imminent. The key issue to assess is how imminent the threat actually is and what signs from the enemy can be taken as a signal of hostile intent. The standard case of justified preemption, in Michael Walzer's *Just and Unjust Wars*, was the Israeli preemptive strike of June 1967 against Egypt and the Arab states. It was legitimate, according to Walzer, because of clear evidence that Arab countries were mobilizing for attack.[31] But this case tells us little about how to evaluate when a covert weapons of mass destruction program has become an imminent danger. Nor does it tell us when to preempt in the case of terrorism, where by definition the signs of imminent attack will be concealed from all but the most determined intelligence service, and where, even in the case of covert transfer of weapons from states to groups, it may be all but impossible for a vulnerable state to acquire advance knowledge of the transfer.

At the same time, a third issue—who decides when preemptive action is justified—adds another dimension of complexity. Under UN Charter rules, the Security Council is supposed to decide whether to authorize force, but its rules do not allow preemption, and even if ways can be found to get around them, through a presentation of the problem as a "threat to international peace and security," any state that feels itself threatened and contemplates preemptive force is not going to hand its right of self-defense over to a committee of other states, no matter how august. While the United States is castigated for its unilateralism, all states are likely to insist on a unilateral right of response to a threat from weapons of mass destruction. Hence while simple prudence suggests that any state should seek international legitimacy before using force and should secure as many allies as possible, it cannot cede its right to make final judgments about its national security to any other state or international organization. Even if it fails to convince other states that a threat requires preemption, it would be justified in going it alone—but only, of course, if the threat turns out to be real.

The intense debate about the legitimacy of the invasion of Iraq indicates that the supposed universal interest of states in effective institutions against proliferation is extraordinarily difficult to translate into universal action. The United States simply disagreed with its usual allies about the extent of the danger posed by Iraq's weapons programs, and while these allies were unable to prevent the United States from using force, their opposition did impose substantial costs on American action: first, it was perceived as illegitimate; and second, the costs of war and of postwar reconstruction were not shared but loaded chiefly onto the backs of American taxpayers. If only to increase legitimacy and reduce cost, multilateral agreement on the use of force is preferable to unilateral action. Yet further unilateral action is inevitable, given the extent to which the United States remains the first-order target for Al Qaeda and other Islamist groups.[32]

The category of such states whose conduct could possibly justify preemptive war is very small. Even states with imperial capabilities know that it is in their interest to respect the sovereignty of other states most of the time, for the alternative is endless war. Besides, preemptive war is impossible against those who already possess such weapons, or who could, before defeat, inflict such damage on others as to impose prohibitive cost on preemptive action.

So preemptive war is going to be a rare occurrence, but even so it would be a lesser evil. It will kill people and cause humanitarian harms even if it succeeds in eliminating a dangerous regime and confiscating weapons of mass destruction. As a lesser evil, preemptive war should be strictly constrained: it needs to be authorized in conditions of genuinely democratic disclosure; states proposing preemption must make a sincere attempt to secure multilateral support; preemption can be justified only as a last resort, once attempts to disarm states through coercive inspection, diplomatic inducements, and other peaceful means have failed; and, finally, preemption must not leave things worse than before the action was contemplated. If a tyrannical state is overthrown, a democratic regime must be put in place. If military action is taken, it must not trigger a wider war. While these conditions are clear enough in theory, judging whether they have been met depends on two crucially difficult anticipatory judgments: is the threat so real that the risk is justified, and are the future benefits of action likely to outweigh the all too evident short-term harms? The effort to get these judgments right and to make them in good faith exposes any democracy and its leaders to enormous moral hazard. The costs of error—when weapons of mass destruction are actually there—could be incalculable.

IV

Terrorism is disorienting to a liberal democracy because, first, it seems to set at naught its capabilities and the strengths that derive from its liberty. It is also disorienting because free peoples used to living at peace have difficulty admitting that they are actually faced with evil. This brings me, as I reach my conclusion, to the uses of ethical discussions like this one. Ethics matter, not just to constrain the means we use, but to define the identity we are defending and to name the evil we are facing. The point of ethics is to enable us to encounter the reality of evil without succumbing to its logic, to combat it with constitutionally regulated lesser evils, without falling prey to greater ones.

A liberal democracy is more than a set of institutional procedures and rights guarantees for the adjudication of conflict and the regulation of violence. Why would we keep faith with such a political system? Why would we care about it if it were procedure alone? We care about it because the procedures protect the rights of each human being who belongs. We care about rights because we believe that each human life is intrinsically worth protecting and preserving. We use rights to set limits to what majorities can do because we believe that the greatest good of the greatest number alone should not decide all political questions. If majorities must prevail as a matter of necessity, those individuals whose rights or interests are harmed are entitled to compensation and redress. We believe that the suffrage of our fellow citizens must be sought, one by one, and their opinions secured by means of argument rather than coercion or bribery. Their rights to due process of law, to basic dignity in treatment, are independent of conduct and irrevocable under any circumstance. We believe that even our enemies deserve to be treated as human beings.

These are just some of the things we believe, and they are not easy to live by. They impose substantial constraints on those who exert power in our name just as they impose constraints on our passions as citizens and individuals.

The major ethical problem in liberal democracies is not the absence or loss of stable, clear ethical values, but simply living within the real constraints of the values we have. These values are not relative, at least not for us, because they are the minimum conditions of our existence as free peoples.

Since these are principles we never fully live up to, they create a form of society that is required as a condition of its existence to engage in a constant, institutionalized process of self-justification. Measured against these standards of what is due each and every member, all liberal democratic societies fail and moreover know that they fail. So they are unique among forms of government in that they are, in the words of Lezsek Kolakowski, "under endless trial," and if they do not accept this burden of justification, they are failing to live the ethical life they themselves prescribe.[33]

Societies under the endless trial of self-justification are apt to feel guilty about their success. But our success is not a fact to feel guilty about, and the failure of other societies is not our fault. It is an illusion, dear to liberal democrats everywhere, especially to Americans, to believe that we are responsible for all the evils of the world and that we are in a position to cure them, if only we possessed the will to do so. Certainly we have a responsibility to work toward relieving the global burden of injustice. But we should be clear that we are doing so for reasons of justice, not in the delusive hope of greater security. Having responded to injustice with justice, we have no right to expect peace and good feeling in return. This is to misunderstand evil, to forget terrorism's essential connection to nihilism, its indifference to the suffering it purports to represent, its contempt for our gestures at reparation.

The success of liberal democracy should not be held as an accusation against us, nor are we entitled to claim it as a vindication of our superiority. The fact that we have succeeded in becoming both rich and free may be too much the result of a particular history and contingent good fortune for us to believe our life is a model for other peoples in other cultures. But the fact that our values may not have universal application does not make them any less compulsory for us.

The challenge of an ethical life in liberal democracy is to live up, as individuals, to the engagements expressed in our constitutions and to seek to ensure that these engagements are kept in respect of the least advantaged of our fellow citizens. The task is also to ensure that each of us actually believes in our society as much of the time as possible. In an age in which individuals are monstrously empowered, by technology and freedom, to bring Armageddon down upon their fellow human beings, it is suddenly no longer a minor matter that some of our fellow citizens, and some of the noncitizens who live among us, happen not to believe in liberal democracy but instead profess a variety of paranoias pretending to be politics. The existence of wild, vengeful, and deluded political opinions, if married to lethal technology in the possession of a single individual, suddenly becomes a threat to us all. I am haunted, as I think we all might be, by the specter of the superempowered loner as the cruel nemesis of the very moral care our society lavishes on the idea of the individual.

It is a condition of our freedom that we cannot compel anyone to believe in the premises of a liberal democracy. Either these premises freely convince others or they are useless. They cannot be imposed, and we violate everything we stand for if we coerce those who do not believe what we do. In any event, we cannot preemptively detain all the discontent in our midst.

So we are stuck, as we should be, with persuasion, with the duty, now more urgent than at any time in our history, to persuade each and every person who lives among us, whether as citizen or as visitor, of two perfectly plain propositions: that we are committed to respect their dignity, and that if they fail to respect ours, we will defend ourselves. The threat of terror, the possibility of a terrorist outcome if we fail to convince one of these superempowered loners, makes the burden of self-justification that falls upon every citizen as a condition of membership in a liberal society heavier than it has ever been. We must be able to defend ourselves—with force of arms, but even more with force of argument. For arms without argument are used in vain. Since I believe in the arguments, since I believe that human beings are unique in their capacity to be persuaded, changed, even redeemed by good ones, I do not doubt that we will prevail.

PREFACE

1. In writing this book, I benefited greatly from advance view of two important contributions to the discussion, Jean Bethke Elshtain's *Just War against Terror: The Burden of American Power in a Violent World* (New York: Basic Books, 2003) and Benjamin R. Barber, *Fear's Empire: War, Terrorism and Democracy in an Age of Interdependence* (New York: Norton, 2003). Also William F. Schulz, *In Our Own Best Interest: How Defending Human Rights Benefits Us All* (Boston: Beacon Press, 2002); William Schulz, *Tainted Legacy: 9/11 and the Ruin of Human Rights* (New York: Thunder's Mouth Press/Nation Books, 2003); Nat Hentoff, *The War on the Bill of Rights and the Gathering Resistance* (New York: Seven Stories Press, 2003); Richard C. Leone and Greg Anrig, Jr., eds., *The War on Our Freedoms: Civil Liberties in an Age of Terrorism* (New York: BBS Public Affairs, 2003); Cynthia Brown, ed., *Lost Liberties: Ashcroft and the Assault on Personal Freedom* (New York: New Press, 2003); David Cole, *Enemy Aliens: Double Standards and Constitutional Freedoms in the War on Terrorism* (New York: New Press, 2003); Nancy Chang and Center for Constitutional Freedoms, *Silencing Political Dissent: How Post September 11 Anti-Terrorism Measures Threaten Our Civil Liberties* (New York: Seven Stories Press, 2002); Stephen J. Schulhofer, *The Enemy Within: Intelligence Gathering, Law Enforcement and Civil Liberties in the Wake of September 11* (New York: Century Foundation Press, 2002); Barbara Olshansky and Greg Ruggiero, *Secret Trials and Executions: Military Tribunals and the Threat to Democracy* (New York: Seven Stories Press, 2002); Richard Delgado, *Justice at War: Civil Liberties and Civil Rights during Times of Crisis* (New York: New York University Press, 2003); Ronald Dworkin, *Freedom's Law: The Moral Reading of the American Constitution* (Cambridge: Harvard University Press, 1997); Richard Posner, *Law, Pragmatism, and Democracy* (Cambridge: Harvard University Press, 2003); Ronald Dworkin, "Terror and the Attack on Civil Liberties," *New York Review of Books*, November 6, 2003; Ronald Dworkin, "The Threat to Patriotism," *New York Review of Books*, February 28, 2002; Ronald Dworkin, "The Trouble with Tribunals," *New York Review of Books*, April 25, 2002; Aryeh Neier, "The Military Tribunals on Trial," *New York Review of Books*, February 14, 2002; Lawyers Committee for Human Rights, *A Year of Loss: Re-examining Civil Liberties since September 11*, September 5, 2002; Lawyers Committee for Human Rights, *Imbalance of Powers: How Changes to U.S. Law and Policy Since 9/11 Erode Human Rights and Civil Liberties*, March 2003 (both Lawyer's Committee reports can be found at http://www.lchr.org/us_law/loss/loss_main.htm [accessed December 4, 2003]); ACLU Testimony at a Hearing on "America after 9/11:

Freedom Preserved or Freedom Lost?" before the Senate Judiciary Committee, submitted by Nadine Strossen, President, and Timothy H. Edgar, Legislative Counsel, November 18, 2003 (http://judiciary.senate.gov/schedule_all.cfm [accessed December 4, 2003]); American Civil Liberties Union, *Seeking Truth from Justice: PATRIOT Propaganda*, July 2003 (http://www.aclu.org/Safeand Free/SafeandFree.cfm?ID=13099&c=206 [accessed December 4, 2003]); ACLU, *Freedom under Fire: Dissent in Post 9.11 America*, May 2003 (http://www.aclu. org/SafeandFree/SafeandFree.cfm?ID=12581&c=206 [accessed December 4, 2003]); Amnesty International, USA, *The Threat of a Bad Example: Undermining International Standards as "War on Terror" Detentions Continue*, August 19, 2003 (http://web.amnesty.org/library/Index/ENGAMR511142003 [accessed December 4, 2003]); Human Rights Watch, *Presumption of Guilt: Human Rights Abuses of Post–September 11 Detainees*, August 2002 (http://www.hrw.org/ reports/2002/us911/ [accessed December 4, 2003]); Human Rights Watch, *Dangerous Dealings: Changes in U.S. Military Assistance after September 11*, February 15, 2002 (http://www.hrw.org/reports/2002/usmil/ [accessed December 4, 2003]).

CHAPTER ONE
DEMOCRACY AND THE LESSER EVIL

1. Cass R. Sunstein, *Designing Democracy: What Constitutions Do* (New York: Oxford University Press, 2001), 6–8, 13–47. Dennis Thompson and Amy Gutmann, *Democracy and Disagreement* (Cambridge: Harvard University Press, Belknap Press, 1996), 41–49.

2. John Hart Ely, *Democracy and Distrust: A Theory of Judicial Review* (Cambridge: Harvard University Press, 1980), 4: "thus the central function, and it is at the same time the central problem, of judicial review: a body that is not elected or otherwise politically responsible in any significant way is telling the people's elected representatives that they cannot govern as they'd like. . . . This in America is a charge that matters."

3. William H. Rehnquist, *All the Laws but One: Civil Liberties in Wartime* (New York: Knopf, 1998), 222.

4. *The Federalist* No. 51, http://memory.loc.gov/const/fed/fedpapers.html (accessed December 4, 2003).

5. For an account of how a Supreme Court seeks to balance the two meanings in times of terrorism, see A. Barak, "A Judge on Judging: The Role of a Supreme Court in a Democracy," *Harvard Law Review* 116, no. 1 (November 2002): 16–162, and especially 36–46 and 148–60.

6. Ronald Dworkin, "Philosophy and Monica Lewinsky," *New York Review of Books*, March 9, 2000; Ronald Dworkin, "Posner's Charges: What I Actually Said" (2000), http://www.nyu.edu/gsas/dept/philo/faculty/dworkin/ (ac-

cessed December 4, 2003). Ronald Dworkin, *Freedom's Law: The Moral Reading of the American Constitution* (Cambridge: Harvard University Press, 1996), vs. Richard Posner, *The Problematics of Moral and Legal Theory* (Cambridge: Harvard University Press, Belknap Press, 1999).

7. Peter Irons, *Justice at War* (New York: Oxford University Press, 1983), 9–13, 57–64. David Cole, "An Ounce of Detention," *American Prospect*, September 9, 2003.

8. *USA Today*/CNN Gallup Poll Results (August 2003), http://www.life andliberty.gov/subs/s_people.htm (accessed December 4, 2003). To the question "Do you think the Bush Administration has gone too far, has been about right or has not gone far enough in restricting civil liberties in order to fight terrorism?" between 55 and 60 percent of respondents say "about right," the numbers remaining stable since June 2002. Forty-eight percent of the sample believe that the Patriot Act gets the balance between liberty and security "about right."

9. David Cole, *Enemy Aliens* (New York: New Press, 2003).

10. For the idea of an enemy of the human race, see the discussion in Hannah Arendt, *Eichmann in Jerusalem: A Report on the Banality of Evil* (New York: Viking, 1963).

11. Ronald Dworkin, "Terror and the Attack on Civil Liberties," *New York Review of Books*, November 6, 2003.

12. Cole. *Enemy Aliens.*

13. *U.S. Justice Department Inspector General Report on Administrative Detention* (June 2003), http://www.usdoj.gov/oig/special/03-06/index.htm (accessed December 4, 2003).

14. Robert D. Marcus and Anthony Marcus, eds., "The Army-McCarthy Hearings, 1954," in *American History through Court Proceedings and Hearings*, vol. 2 (St. James, N.Y.: Brandywine Press, 1998), 136–51.

15. Dennis F. Thompson, *Political Ethics and Public Office* (Cambridge: Harvard University Press, 1987), 118; also Dennis Thompson, "Democratic Secrecy," *Political Science Quarterly* 114, no. 2 (Summer 1999): 181–93. See also *U.S. Senate Final Report of the Select Committee to Study Governmental Operations with Respect to Intelligence Activities* (Washington, D.C.: U.S. Government Printing Office, 1976), 11–14.

16. *Israeli Supreme Court Judgment on the Interrogation Methods Applied by the GSS* (September 6, 1999), http://www.us-israel.org/jsource/Society_& _Culture/GSS.html (accessed December 4, 2003):

> Moreover, the "necessity" defense has the effect of allowing one who acts under the circumstances of "necessity" to escape criminal liability. The "necessity" defense does not possess any additional normative value. In addition, it does not authorize the use of physical means for the purposes of allowing investigators to execute their

duties in circumstances of necessity. The very fact that a particular act does not constitute a criminal act (due to the "necessity" defense) does not in itself authorize the administration to carry out this deed, and in doing so infringe upon human rights.

17. Michael Ignatieff, *Virtual War: Kosovo and Beyond* (New York: Metropolitan, 2000), conclusion.

18. Euripides, *Medea*, trans. Rex Warner (New York: Dover Publications, 1993), 40.

19. Niccolò Machiavelli, *The Prince*, trans. and ed. Robert M. Adams (New York: Norton, 1977), 44–45, "On the Reasons Why Men Are Praised or Blamed—Especially Princes": "And again, he need not make himself uneasy at incurring a reproach for those vices without which the state can only be saved with difficulty, for if everything is considered carefully, it will be found that something which looks like virtue, if followed, would be his ruin; whilst something else, which looks like vice, yet followed brings him security and prosperity." Isaiah Berlin, "The Originality of Machiavelli," in *Against the Current* (New York: Viking, 1980).

20. Isaiah Berlin, "Two Concepts of Liberty" in *Four Essays on Liberty* (Oxford: Oxford University Press, 1969), 165:

> If I wish to preserve my liberty, it is not enough to say that it must not be violated unless someone or other—the absolute ruler, or the popular assembly, or the King in Parliament, or the judges, or some combination of authorities, or the laws themselves—for the laws may be oppressive—authorizes its violation. I must establish a society in which there must be some frontiers of freedom which nobody should be permitted to cross. Different names or natures may be given to the rules that determine these frontiers: they may be called natural rights, or the word of God, or Natural Law, or the demands of utility or of the "permanent interests of man"; I may believe them to be valid *a priori*, or assert them to be my own ultimate ends, or the ends of my society or culture. What these rules or commandments will have in common is that they are accepted so widely, and are grounded so deeply in the actual nature of men as they have developed through history, as to be, by now, an essential part of what we mean by being a normal human being. Genuine belief in the inviolability of a minimum extent of individual liberty entails some such absolute stand. For it is clear that it has little to hope for from the rule of majorities; democracy as such is logically uncommitted to it, and historically has at times failed to protect it, while remaining faithful to its own principles. Few governments, it has been observed, have found much difficulty in causing their subjects to generate any will that the government wanted. "The triumph of despotism is to force the slaves to declare themselves free." It may need no force; the slaves may proclaim their freedom quite sincerely: but they are none the less slaves. Perhaps the chief value for liberals of political—"positive"—rights, of participating in the government, is as a means for protecting what they hold to be an ultimate value, namely individual—"negative"—Liberty.

21. Michael Ignatieff, "Genocide: An Essay," in Simon Norfolk, *For Most of It I Have No Words* (London: Dewi Lewis, 1998).

22. John Stuart Mill, "On Liberty" (1869), in *On Liberty*, ed. Edward Alexander (Peterborough, Ont.: Broadview Press, 1999), pp. 51–52:

> The object of this Essay is to assert one very simple principle, as entitled to govern absolutely the dealings of society with the individual in the way of compulsion and control, whether the means used be physical force in the form of legal penalties, or the moral coercion of public opinion. That principle is that the sole end for which mankind are warranted, individually or collectively, in interfering with the liberty of action of any of their number, is self-protection. That the only purpose for which power can be rightfully exercised over any member of a civilized community, against his will, is to prevent harm to others. His own good, either physical or moral, is not a sufficient warrant. He cannot rightfully be compelled to do or forbear because it will be better for him to do so, because it will make him happier, because, in the opinions of others, to do so would be wise, or even right. These are good reasons for remonstrating with him, or reasoning with him, or persuading him, or entreating him, but not for compelling him, or visiting him with any evil in case he do otherwise. To justify that, the conduct from which it is desired to deter him, must be calculated to produce evil to some one else. The only part of the conduct of any one, for which he is amenable to society, is that which concerns others. In the part which merely concerns him, his independence is, of right, absolute. Over himself, over his own body and mind, the individual is sovereign.

23. See my *A Just Measure of Pain: Penitentiaries in the Industrial Revolution* (New York: Pantheon, 1978) for a discussion of Beccarian and post-Beccarian theories of punishment in the European Enlightenment.

24. Hannah Arendt, "Personal Responsibility under Dictatorship," in *Responsibility and Judgment*, ed. Jerome Kohn (New York: Schocken Books, 2003), 44.

25. Daniel Ellsberg, *Secrets: A Memoir of Vietnam and the Pentagon Papers* (New York: Viking, 2002). For a whistle-blower's career in the CIA, see Robert Baer, *See No Evil: The True Story of a Ground Soldier in the CIA's War on Terrorism* (New York: Crown Publishers, 2002).

26. See Michael Ignatieff, ed., *American Exceptionalism and Human Rights* (Princeton: Princeton University Press, 2004).

CHAPTER TWO
THE ETHICS OF EMERGENCY

1. Rein Mullerson, "Jus ad Bellum: Plus Ça Change (le Monde) Plus C'est la Même Chose (le Droit)?," *Journal of Conflict and Security Law* 7, no.2 (2002): 149–90.

2. Gabriel L. Negretto and José Antonio Aguilar Rivera, "Liberalism and Emergency Powers in Latin America: Reflections on Carl Schmitt and the Theory of Constitutional Dictatorship," *Cardozo Law Review*, 21 (2000): 1797.

3. Kathleen Sullivan, Tanner Lectures, delivered at Harvard University, 2001–2, published as *The Tanner Lectures on Human Values* (Salt Lake City: University of Utah Press, 2002).

4. John Locke, *Second Treatise on Government* (Indianapolis: Hackett, 1980), chap. 14, "Of Prerogative," sec. 160.

5. Pasquale Pasquino, "Locke on King's Prerogative," *Political Theory* 26, no. 2 (April 1998): 198–208.

6. On the distinction between liberal and republican attitudes to prerogative power, see Negretto and Aguilar Rivera, "Liberalism and Emergency Powers in Latin America."

7. Abraham Lincoln, letter to Erastus Corning and others, June 12, 1863, in *Abraham Lincoln, Slavery and the Civil War: Selected Writings and Speeches*, ed. Michael P. Johnson (Boston: Bedford/St. Martin's, 2001), 247.

8. *Ex parte Milligan*, U.S. Supreme Court, 71 U.S. 2 (1866), http://www.law.uchicago.edu/tribunals/milligan.html (accessed December 4, 2003).

9. Mark E. Neely Jr., *The Fate of Liberty: Abraham Lincoln and Civil Liberties* (New York: Oxford University Press, 1991), 179–84.

10. William H. Rehnquist, *All the Laws but One: Civil Liberties in Wartime* (New York: Knopf, 1998).

11. Jack Goldsmith and Cass R. Sunstein, "Military Tribunals and Legal Culture: What a Difference Sixty Years Makes" (June 2002) http://www.law.uchicago.edu/academics/publiclaw/index.html (accessed December 4, 2003).

12. On Lincoln's impact on presidential prerogative, see Larry Arnhart, "The Godlike Prince: John Locke, Executive Prerogative and the American Presidency," *Presidential Studies Quarterly* 9, no. 2 (Spring 1979): 121–30.

13. Oren Gross, "Chaos and Rules: Should Responses to Violent Crises Always Be Constitutional?" *Yale Law Journal* 112 (March 2003): 1101.

14. *Amnesty International (Canada) Protecting Human Rights and Providing Security: Comments with Respect to Bill C-36* (Ottawa, 2001), http://www.amnesty.ca/sept11/brief.PDF (accessed December 4, 2003).

15. David Cole and James X. Dempsey, *Terrorism and the Constitution: Sacrificing Civil Liberties in the Name of National Security* (New York: New Press, 2002).

16. Negretto and Aguilar Rivera, "Liberalism and Emergency Powers in Latin America." See also Brian Loveman, *The Constitution of Tyranny: Regimes of Exception in Spanish America* (Pittsburgh: University of Pittsburgh Press, 1993). Juan Linz and Alfred Stepan, *The Breakdown of Democratic Regimes* (Baltimore: Johns Hopkins University Press, 1978).

17. U.S. Constitution, Article 1, Section 9.

18. Estonia Constitution, 1991, Articles 129, 130, 131, http://www.oefre
.unibe.ch/law/icl/en00000_.html (accessed December 4, 2003):

> In the case of a threat to the Consitutional system of government, the Parliament
> may declare, on proposal by the President of the Republic or the Government of the
> Republic and with a majority of its complement, a state of emergency in the whole
> country, with a duration of no longer than three months. Regulations for a state of
> emergency shall be determined by law. During a state of emergency or a state of
> war, the rights and liberties of persons may be restricted, and obligations placed
> upon them, in the interests of national security and public order, in the cases, and
> in accordance with procedures prescribed by law. Rights and liberties determined
> by Article 8, Articles 11–18, Article 20 (3), Article 22, Article 23, Article 24 (2) and
> (4), Article 5, Article 27, Article 28, Article 36 (2), Article 40, Article 41, Article 9 and
> Article 51 (1) may not be restricted.
>
> During a state of emergency or a state of war there shall be no elections for the
> Parliament, the President of the Republic or representative bodies of local govern-
> ment, nor can their authority be terminated.
>
> The authority of the Parliament, the President of the Republic, and representative
> bodies of local government shall be extended if they should end during a state of
> emergency or state of war, or within three months of the end of a state of emergency
> or state of war. In these cases, new elections shall be declared within three months
> of the end of a state of emergency or a state of war.

Constitution of the Republic of Serbia, 1995, Articles 67, 89, http://unpan1.un
.org/intradoc/groups/public/documents/untc/unpan003694.htm   (accessed
December 4, 2003):

> In times of an immediate threat of war, the state of war or major natural disaster, it
> shall be possible to restrict by law the disposal, or establish a special way of use, of
> the part of resources belonging to legal entities and individuals, for the duration of
> the emergency.
>
> The President of the Republic shall:
>
> at the proposal of the Government, if the security of the Republic of Serbia, the
> freedoms and rights of man and citizen or the work of State bodies and agencies
> are threatened in a part of the territory of the Republic of Serbia, proclaim the state
> of emergency, and issue acts for taking measures required by such circumstances,
> in accordance with the Constitution and law;
>
> The National Assembly may not be dissolved during a state of war, an immediate
> threat of war or a state of emergency.

19. On Ulysess and the Sirens and on precommitment in general and in relation to constitutions and rights regimes, see Jon Elster, *Ulysses Unbound: Studies
in Rationality, Precommitment and Constraints* (Cambridge: Cambridge University Press, 2000), especially 104; see also his *Ulysses and the Sirens: Studies in*

Rationality and Irrationality (Cambridge: Cambridge University Press, 1979), 36–40; see also Homer, *The Odyssey*, bk. 12, lines 36–60.

20. Ronald Dworkin, "The Threat to Patriotism," in *Understanding September 11*, ed. Craig Calhoun et al. (New York: New Press, 2002), 273–85.

21. Abraham Lincoln, "Special Message to Congress," July 4, 1861 (Washington, D.C.: Library of America, 1989), 253.

22. For an extended treatment of this, see Michael Ignatieff, ed., *American Exceptionalism and Human Rights* (Princeton: Princeton University Press, 2004).

23. Sanford Levinson, " 'Precommitment' and 'Post-Commitment': The Ban on Torture in the Wake of September 11" (Paper delivered at Princeton University, November 21, 2002).

24. Ronald Dworkin, *Freedom's Law: The Moral Reading of the Constitution* (Cambridge: Harvard University Press, 1996), introduction; Richard A. Posner, *Law, Pragmatism, and Democracy* (Cambridge: Harvard University Press, 2003), especially chap. 8.

25. Posner, *Law, Pragmatism, and Democracy*, 299.

26. John P. Roche, "Executive Power and Domestic Emergency: The Quest for Prerogative," *Western Political Quarterly* 5, no. 4 (December 1952): 608.

27. Lincoln, "Special Message to Congress," July 4, 1861.

28. Roche, "Executive Power and Domestic Emergency."

29. Clinton L. Rossiter, *Constitutional Dictatorship: Crisis Government in Modern Democracies* (Princeton: Princeton University Press, 1948).

30. Ibid.

31. Oren Gross, "The Normless and Exceptionless Exception: Carl Schmitt's Theory of Emergency Powers and the 'Norm-Exception' Dichotomy," *Cardozo Law Review* 21 (2000): 1825.

32. Prevention of Terrorism (Temporary Provisions) Act 1989, Section 27:5, http://www.hmso.gov.uk/acts/acts1989/Ukpga_19890004_en_1.htm (accessed December 4, 2003): "The provisions of Parts I to V of this Act and of subsection (6)(c) below shall remain in force until 22nd March 1990 and shall then expire unless continued in force by an order under subsection (6) below." Section 27:6: "The Secretary of State may by order made by statutory instrument provide— (a) that all or any of those provisions which are for the time being in force (including any in force by virtue of an order under this paragraph or paragraph (c) below) shall continue in force for a period not exceeding twelve months from the coming into operation of the order; (b) that all or any of those provisions which are for the time being in force shall cease to be in force; or (c) that all or any of those provisions which are not for the time being in force shall come into force again and remain in force for a period not exceeding twelve months from the coming into operation of the order." There are no such clauses in UK Terrorism Act 2000, http://www.hmso.gov.uk/acts/acts2000/20000011.htm (accessed December 4, 2003).

33. *Yaser Esam Hamdi v. Donald Rumsfeld*, U.S. Court of Appeal for the Fourth Circuit 296 F.3d 278; 2002 U.S. App. LEXIS 14012 (4th Cir. July 12, 2002), http://faculty.maxwell.syr.edu/tmkeck/Cases/HamdivRumsfeld2002.htm (accessed December 4, 2003); *Jose Padilla v. Donald Rumsfeld*, U.S. District Court for the Southern District of New York 243 F. Supp. 2d 42; 2003 U.S. Dist. LEXIS 3471, March 11, 2003, http://faculty.maxwell.syr.edu/tmkeck/Cases/Padillav Rumsfeld2003.htm (accessed December 4, 2003).

34. Linda Greenhouse, "Justices to Hear Case of Detainees at Guantanamo," *New York Times*, November 11, 2003. Linda Greenhouse, "It's Question of Federal Turf," *New York Times*, November 12, 2003.

35. Elster, *Ulysses Unbound*.

36. Robert H. Jackson's dissenting opinion in *Terminiello v. City of Chicago* 337 U.S. 1 (1949), http://caselaw.lp.findlaw.com/scripts/getcase.pl?court= US&vol=337&invol=1 (accessed December 4, 2003).

37. On Schmitt, see Mark Lilla, *The Reckless Mind: Intellectuals in Politics* (New York: New York Review of Books, 2001), 47–77. See also the biographical essay on Schmitt, Gopal Balakrishnan, *The Enemy: An Intellectual Portrait of Carl Schmitt* (London: Verso, 2000).

38. On the Weimar Constitution, see Wolfgang Mommsen, *Max Weber and German Politics, 1890–1920*, trans. Michael Steinberg (Chicago: University of Chicago Press, 1984), chap. 9.

39. Carl Schmitt, *Political Theology: Four Chapters on the Concept of Sovereignty* (Cambridge: MIT Press, 1985), 1.

40. Gross, "The Normless and Exceptionless Exception."

41. Locke, *Second Treatise on Government*, chap. 14, sec. 168, http://www .swan.ac.uk/poli/texts/locke/locke13.html (accessed December 4, 2003).

42. See Michael Ignatieff, *Human Rights as Politics and Idolatry* (Princeton: Princeton University Press, 2001), for a fuller discussion, in chap. 1, of the role of the Holocaust as the Ground Zero, or starting point, for postwar European human rights.

43. Rehnquist, *All the Laws but One*, 9. The most famous use of the phrase "higher law" in American politics came in 1850 when William H. Seward used the phrase "a higher law than the Constitution" to justify his opposition to the extension of slavery into the U.S. territories.

44. *Lawless v. Ireland* (1961), in *European Human Rights Report* 1 (London: European Law Centre, 1979), 15, para. 22.

45. *Aksoy v. Turkey* (1997), in *European Human Rights Report* 23:553.

46. *The Vienna Declaration and Programme of Action, June 14–25* (June 1993), http://www.unhchr.ch/huridocda/huridoca.nsf/(Symbol)/ A.CONF.157.23.En?OpenDocument (accessed December 4, 2003): "All human rights are universal, indivisible and interdependent and interrelated. The international community must treat human rights globally in a fair and equal manner, on the same footing, and with the same emphasis. While the significance

of national and regional particularities and various historical, cultural and religious backgrounds must be borne in mind, it is the duty of States, regardless of their political, economic and cultural systems, to promote and protect all human rights and fundamental freedoms."

47. Michael K. Addo and Nicholas Grief, "Does Article 3 of the European Convention on Human Rights Enshrine Absolute Rights?" *European Journal of International Law* 4 (1998): 510–24.

48. Amartya Sen, *Development as Freedom* (New York: Knopf, 1999), 152–54, 180–82.

49. Brian Simpson, *Human Rights and the End of Empire: Britain and the Genesis of the European Convention* (Oxford: Oxford University Press, 2001); Andrew Moravcsik, "The Origins of International Human Rights Regimes: Democratic Delegation in Postwar Europe," *International Organization* 54, no. 2 (Spring 2000): 217–52.

50. Jonathan Black-Branch, "The Derogation of Rights under the UK Human Rights Act: Diminishing International Standards," *Statute Law Review* 22, no. 1 (2001): 71–81. This article points out that the UK legislation incorporating the European Convention into UK law does not include the derogation procedures under the Convention itself, thus rendering all rights derogable following legislation.

51. Albert O. Hirschman, *Exit, Voice, and Loyalty: Responses to Declines in Firms, Organizations and States* (Cambridge: Harvard University Press, 1970).

52. R. St. J. MacDonald, "Derogations under Article 15 of the European Convention on Human Rights," *Columbia Journal of Transnational Law* 36 (1997): 225–67: "There are no sanctions against a state that fails to execute a judgement, short of suspension from the Council [of Europe]."

53. "A Conundrum for Austria—and for Europe," *Economist*, February 3, 2000; the European Union–commissioned *Report by Martti Ahtisaari, Jochen Frowein, and Marcelino Oreja* (adopted in Paris on September 8, 2000), http://www.virtual-institute.de/en/Bericht-EU/report.pdf (accessed December 4, 2003). The authors "received a mandate from the XIV through the President of the European Court of Human Rights to 'deliver, on the basis of a thorough examination, a report covering: the Austrian government's commitment to the common European values, in particular concerning the rights of minorities, refugees and immigrants; the evolution of the political nature of the FPO.' "

54. "Parliament in Italy Passes Immunity Law for Berlusconi," *New York Times*, June 18, 2003; UN Commission on Human Rights, Report of the Special Commissioner on the Independence of Judges and Lawyers, *Civil and Political Rights, Including the Questions of: Independence of Judiciary, Administration of Justice, Impunity* (January 31, 2003), http://www.unhchr.ch/Huridocda/Huridoca.nsf/0/e27d4ccdfc6ef9a3c1256cf400570613?Opendocument (accessed December 4, 2003).

55. Subrata Roy Chowdhury, *Rule of Law in a State of Emergency: The Paris Minimum Standards of Human Rights Norms in a State of Emergency* (London: Pinter Publishers, 1989).

56. The Inter-American Court of Human Rights has ruled that while habeas corpus was not listed as one of the nonderogable rights in times of emergency under the American Convention on Human Rights, it could not be suspended in an emergency. See Advisory Opinion No. 8, *Habeus Corpus in Emergency Situations*, I/A Court H.R. Series A No.8 (1987), http://www1.umn.edu /humanrts/iachr/b_11_4h.htm (accessed December 4, 2003).

57. John E. Finn, *Constitutions in Crisis: Political Violence and the Rule of Law* (New York: Oxford University Press, 1991), 32.

58. International Covenant for Civil and Political Rights, Article 4, http:// www.hrweb.org/legal/undocs.html (accessed December 4, 2003).

59. Ibid.

60. Laura K. Donohue, *Counter-Terrorist Law and Emergency Powers in the United Kingdom, 1922–2000* (Dublin: Irish Academic Press, 2001).

61. In 2001, the UK government informed the Council of Europe that it was derogating from its European Convention obligations in relation to the detention of terrorist suspects. See www.hmso.govt.uk.si/si2001/20013644.htm (accessed December 4, 2003); Laura K. Donohue, "Civil Liberties, Terrorism and Liberal Democracy: Lessons from the United Kingdom" (Discussion Paper 2000-05, John F. Kennedy School of Government, Harvard University, August 2000), http://bcsia.ksg.harvard.edu/publication.cfm?program=CORE&ctype =paper&item_id=79 (accessed December 4, 2003).

62. Kenneth Roth, "US: New Military Commissions Threaten Rights, Credibility," *Human Rights Watch*, November 15, 2001. "The Executive Order raises important concerns regarding U.S. obligations under the International Covenant on Civil and Political Rights (ICCPR), which the U.S. ratified in 1992. Article 4 of the ICCPR does permit a state to take measures derogating from its obligations under the Covenant in time of public emergency that threatens the life of the nation and is officially proclaimed. The U.S. declaration of a national emergency on September 14 may be considered to have met that condition, although to our knowledge the required formal notification of the U.N. Secretary-General has not occurred"; Louise Doswald-Beck, secretary-general of International Commission of Jurists, "Open Letter to President Bush on Military Commissions" (December 6, 2001), http://www.icj.org/news.php3?id_article =2609&lang=en (accessed December 4, 2003): "It remains unclear as to whether your Government considers itself to be under a state of emergency within the meaning of article 4 of the ICCPR, which would allow for the United States to undertake measures in derogation of some provisions of the ICCPR. Certainly no notification of such a state of emergency has been provided to the United Nations Secretary-General, as required under article 4 (3) of the ICCPR. If the

United States were to proclaim a state of emergency, such emergency would have to be of such gravity as to threaten the life of the nation. Any derogating measure undertaken would have to be strictly required by the exigencies of the emergency situation."

63. Ronald J. Daniels, Patrick Macklem, and Kent Roach, eds., *The Security of Freedom: Essays on Canada's Anti-Terrorism Bill* (Toronto: University of Toronto Press, 2001), 131–72.

64. Andrew Sabl, "Looking Forward to Justice: Rawlsian Civil Disobedience and Its Non-Rawlsian Lesson," *Journal of Political Philosophy* 9, no. 3 (November 2001): 307–30.

CHAPTER THREE
THE WEAKNESS OF THE STRONG

1. Brian Loveman, *The Constitution of Tyranny: Regimes of Exception in Latin America* (Pittsburgh: University of Pittsburgh Press, 1993), chap. 1; "National Strategy for Homeland Security," U.S. Government Office of Homeland Security (July 2002), http://www.whitehouse.gov/homeland/book/ (accessed December 4, 2003).

2. Sue Ann Presley, "Site of Crash is 'Hallowed Ground,' " *Washington Post*, September 11, 2002; "White House Target of Flight 93, Officials Say," CNN.com (accessed December 4, 2003), May 23, 2002; Oliver Burkeman, "Al-Qaida Captive May Have Been Planning Fifth Hijack," *Guardian*, October 12, 2002.

3. Harold Hongju Koh, "The Spirit of the Laws," *Harvard International Law Journal* 43 (2002): 23: "In the days since, I have been struck by how many Americans—and how many lawyers—seem to have concluded that, somehow, the destruction of four planes and three buildings has taken us back to a state of nature in which there are no laws or rules. In fact, over the years, we have developed an elaborate system of domestic and international laws, institutions, regimes, and decision-making procedures precisely so that they will be consulted and obeyed, not ignored, at a time like this."

4. Robert K. Murray, *Red Scare: A Study in National Hysteria, 1919–1920* (New York: McGraw Hill, 1955).

5. It was not until May 1920 that the National Popular Government League—a civil liberties group composed of figures like Felix Frankfurter and Zechariah Chafee—released its *Report upon the Illegal Practices of the United States Department of Justice*. See Murray, *Red Scare*, 255.

6. Eric Lichtau, "U.S. Uses Terror Law to Pursue Crimes from Drugs to Swindling," *New York Times*, September 28, 2003.

7. See Department of Justice, www.lifeandliberty.govs/subs_people.htm (accessed December 4, 2003) for evidence of poll support of government positions on civil liberties. For critical evaluation of the data, see Alan F. Kay,

"Catching Commercial Pollsters with Hands in the Cookie Jar," *Polling Critic* (September 18, 2003), www.cdi.org/polling/26-patriot-act-cfm (accessed December 4, 2003).

8. David A. Charters, "Democracy and Counter-Terrorism, Policy and Practice: Past and Present" (Paper presented at CASIS 2002, International Conference on the New Intelligence Order: Knowledge for Security and International Relations, Ottawa, September 2002).

9. Paul Berman, *Terror and Liberalism* (New York: Norton, 2003); Lawrence Wright, "The Man behind Bin-Laden," *New Yorker*, September 16, 2002.

10. See Franco Venturi, *Roots of Revolution* (New York: Knopf, 1960), 284–302, 587–679.

11. The intellectual and cultural atmosphere of Russian nihilism is well captured in Joseph Frank, *Dostoevsky: The Mantle of the Prophet, 1871–1881* (Princeton: Princeton University Press, 2002), 66–67.

12. Geoffrey Hosking, *Russia and the Russians: A History* (Cambridge: Harvard University Press, Belknap Press, 2001), 308–19; Orlando Figes, *A People's Tragedy: A History of the Russian Revolution* (New York: Viking, 1997); Dominique Venner, *Histoire du terrorisme* (Paris: Pygmalion, 2002).

13. On Stolypin, see Figes, *A People's Tragedy*. See Michael Ignatieff, *The Russian Album* (London: Chatto and Windus, 1987).

14. As quoted in Venturi, *Roots of Revolution*, 633.

15. Venner, *Histoire du terrorisme*, 28–29.

16. Theda Skocpol, *States and Social Revolutions: A Comparative Analysis of France, Russia and China* (Cambridge: Cambridge University Press, 1979), 47.

17. John E. Finn, *Constitutions in Crisis: Political Violence and Rule of Law* (New York: Oxford University Press, 1991), 139–78; and M. Rainer Lepsius, "From Fragmented Party Democracy to Government by Emergency Decree and National Socialist Takeover: Germany," in *The Breakdown of Democratic Regimes*, ed. Juan J. Linz and Alfred Stepan (Baltimore: Johns Hopkins University Press, 1978), 34–79.

18. Richard J. Evans, *The Coming of the Third Reich* (London: Penguin, 2003), 74, 193–94.

19. Finn, *Constitutions in Crisis*, 139.

20. Evans, *The Coming of the Third Reich*, 97–102.

21. Loveman, *The Constitution of Tyranny*, and Linz and Stepan, *The Breakdown of Democratic Regimes*.

22. David Scott Palmer, "Democracy and Its Discontents in Fujimori's Peru," *Current History* 99 (February 2000): 60–65. James F. Rochlin, *Vanguard Revolutionaries in Latin America: Peru, Colombia, Mexico* (Boulder, Colo.: Lynne Rienner Publishers, 2003), 37–39, 43, 70–71. Kees Koonings and Dirk Kruijt, eds., *Societies of Fear: The Legacy of Civil War, Violence and Terror in Latin America* (London: Zed Books, 1999), 4–27, 141–67.

23. Michael Taussig, *Law in a Lawless Land: Diary of a Limpieza* (New York: New Press, 2003).

24. Robert I. Rotberg, ed., *Creating Peace in Sri Lanka: Civil War and Reconciliation* (Cambridge, Mass.: World Peace Foundation and the Belfer Center for Science and International Affairs; Washington, D.C.: Brookings Institution Press, 1999); *Neelan Tiruchelvam, 1944–1999: Sri Lankan Visionary and World Citizen. Selected Tributes* (Colombo: International Centre for Ethnic Studies, 2000).

25. Israel Supreme Court judgments, especially 1998 judgment on the methods used by the GSS; Israeli Supreme Court Judgment Regarding "Assigned Residence" (HCJ 7015/02; 7019/02), Israeli Supreme Court Judgment Regarding Use of Civilians as Human Shields (HCJ 2941/02), Israeli Supreme Court Judgment Regarding Civilian Targets in West Bank Region (HCJ 3022/02), Israeli Supreme Court Judgment Regarding the Detention Condition in "Kzoit" Camp (HCJ 5591/02), Israeli Supreme Court Judgment Regarding Operation Defensive Shield (HCJ 3116/02) Israeli Supreme Court Judgment Regarding Destruction of Houses (HCJ 2977/02).

26. War Resisters' International, "Conscientious Objection to Military Service in Israel: An Unrecognised Human Right. Report for the Human Rights Committee in Relation to Article 18 of the International Covenant on Civil and Political Rights" (January 31, 2003), http://www.wri-irg.org/co/co-isr-03.htm (accessed December 4, 2003).

27. Peter J. Katzenstein, "Left-Wing Violence and State Response: United States, Germany, Italy and Japan, 1960s-1990s" (Working paper for the Institute for European Studies, January 1998).

28. Yonah Alexander and Dennis A. Pluchinsky, *Europe's Red Terrorists: The Fighting Communist Organizations* (London: Frank Cass, 1992).

29. Robert C. Meade, *Red Brigades: The Story of Italian Terrorism* (New York: St. Martin's Press, 1990), 208–17.

30. Paddy Woodworth, *Dirty War, Clean Hands: ETA, the GAL and Spanish Democracy* (Cork: Cork University Press, 2001).

31. Paddy Woodworth, "Why Do They Kill? The Basque Conflict in Spain," *World Policy Journal*, Spring 2001.

32. "The Compton Report: Report of the Enquiry into Allegations against the Security Forces of Physical Brutality in Northern Ireland Arising Out of Events on the 9th August, 1971" (November 1971); "The Hunt Report: Report of the Advisory Committee on Police In Northern Ireland" (1969); "The Gardiner Report: Report of a Committee to Consider, in the Context of Civil Liberties and Human Rights, Measures to Deal with Terrorism in Northern Ireland" (January 1975); "The Scarman Report: Report of a Tribunal of Inquiry into Violence and Civil Disturbances in Northern Island" (April 1972) (all four reports can be found at http://cain.ulst.ac.uk/issues/policy/polic.htm [accessed December 4, 2003]); D. G. Boyce, "Water for the Fish: Terrorism and Public Opin-

ion," in *Terrorism in Ireland*, ed. Yonah Alexander and Alan O'Day (New York: St. Martin's Press, 1984), 149–70.

33. Sir John Stevens, commissioner of the Metropolitan Police Service, "Stevens Enquiry" (April 17, 2003), http://cain.ulst.ac.uk/issues/collusion /stevens3/stevens3summary.htm (accessed December 4, 2003).

34. The Political Parties Law that allows for the banning of the Batasuna party was passed in June 2002. The law's official name is the Ley Orgánica 6/ 2002, de 27 de junio, de Partidos Políticos, http://www.igsap.map.es/cia /dispo/lo6-02.htm (accessed December 4, 2003).

35. Matthew Tempest, "Fourth Suspension for Stormont," *Guardian*, October 14, 2002; "Suspension of Devolved Government in Northern Ireland: Joint Statement by the Prime Minister and the Taoiseach" (October 14, 2002), http://www.britainusa.com/nireland/xq/asp/SarticleType.21/Article_ID.664 /qx/articles_show.htm (accessed December 4, 2003).

36. John Gray, *A False Dawn: The Delusions of Global Capitalism* (London: Granta Books, 1998); Amitai Etzioni, *The New Golden Rule: Community and Morality in a Democratic Society* (New York: Basic Books, 1996).

37. Donatella della Porta, *Social Movements, Political Violence, and the State: A Comparative Analysis of Italy and Germany* (New York: Cambridge University Press, 1995).

38. Elaine Scarry, *Who Defended the Country?* (Boston: Beacon Press, 2003).

39. For the distinction between ethnic and civic nationalism or patriotism, see Michael Ignatieff, *Blood and Belonging: Journeys into the New Nationalism* (New York: Metropolitan, 1994), chap. 1.

40. For a critique of the civic and ethnic distinction, see Bernard Yack, "The Myth of the Civic Nation," *Critical Review* 10, no. 2 (Spring 1996): 193–213.

41. Jack Goldsmith and Cass R. Sunstein, "Military Tribunals and Legal Culture: What a Difference Sixty Years Makes" (June 2002), http://www.law .uchicago.edu/academics/publiclaw/index.html (accessed December 4, 2003).

42. Woodworth, *Dirty War, Clean Hands*.

43. "European Court of Human Rights Judgment in Case of *McCann and others v. United Kingdom*" (September 27, 1995), in *European Human Rights Report* 21 (1996), 97.

44. U.S. Senate Committee on Governmental Affairs, *Summary of Legislation to Establish a Department of Homeland Security* (December 2002), http:// www.senate.gov/~gov_affairs/homelandlawsummary.pdf (accessed December 4, 2003): "Labor-Management Relations. (Section 842) Existing law allows the President by executive order to exclude an agency from coverage under collective-bargaining law if the President determines such law cannot be applied consistent with national security. Section 842 allows such an executive order for an agency transferred to the Department if the mission and responsibilities of the agency materially change. However, the President may waive that condition if he determines its application would have a substantial ad-

verse impact on the Department's ability to protect homeland security and if he provides Congress a written explanation 10 days in advance"; David Firestone, "Lawmakers Move toward Compromise Curbing Worker Rights in New Department," *New York Times*, November 12, 2002.

45. Sara Kehaulani Goo, "An ID with a High IQ: 'Smart Cards' Are in Demand as Concerns about Security Rise, but Privacy Issues Loom," *Washington Post*, February 23, 2003; Testimony of Katie Corrigan, ACLU Legislative Council on the Establishment of a National ID Card (November 16, 2001), http://archive.aclu.org/congress/l111601a.html (accessed December 4, 2003).

46. Alan Travis, "Ten Thousand to Test Eye Scan and Fingerprint Scheme," *Guardian*, November 12, 2003.

47. Amitai Etzioni, *The Limits of Privacy* (New York: Basic Books, 1999), chap. 4.

48. Ronald J. Daniels, Patrick Macklem, and Kent Roach, eds., *The Security of Freedom: Essays on Canada's Anti-Terrorism Bill* (Toronto: University of Toronto Press, 2001).

49. Ian Cuthbertson, "Whittling Liberties," *World Policy Journal* 18, no. 4 (Winter 2001).

CHAPTER FOUR
THE STRENGTH OF THE WEAK

1. Omar Malik, *Enough of the Definition of Terrorism* (London: Royal Institute of International Affairs, 2000).

2. Robert Jay Lifton, *Destroying the World to Save It: Aum Shinrikyo, Apocalyptic Violence and the New Global Terrorism* (New York: Henry Holt and Co., 1999).

3. Barry Goldwater's Acceptance Speech, Republican Presidential Nomination (Republican National Convention, Cow Palace, San Francisco, 1964): "I would remind you that extremism in the defense of liberty is no vice! And let me remind you also that moderation in the pursuit of justice is no virtue," in William Rentschler, "Barry Goldwater: Icon of Political Integrity," *USA Today*, March 2000, http://www.findarticles.com/cf_dls/m1272/2658_128/60868329/p6/article.jhtml?term (accessed December 4, 2003).

4. Richard Hofstadter, *The Paranoid Style in American Politics and Other Essays* (Cambridge: Harvard University Press, 1996); Daniel Levitas, *The Terrorist Next Door: The Militia Movement and the Radical Right* (New York: Thomas Dunne Books, 2002), 2–4, 315–24; Garry Wills, *A Necessary Evil: A History of American Distrust of Government* (New York: Simon and Schuster, 1999), 263–66.

5. Fred Schauer, "The Exceptional First Amendment," in *American Exceptionalism and Human Rights*, ed. Michael Ignatieff (Princeton: Princeton University Press, 2004).

6. Michael Ignatieff, "The Torture Wars," *New Republic*, April 22, 2002, 40–43; Paul Aussaresses, *Services speciaux: Algerie 1955–1957* (Paris: Perrin, 2001).

7. Joseph Frank, *Dostoevsky: The Mantle of the Prophet, 1871–1881* (Princeton: Princeton University Press, 2002).

8. Margaret MacMillan, *Paris 1919: Six Months That Changed the World* (New York: Random House, 2001), 11–14; "Of all the ideas Wilson brought to Europe, this concept of self-determination was, and has remained, one of the most controversial and opaque. During the Peace Conference, the head of the American mission in Vienna sent repeated requests to Paris and Washington for an explanation of the term. No answer ever came. It has never been easy to determine what Wilson meant. 'Autonomous development,' 'the right of those who submit to authority to have a voice in their own governments,' 'the rights and liberties of small nations,' a world made safe 'for every peace-loving nation which, like our own, wishes to live its own life, determine its own institutions': the phrases had poured out from the White House, an inspiration to peoples around the world. But what did they add up to? Did Wilson merely mean, as sometimes appeared, an extension of democratic self-government? Did he really intend that any people who called themselves a nation should have their own state? In a statement he drafted, but never used, to persuade the American people to support the peace settlements, he stated, 'We say now that all these people have the right to live their own lives under governments which they themselves choose to set up. That is the American principle.' . . . The more Wilson's concept of self-determination is examined, the more difficulties appear. Lansing asked himself: When the President talks of 'self-determination' what unit has he in mind? Does he mean a race, a territorial area, or a community?' 'It will raise hopes which can never be realized. It will, I fear, cost thousands of lives. In the end it is bound to be discredited, to be called the dream of an idealist who failed to realize the danger until it was too late to check those who attempt to put the principle into force' " (pp. 71, 75).

9. Paul Aussaresses and Robert L. Miller, *Battle of the Casbah: Terrorism and Counter-Terrorism in Algeria, 1955–57* (New York: Gazelle, 2000); Alastair Horne, *A Savage War of Peace* (London: Papermac, 1996), 99–104, 128–46.

10. Monica Toft, *The Geography of Ethnic Conflict: Identity, Interests, and the Indivisibility of Territory* (Princeton: Princeton University Press, 2003).

11. A typical Hamas statement is the following: "We will never recognize Israel, but it is possible that a truce could prevail between us for days, months or years." Mahmud al Zahar, Hamas leader in Gaza, quoted in Robert A. Pape, "The Strategic Logic of Suicide Terrorism," *American Political Science Review* 97, no. 3 (August 2003): 348.

12. Mary Ann Glendon, *Rights Talk: The Impoverishment of Political Discourse* (New York: Free Press, 1991), 9.

13. International Covenant on Civil and Political Rights and International Covenant on Economic, Social and Cultural Rights, Article 1 of each: "All peoples have the right to self-determination. By virtue of that right they freely

determine their political status and freely pursue their economic, social and cultural development."

14. John Locke, *Two Treatises of Government*, ed. Peter Laslett (Cambridge: Cambridge University Press, 1988), "On the Dissolution of Government," 406–28.

15. Thomas Jefferson, Declaration of Independence, July 4, 1776: "We hold these Truths to be self-evident, that all Men are created equal, that they are endowed by their Creator with certain unalienable Rights, that among these are Life, Liberty and the Pursuit of Happiness—That to secure these Rights, Governments are instituted among Men, deriving their just Powers from the Consent of the Governed, that whenever any Form of Government becomes destructive of these Ends, it is the Right of the People to alter or to abolish it, and to institute new Government, laying its Foundation on such Principles, and organizing its Powers in such Form, as to them shall seem most likely to effect their Safety and Happiness. Prudence, indeed, will dictate that Governments long established should not be changed for light and transient Causes; and accordingly all Experience hath shewn, that Mankind are more disposed to suffer, while Evils are sufferable, than to right themselves by abolishing the Forms to which they are accustomed. But when a long Train of Abuses and Usurpations, pursuing invariably the same Object, evinces a Design to reduce them under absolute Despotism, it is their Right, it is their Duty, to throw off such Government, and to provide new Guards for their future Security."

16. Tony Honore, "The Right to Rebel," *Oxford Journal of Legal Studies* 8, no. 1 (1988): 34–54; see also David Miller, "The Use and Abuse of Political Violence," *Political Studies* 32 (1984): 401–19.

17. United Nations General Assembly Resolution 1514 (December 14, 1960): "Declaration on the Granting of Independence to Colonial Countries and Peoples," http://www.unhchr.ch/html/menu3/b/c_coloni.htm (accessed December 4, 2003):

> The General Assembly, *Mindful of* the determination proclaimed by the peoples of the world in the Charter of the United Nations to reaffirm faith in fundamental human rights, in the dignity and worth of the human person, in the equal rights of men and women and of nations large and small and to promote social progress and better standards of life in larger freedom, *Conscious of* the need for the creation of conditions of stability and well-being and peaceful and friendly relations based on respect for the principles of equal rights and self-determination of all peoples, and of universal respect for, and observance of, human rights and fundamental freedoms for all without distinction as to race, sex, language or religion, *Recognizing* the passionate yearning for freedom in all dependent peoples and the decisive role of such peoples in the attainment of their independence, *Aware of* the increasing conflicts resulting from the denial of or impediments in the way of the freedom of such peoples, which constitute a serious threat to world peace, *Considering* the important

role of the United Nations in assisting the movement for independence in Trust and Non-Self-Governing Territories, *Recognising* that the peoples of the world ardently desire the end of colonialism in all its manifestations, *Convinced* that the continued existence of colonialism prevents the development of international economic co-operation, impedes the social, cultural and economic development of dependent peoples and militates against the United Nations ideal of universal peace, *Affirming* that peoples may, for their own ends, freely dispose of their natural wealth and resources without prejudice to any obligations arising out of international economic co-operation, based upon the principle of mutual benefit, and international law, *Believing* that the process of liberation is irresistible and irreversible and that, in order to avoid serious crises, an end must be put to colonialism and all practices of Segregation and discrimination associated therewith, *Welcoming* the emergence in recent years of a large number of dependent territories into freedom and independence, and recognizing the increasingly powerful trends towards freedom in such territories which have not yet attained independence, *Convinced* that all peoples have an inalienable right to complete freedom, the exercise of their sovereignty and the integrity of their national territory, *Solemnly proclaims* the necessity of bringing to a speedy and unconditional end colonialism in all its forms and manifestations; And to this end Declares that:

1. The subjection of peoples to alien subjugation, domination and exploitation constitutes a denial of fundamental human rights, is contrary to the Charter of the United Nations and is an impediment to the promotion of world peace and co-operation.

2. All peoples have the right to self-determination; by virtue of that right they freely determine their political status and freely pursue their economic, social and cultural development.

3. Inadequacy of political, economic, social or educational preparedness should never serve as a pretext for delaying independence.

4. All armed action or repressive measures of all kinds directed against dependent peoples shall cease in order to enable them to exercise peacefully and freely their right to complete independence, and the integrity of their national territory shall be respected.

5. Immediate steps shall be taken, in Trust and Non-Self-Governing Territories or all other territories which have not yet attained independence, to transfer all powers to the peoples of those territories, without any conditions or reservations, in accordance with their freely expressed will and desire, without any distinction as to race, creed or colour, in order to enable them to enjoy complete independence and freedom.

6. Any attempt aimed at the partial or total disruption of the national unity and the territorial integrity of a country is incompatible with the purposes and principles of the Charter of the United Nations.

7. All States shall observe faithfully and strictly the provisions of the Charter of the United Nations, the Universal Declaration of Human Rights

and the present Declaration on the basis of equality, non-interference in the internal affairs of all States, and respect for the sovereign rights of all peoples and their territorial integrity.

UN General Assembly Resolution 2908, "Implementation of the Declaration on the Granting of Independence to Colonial Countries and Peoples" (November 2, 1972), http://www.un.org/documents/ga/res/27/ares27.htm (accessed December 4, 2003):

Deeply concerned that twelve years after the adoption of the Declaration many Terrorities are still under colonial and alien domination and that millions of oppressed persons live under conditions of ruthless and blatant colonialist and racialist repression, *Deeply deploring* the continued refusal of the colonial Powers, especially Portugal and South Africa, to implement the Declaration and other relevant resolutions on decolonization, particularly those relating to the territories under Portuguese domination, Namibia and Southern Rhodesia, *Strongly deploring* the policies of those States which, in defiance of the relevant resolutions of the Security Council, the General Assembly and the Special Committee on the Situation with regard to the Implementation of the Declaration on the Granting of Independence to Colonial Countries and Peoples, continue to co-operate with the governments of Portugal and South Africa and with the illegal racist minority regime in Southern Rhodesia, . . . 5. *Reaffirms* that the continuation of colonialism in all its forms and manifestations—including racism, apartheid and activities of foreign economic and other interests which exploit colonial peoples, as well as the waging of colonial wars to suppress the national liberation movements of the colonial Territories in Africa—is incompatible with the Charter of the UN, the Universal Declaration of Human Rights and the Declaration on the granting of Independence to Colonial Countries and Peoples and poses a threat to international peace and security; 6. *Reaffirms* its recognition of the legitimacy of the struggle of the colonial peoples and peoples under alien domination to exercise their right to self-determination and independence by all the necessary means at their disposal, and notes with satisfaction the progress made by the national liberation movements of the colonial Territories, particularly in Africa, both through their struggle and through reconstruction programmes, towards the national independence of their countries; . . . 8. *Urges* all states and the specialized agencies and other organizations within the United Nations system to provide moral and material assistance to all peoples struggling for their freedom and independence in the colonial Territories and to those living under alien domination—in particular to the national liberation movements of the Territories in Africa—in consultation, as appropriate, with the OAU; 9. *Requests* all States, directly and through their action in the specialized agencies and other organization within the United Nations system, to withhold or continue to withhold assistance of any kind from the Governments of Portugal and South Africa and from the illegal racist minority regime in Southern Rhodesia until they renounce their policy of colonial domination and racial discrimination.

18. Hurst Hannum, *Autonomy, Sovereignty and Self-Determination* (Philadelphia: University of Pennsylvania Press, 1990), 14–26.

19. Adam Roberts and Richard Guelff, *Documents on the Laws of War* (Oxford: Oxford University Press, 2000).

20. Christopher Greenwood, "Terrorism and Humanitarian Law—the Debate over Additional Protocol 1," in *Terrorism*, ed. Conor Gearty (Aldershot: Dartmouth, 1996), 187–207.

21. Eitan Felner and Michael Ignatieff, "Human Rights Leaders in Conflict Zones: A Case Study of the Politics of 'Moral Entrepreneurs' " (Carr Center Case Study and forthcoming Center for Public Leadership Working Paper, August 2003).

22. Michael Walzer, *Just and Unjust Wars*, 3d ed. (New York: Basic Books, 2000), chaps. 9–10.

23. Che Guevara, *Oeuvres I: Textes militaires* (Paris: Maspero, 1968), 98, cited in Jacques Freymond and Thierry Hentsch, *On Mediating Violence: Armed Political Movements and Humanitarian Principals* (Geneva: ICRC, 1973).

24. Mao Tse-Tung, "On Protracted War," in *Selected Works of Mao Tse-tung* (Peking: Foreign Language Press, 1967):

This is the so-called theory that "weapons decide everything," which constitutes a mechanical approach to the question of war and a subjective and one-sided view. Our view is opposed to this; we see not only weapons but also people. Weapons are an important factor in war, but not the decisive factor; it is people, not things, that are decisive. The contest of strength is not only a contest of military and economic power, but also a contest of human power and morale. Military and economic power is necessarily wielded by people. If the great majority of the Chinese, of the Japanese and of the people of other countries are on the side of our War of Resistance Against Japan, how can Japan's military and economic power, wielded as it is by a small minority through coercion, count as superiority? And if not, then does not China, though wielding relatively inferior military and economic power, become the superior? There is no doubt that China will gradually grow in military and economic power, provided she perseveres in the War of Resistance and in the united front. As for our enemy, weakened as he will be by the long war and by internal and external contradictions, his military and economic power is bound to change in the reverse direction. In these circumstances, is there any reason why China cannot become the superior? And that is not all. Although we cannot as yet count the military and economic power of other countries as being openly and to any great extent on our side, is there any reason why we will not be able to do so in the future? If Japan's enemy is not just China, if in future one or more other countries make open use of their considerable military and economic power defensively or offensively against Japan and openly help us, then will not our superiority be still greater? Japan is a small country, her war is reactionary and barbarous, and she will become more and more isolated internationally; China is a large country, her

war is progressive and just, and she will enjoy more and more support internationally. Is there any reason why the long-term development of these factors should not
definitely change the relative position between the enemy and ourselves? (143–44)

A national revolutionary war as great as ours cannot be won without extensive and
thoroughgoing political mobilization. Before the anti-Japanese war there was no political mobilization for resistance to Japan, and this was a great drawback, as a result
of which China has already lost a move to the enemy. After the war began, political
mobilization was very far from extensive, let alone thoroughgoing. It was the enemy's gunfire and the bombs dropped by enemy aeroplanes that brought news of
the war to the great majority of the people. That was also a kind of mobilization,
but it was done for us by the enemy, we did not do it ourselves. Even now the
people in the remoter regions beyond the noise of the guns are carrying on quietly
as usual. This situation must change, or otherwise we cannot win in our life-and-
death struggle. We must never lose another move to the enemy; on the contrary, we
must make full use of this move, political mobilization, to get the better of him. This
move is crucial; it is indeed of primary importance, while our inferiority in weapons
and other things is only secondary. The mobilization of the common people
throughout the country will create a vast sea in which to drown the enemy, create
the conditions that will make up for our inferiority in arms and other things, and
create the prerequisites for overcoming every difficulty in the war. To win victory,
we must persevere in the War of Resistance, in the united front and in the protracted
war. But all these are inseparable from the mobilization of the common people. (155)

We, on the contrary, maintain that these strong points of the Japanese army can be
destroyed and that their destruction has already begun. The chief method of destroying them is to win over the Japanese soldiers politically. We should understand, rather than hurt, their pride and channel it in the proper direction and, by
treating prisoners of war leniently, lead the Japanese soldiers to see the anti-popular
character of the aggression committed by the Japanese rulers. (177)

25. Human Rights Watch, *Sowing Terror: Atrocities against Civilians in Sierra
Leone* 10, no. 3 (July 1998); Mark Doyle, "Sierra Leone: Rebels Profit from Terror
Tactics," *Guardian*, July 9, 1999.

26. Cited at www.anc.org.za/ancdocs/history/mk/geneva.html (accessed
December 4, 2003).

27. I documented some of these abuses in a BBC documentary, *Getting Away
with Murder* (BBC 2 Television Correspondent Series, 1999).

28. "Further Submissions and Responses by the ANC to Questions Raised
by the Commission for Truth and Reconciliation" (May 12, 1997), at www.anc
.org.za/ancdocs/misc/trc2 (accessed December 4, 2003).

29. Freymond and Hentsch, *On Mediating Violence*.

30. Human Rights Watch, *The Sri Lankan Conflict and Standards of Humanitarian Law* (April 1992), http://www.hrw.org/reports/pdfs/S/SRILANKA
/SRILANKA924.PDF (accessed December 4, 2003).

31. Physicians for Human Rights, *Endless Brutality: Ongoing Human Rights Violations in Chechnya* (January 23, 2001), http://www.phrusa.org/research/chechnya/chech_rep.html (accessed December 4, 2003). Amnesty International, *Russian Federation: Human Rights Report* (January 2002), http://web.amnesty.org/web/ar2002.nsf/eur/russian+federation!Open (accessed December 4, 2003). Human Rights Watch, *Human Rights Watch Briefing Paper to the Fifty-ninth Session of the UN Commission on Human Rights on the Human Rights Situation in Chechnya* (April 7, 2003), http://www.hrw.org/backgrounder/eca/chechnya/ (accessed December 4, 2003).

32. Somini Sengupta, "Terror Persists as Congolese Await UN Force," *New York Times*, June 4, 2003. Lynne Duke, "Whispers of Genocide, and Again, Africa Suffers Alone," *Washington Post*, June 29, 2003.

33. ABC/PBS Interview with Osama bin Laden, May 1998; Osama bin Laden's October 7, 2001, statement; Mohamed Atta's "Suicide Note," published September 29, 2001, http://abcnews.go.com/sections/world/DailyNews/attaletter_1.html (accessed December 4, 2003).

34. Pape, "The Strategic Logic of Suicide Terrorism," 343–61.

35. UNDP, Arab Human Development Report, 2003: "Building a Knowledge Society" (New York: UNDP, Regional Bureau for Arab States, 2003); UNDP, Arab Human Development Report, 2002: "Creating Opportunities for Future Generations" (New York: UNDP, Regional Bureau for Arab States, 2003).

36. George Bush, "President Bush Discusses Freedom in Iraq and the Middle East" (Speech at the Twentieth Anniversary of the National Endowment of Democracy, U. S. Chamber of Commerce, Washington, D.C., November 6, 2003).

37. Noah Feldman, *After Jihad: America and the Struggle for Islamic Democracy* (New York: Farrar, Straus and Giroux, 2003); Noah Feldman, "A New Democracy: Enshrined in Faith," *New York Times*, November 13, 2003.

38. Paddy Woodworth, *Dirty War, Clean Hands: ETA, the GAL and Spanish Democracy* (Cork: Cork University Press, 2001).

39. Laura K. Donohue, *Counter-Terrorist Law and Emergency Powers in the United Kingdom, 1922–2000* (Dublin: Irish Academy Press, 2001); R. F. Foster, *Modern Ireland, 1600–1972* (New York: Viking Penguin, 1988).

40. *Neelan Tiruchelvam, 1944–1999: Sri Lankan Visionary and World Citizen: Selected Tributes* (Colombo: International Centre for Ethnic Studies, 2000).

41. Michael Rubner, "The Oslo Peace Process through Three Lenses," *Middle East Policy* 6, no. 2 (October 1998).

42. Human Rights Watch, *Human Rights and Algeria's Presidential Elections* (April 1999), http://www.hrw.org/backgrounder/mena/algeria-election-0499.htm (accessed December 4, 2003). James Ciment, *Algeria: The Fundamentalist Challenge* (New York: Facts on File, 1997), 169–97.

43. J. Bowyer Bell, *Terror Out of Zion: Irgun Zvai Leumi, LEHI, and the Palestinian Underground, 1929–1949* (New York: St. Martin's Press, 1977), 169–73.

44. Larry Collins and Dominique Lapierre, *O Jerusalem* (New York: Simon and Schuster, 1972), 272–81, 337: "As the French and Belgians had repeated to each other on the highways of their exodus, stories of German soldiers raping nuns and slaughtering children, so the Arabs nourished theirs with the images of the atrocities of Deir Yassin."

45. Caleb Carr, *The Lessons of Terror* (New York: Random House, 2002), 213–15; Michael Ignatieff, "Barbarians at the Gate," *New York Times Book Review*, February 17, 2002.

46. International Crisis Group, *Islamic Social Welfare Activism in the Palestinian Territories: A Legitimate Target?* (April 2, 2003), http://www.reliefweb.int /library/documents/2003/icg-opt-02apr.pdf (accessed December 4, 2003). Neil MacFarquhar, "To U.S., a Terrorist Group, to Lebanese, a Social Agency," *New York Times*, December 28, 2001.

47. "Court Move for Total Batasuna Ban," CNN, September 4, 2002; "Basque Party to Fight Ban," BBC News, August 29, 2002; "Police Storm Basque Separatists' Headquarters," *Guardian*, August 28, 2002;"Bill Bans ETA Political Wing," *Agence France Press*, June 26, 2002. See also Council of Europe, Political Affairs Committee, Doc. 9526, "Restrictions on Political Parties in the Council of Europe Member States" (July 17, 2002), http://assembly.coe.int /Documents/WorkingDocs/doc02/EDOC9526.htm (accessed December 4, 2003). See also Anthony Richards, "Terrorist Groups and Political Fronts: The IRA, Sinn Fein, the Peace Process and Democracy," *Terrorism and Political Violence* 13, no. 4 (Winter 2001): 72–89; John Finn, "Electoral Regimes and the Proscription of Anti-Democratic Parties," *Terrorism and Political Violence* 12, nos. 3–4 (Autumn/Winter 2000): 51–77.

48. Finn, "Electoral Regimes and the Proscription of Anti-Democratic Parties"; Council of Europe, "Restrictions on Political Parties"; European Court of Human Rights Judgments on Case of *Refah Partisi (Welfare Party) and Others v. Turkey* (July 31, 2001, and February 13, 2003), HUDOC reference number REF00002693, http://hudoc.echr.coe.int/hudoc/ViewRoot.asp?Item=0&Action =Html&X=1212235211&Notice=0&Noticemode=&RelatedMode=0, and HUDOC reference number REF00004090, http://hudoc.echr.coe.int/hudoc/View Root.asp?Item=0&Action=Html&X=1212234916&Notice=0&Noticemode=& RelatedMode=0 (both accessed December 4, 2003).

49. Letters from the Quebec Authorities requesting the Implementation of the War Measures Act (October 15–16, 1971): Letter from Robert Bourassa, premier of Quebec, Letter from Jean Drapeau, mayor of Montreal, and Lucien Saulnier, chairman of the Executive Committee of the City of Montreal, Letter from M. St. Pierre, director of the police of Montreal, all found at http:// www2.marianopolis.edu/quebechistory/docs/october/letters.htm (accessed

December 4, 2003); Robert Bourassa, *Les Années Bourassa* (Montreal: Éditions Héritage, 1977), chap. l.

50. *European Court of Human Rights Ireland v. United Kingdom (1978)*, 2 EHRR 25.

51. Sir John Stevens, commissioner of the Metropolitan Police Service, "Stevens Enquiry" (April 17, 2003), http://cain.ulst.ac.uk/issues/collusion /stevens3/stevens3summary.htm (accessed December 4, 2003).

52. Israeli Supreme Court Judgment on the Interrogation Methods applied by the GSS, September 6, 1999; Israeli Supreme Court Judgment Regarding "Assigned Residence" (HCJ 7015/02; 7019/02); Israeli Supreme Court Judgment Regarding Use of Civilians as Human Shields (HCJ 2941/02); Israeli Supreme Court Judgment Regarding Civilian Targets in West Bank Region (HCJ 3022/02); Israeli Supreme Court Judgment Regarding the Detention Condition in "Kzoit' Camp (HCJ 5591/02); Israeli Supreme Court Judgment Regarding Operation Defensive Shield (HCJ 3116/02); Israeli Supreme Court Judgment Regarding Destruction of Houses (HCJ 2977/02). Specific weblinks to the judgments are: HCJ 7019/02—http://www.btselem.org/search.asp ?Lang=en-us&txtSearch=HCJ%207019/02; HCJ 3022/02—http://www.adalah .org/features/opts/3116decision-eng.doc; HCJ 5591/02—http://www.hamoked .org.il/items/20_Aa1_3278-02_eng.pdf; HCJ 3116/02— http://www.adalah .org/features/opts/3116decision-eng.doc; HCJ 2977/02—http://www.adalah .org/features/opts/2977decision-eng.doc (all accessed December 4, 2003).

CHAPTER FIVE
THE TEMPTATIONS OF NIHILISM

1. On anarchist violence in the 1890s, see Dominique Venner, *Histoire du terrorisme* (Paris: Pygmalion, 2002), 13–17.

2. Joseph Conrad, *The Secret Agent* (New York: Modern Library), 55–67.

3. M. Bakunin and S. Nechaev, *Catechism of a Revolutionary* (1868), in *Imperial Russia: A Source Book, 1700–1917*, ed. Basil Dmytryshyn (Hinsdale, Ill.: Dryden Press, 1977); Ivan Turgenev, *Fathers and Sons* (Harmondsworth: Penguin, 1975). Turgenev's character Bazarov is a portrait of a nihilist not as a terrorist but as a materialist cynic, hostile to the *bien pensant* liberal commonplaces of his time.

4. Joseph Frank, *Dostoevsky: The Mantle of the Prophet, 1871–1881* (Princeton: Princeton University Press, 2002), chaps. 4, 26; pp. 65–86, 475–96.

5. Fyodor Dostoevsky, *The Devils*, trans. David Magarshak (London: Penguin Classics, 1953), pt. 1, chap. 4, p. 106.

6. The best account of Islamic terrorist motivation is Jessica Stern, *Terror in the Name of God: Why Religious Militants Kill* (New York, Harper Collins, 2003).

7. Hays Parks Memorandum on Executive Order 12333 and Assassination, 1989; found through Carr Center program on the Use of Force, http://www

.ksg.harvard.edu/cchrp/Use%20of%20Force/October%202002/Parks_final.pdf (accessed December 4, 2003).

8. Peter Taylor, *Behind the Mask: The IRA and Sinn Fein* (New York: TV Books, 1997); Tim Pat Coogan, *The IRA: A History* (New York: Palgrave MacMillan, 2002).

9. Mark Juergensmeyer, *Terror in the Mind of God: The Global Rise of Religious Violence* (Berkeley and Los Angeles: University of California Press, 2000).

10. John Esposito, *Unholy War: Terror in the Name of Islam* (Oxford: Oxford University Press, 2002), 26–70. John Kelsay and James Turner Johnson, eds., *Just War and Jihad: Historical and Theoretical Perspectives on War and Peace in Western and Islamic Traditions* (New York: Greenwood Press, 1991).

11. Juergensmeyer, *Terror in the Mind of God*; Stern, *Terror in the Name of God*.

12. ABC/PBS John Miller, interview with Osama bin Laden, Afghanistan, May 1998.

13. Ibid.; Rohan Gunaratna, *Inside Al Qaeda: Global Network of Terror* (New York: Columbia University Press, 2002).

14. Ehud Sprinzak, "Rational Fanatics," *Foreign Policy*, September/October 2000; Joseph Lelyveld, "All Suicide Bombers Are Not Alike," *New York Times Magazine*, October 28, 2001.

15. Mohamed Atta's "Suicide Note," *New York Times*, September 29, 2001; Pam Belluck, "A Mundane Itinerary on the Eve of Terror," *New York Times*, October 5, 2001.

16. ABC/PBS John Miller, interview with Osama bin Laden, Afghanistan, May 1998.

17. Anti-Defamation League, "September 11 and Arab Media: The Anti-Jewish and Anti-American Blame Game" (November 2001), http://www.adl.org/presrele/ASInt_13/3965_13.asp (accessed December 4, 2003); David Aaronovitch, "The New Anti-Semitism," *Observer*, June 22, 2003.

18. African National Congress, Statement to the Truth and Reconciliation Commission (August 1996). South Africa Truth and Reconciliation Commission, "Findings on the ANC" (October 1998), http://www.anc.org.za/ancdocs/misc/trctoc.html (accessed December 4, 2003).

19. Judy Dempsey, "Jewish Settlers May Raise Stakes," *Financial Times*, October 11, 2000; Human Rights Watch, "Erased in a Moment: Suicide Bombing Attacks against Civilians" (October 2002), 54–57, http://www.hrw.org/reports/2002/isrl-pa/ (accessed December 4, 2003).

20. UN Secretary General's Report Prepared Pursuant to General Assembly Resolution ES10/10 (Report on Jenin) (July 30, 2002), http://www.un.org/peace/jenin/ (accessed December 4, 2003).

21. Fritz Morris, "Security, Intelligence Reform and Civil Liberties in the United States: September 11, 2001, through a Historical Lens" (Unpublished research paper, Carr Center for Human Rights Policy, Kennedy School of Government, Harvard University, June 2002); Select Committee to Study Government

Operations with Respect to Intelligence Activities, U.S. Senate, *Alleged Assassination Plots Involving Foreign Leaders* (Church Committee Report), Interim Report, November 20, 1975 (Washington, D.C.: U.S. Government Printing Office, 1975); William Colby, *Honorable Men: My Life in the CIA* (New York: Simon and Schuster, 1978).

22. Robert Baer, *See No Evil: The True Story of a Ground Soldier in the CIA's War on Terrorism* (New York: Crown Publishers, 2002).

23. Matthew Whitehead, "The Foreign Intelligence Surveillance Act of 1978—a Tool for Security?" (Submitted for ISP-224 Class, Kennedy School of Government, Harvard University, Fall 2002). Philip Shenon, "Paper Court Comes to Life over Secret Tribunal's Ruling on Post-9/11 Powers," *New York Times*, August 27, 2002. Philip Shenon, "Secret Court to Give Senate Wiretap Ruling," *New York Times*, September 12, 2002.

24. Paul Aussaresses and Robert L. Miller, *Battle of the Casbah: Terrorism and Counter-Terrorism in Algeria, 1955–57* (New York: Gazelle, 2000); Alastair Horne, *A Savage War of Peace* (London: Papermac, 1996).

25. Michael Ignatieff, *A Just Measure of Pain: The Penitentiary in the Industrial Revolution* (New York: Pantheon, 1978).

26. Eric J. Hobsbawm, "Barbarism: A User's Guide," in *On History* (New York: New Press, 1997).

27. UN Convention against Torture and Other Cruel, Inhuman or Degrading Treatment or Punishment (adopted and open for signature, ratification and accession by GA resolution 39/46 of December 10, 1984, entry into force June 26, 1987, in accordance with Article 27), http://www.hrweb.org/legal/cat.html (accessed December 4, 2003): "No exceptional circumstances whatsoever, whether a state of war or a threat of war, internal political instability or any other public emergency, may be invoked as a justification of torture."

28. Dana Priest and Barton Gellman, "U.S. Decries Abuse but Defends Interrogations," *Washington Post*, December 26, 2002; Alan Cooperman, "CIA Interrogation under Fire," *Washington Post*, December 28, 2002; Peter Slevin, "U.S. Pledges Not to Torture Terror Suspects," *Washington Post*, June 27, 2003.

29. Mark Bowden, "The Dark Art of Interrogation: A Survey of the Landscape of Persuasion," *Atlantic Monthly*, October 2003.

30. Duncan Campbell, "U.S. Sends Suspects to Face Torture," *Guardian*, March 12, 2002. Rajiv Chandrasekaran and Peter Finn, "U.S. behind Secret Transfer of Terror Suspects," *Washington Post*, March 11, 2002. Priest and Gellman, "U.S. Decries Abuse but Defends Interrogations"; Laura K. Donohue, "The British Traded Rights for Security, Too," *Washington Post*, April 6, 2003.

31. Sanford Levinson, " 'Precommitment' and 'Post-Commitment': The Ban on Torture in the Wake of September 11" (Paper delivered at Conference on Precommitment at the University of Texas Law School, September 20–21, 2002).

32. Alan Dershowitz, "Is There a Torturous Road to Justice?" *Los Angeles Times*, November 8, 2001. Alan Dershowitz, "When All Else Fails, Why Not Tor-

ture?" *American Legion Magazine*, July 2002. Alan Dershowitz, *Why Terrorism Works: Understanding the Threat, Responding to the Challenge* (New Haven: Yale University Press, 2002), 131–64.

33. Israel Supreme Court Judgment on the Interrogation Methods Applied by the GSS, September 1999, Statement of Court President A. Barak, http://www.us-israel.org/jsource/Society_&_Culture/GSS.html (accessed December 4, 2003):

> We shall now turn from the general to the particular. Plainly put, shaking is a prohibited investigation method. It harms the suspect's body. It violates his dignity. It is a violent method which does not form part of a legal investigation. It surpasses that which is necessary. Even the State did not argue that shaking is an "ordinary" investigation method which every investigator (in the GSS or police) is permitted to employ. The submission before us was that the justification for shaking is found in the "necessity" defence. That argument shall be dealt with below. In any event, there is no doubt that shaking is not to be resorted to in cases outside the bounds of "necessity" or as part of an "ordinary" investigation. . . . It was argued before the Court that one of the investigation methods employed consists of the suspect crouching on the tips of his toes for five minute intervals. The State did not deny this practice. This is a prohibited investigation method. It does not serve any purpose inherent to an investigation. It is degrading and infringes upon an individual's human dignity.
>
> To the above, we must add that the "Shabach" position includes all the outlined methods employed simultaneously. Their combination, in and of itself gives rise to particular pain and suffering. This is a harmful method, particularly when it is employed for a prolonged period of time. For these reasons, this method does not form part of the powers of interrogation. It is an unacceptable method.
>
> Our conclusion is therefore the following: According to the existing state of the law, neither the government nor the heads of security services possess the authority to establish directives and bestow authorization regarding the use of liberty infringing physical means during the interrogation of suspects suspected of hostile terrorist activities, beyond the general directives which can be inferred from the very concept of an interrogation. Similarly, the individual GSS investigator—like any police officer—does not possess the authority to employ physical means which infringe upon a suspect's liberty during the interrogation, unless these means are inherently accessory to the very essence of an interrogation and are both fair and reasonable.
>
> This decision opens with a description of the difficult reality in which Israel finds herself security wise. We shall conclude this judgment by re-addressing that harsh reality. We are aware that this decision does not ease dealing with that reality. This is the destiny of democracy, as not all means are acceptable to it, and not all practices employed by its enemies are open before it. Although a democracy must often fight with one hand tied behind its back, it nonetheless has the upper hand. Preserving the Rule of Law and recognition of an individual's liberty constitutes an important

component in its understanding of security. At the end of the day, they strengthen its spirit and its strength and allow it to overcome its difficulties.

34. Lawrence Wright, "The Man behind bin Laden: How an Egyptian Doctor Became a Master of Terror," *New Yorker*, September 16, 2002.

35. Michel Rio, *Parrot's Perch*, trans. Leigh Hafrey (New York: Harcourt Brace Jovanovich, 1983), a novel about torture and its psychic consequences.

36. Jean Amery, *Par-delà le crime et le châtiment, essai pour surmonter l'insurmontable* (1966) (Arles: Actes Sud, 1994).

37. Ibid., 79. See also Owen Bowcott, "September 11 Blamed on Trail of State Torture," *Guardian*, January 30, 2003, on the role of torture in Egyptian prisons.

38. For Primo Levi, see Carole Angier, *The Double Bond: Primo Levi, a Biography* (New York: Viking, 2002).

CHAPTER SIX
LIBERTY AND ARMAGEDDON

1. George Tenet "The Worldwide Threat in 2003: Evolving Dangers in a Complex World," Testimony before the Senate Select Intelligence Committee (February 11 2003), http://www.ceip.org/files/nonprolif/resources/intelligence.asp (accessed December 4, 2003). CIA, *Unclassified Report to Congress on the Acquisition of Technology Relating to Weapons of Mass Destruction and Advanced Conventional Munitions, 1 January through 30 June 2003* (November 2003), http://www.nti.org/e_research/official_docs/cia/cia110303.pdf (accessed December 4, 2003). *Iraq's Weapons of Mass Destruction—The Assessment of the British Government* (September 24, 2002), http://www.number-10.gov.uk/output/Page271.asp (accessed December 4, 2003).

2. Jason Pate, "Anthrax and Mass Casualty Terrorism: What Is the Bioterrorist Threat after September 11?" *U.S. Foreign Policy Agenda*, November 2001.

3. Max Weber, "Politics as Vocation," in *From Max Weber*, ed. H. H. Gerth and C. Wright Mills (New York: Oxford University Press, 1980). On the Peace of Westphalia, see Steven D. Krasner, *Sovereignty: Organized Hypocrisy* (Princeton: Princeton University Press, 1999), 107–15.

4. Matthew Bunn, "Preventing Nuclear Terrorism," Belfer Center for Science and International Affairs, and Nuclear Threat Initiative, Report (October 21, 2003), www.nti.org (accessed December 4, 2003).

5. CNN, "Timeline: UK Ricin Terror Probe" (January 23, 2003), http://www.cnn.com/2003/WORLD/europe/01/15/ricin.timeline/ (accessed December 4, 2003); Helen Gibson, "The Algerian Factor," *TimeEurope*, January 27, 2003.

6. United States Commission on National Security/Twenty-first Century Phase 1 Report, "New World Coming: American Security in the Twenty-first Century" (September 15, 1999), 50–51, http://www.nssg.gov/Reports/New_World_Coming/new_world_coming.htm (accessed December 4, 2003).

7. Oliver Burkeman, "US Scientist Is Suspect in Anthrax Investigation," *Guardian*, February 20, 2002. BBC News, "Anthrax Killer Is US Defence Insider," August 18, 2002.

8. Peter Jennings, "The Kennedy Assassination: Beyond Conspiracy," ABC News Special Report, November 20, 2003.

9. Robert Jay Lifton, *Destroying the World to Save It: Aum Shinrikyo, Apocalyptic Violence and the New Global Terrorism* (New York: Henry Holt and Co., 1999), 25–27, 37–43.

10. Scott Anderson, "The Makeover," *New York Times Magazine*, January 19, 2003.

11. The failed or failing states that might be incapable of denying terrorists safe haven would be the following: Congo, Sierra Leone, Liberia, Somalia, Burundi, Afghanistan, Pakistan, Abkhazia, Georgia, Tajikistan, Kirghizstan, Moldova, and Colombia. Michael Ignatieff, "Intervention and State Failure," *Dissent*, Winter 2002, 115–23; Larry Diamond, "Winning the New Cold War on Terrorism: The Democratic-Governance Imperative" (Institute for Global Democracy Policy Paper #1, 2002), http://www.911investigations.net/docu ment277.html (accessed December 4, 2003); Jeffrey Herbst, "Let Them Fail: State Failure in Theory and Practice, Implications for Policy," in *When States Fail: Causes and Consequences*, ed. Robert Rotberg (Princeton: Princeton University Press, 2004); Gerald B. Helman and Steven R. Ratner, "Saving Failed States," *Foreign Policy*, no. 89 (Winter 1992–93): 3–20.

12. Benjamin R. Barber, *Fear's Empire: War, Terrorism and Democracy* (New York: Norton, 2003).

13. Larry Diamond, "How to Win the War," *Hoover Digest*, no. 1 (Winter 2002); Diamond, "Winning the New Cold War on Terrorism."

14. Noah Feldman, *After Jihad: America and the Struggle for Islamic Democracy* (New York: Farrar, Straus and Giroux, 2003).

15. George Bush, "President Bush Discusses Freedom in Iraq and the Middle East" (Speech at the Twentieth Anniversary of the National Endowment of Democracy, U.S. Chamber of Commerce, Washington, D.C., November 6, 2003).

16. International Crisis Group (ICG), "Pakistan: The Dangers of Conventional Wisdom" (March 12, 2002); ICG, "Pakistan: Madrasas, Extremism and the Military" (July 29, 2002); ICG, "Pakistan: Transition to Democracy" (October 3, 2002); ICG, "Pakistan: Mullahs and the Military" (March 20, 2003), http://www.intl-crisis-group.org/home/index.cfm?id=1267&l=1 (accessed December 4, 2003).

17. UN Security Council Resolutions 1368 (9/12/2001) and 1373 (9/28/2001), http://www.state.gov/p/io/rls/othr/2001/4899.htm and http://www .state.gov/p/io/rls/othr/2001/5108.htm (accessed December 4, 2003).

18. Peter Slevins, "U.N. Vote Removes Sanctions on Libya," *Washington Post*, September 13, 2003. Gary Younge and Brian Whitaker, "Lockerbie Relatives See UN End Libya Sanctions," *Guardian*, September 13, 2003.

19. Tenet, "World-Wide Threats in 2003"; CIA Document on North Korea Nuclear Program, Untitled, November 2002, National Security Archive, http://www.gwu.edu/~~~nsarchiv/NSAEBB/NSAEBB87/nk22.pdf
(accessed December 4, 2003); Larry A. Niksch, "North Korea's Nuclear Weapons Program," *Congressional Research Issue Brief 91141* (August 27, 2003), http://fpc.state.gov/documents/organization/24045.pdf (accessed December 4, 2003).

20. *Small Arms Survey 2002: Counting the Human Cost*, Small Arms Survey, www.smallarmssurvey.org (accessed December 4, 2003), chap. 3, "The Legal-Illicit Link"; Human Rights Watch, "Small Arms and Human Rights: The Need for Global Action. A Briefing Paper for the U.N. Biennial Meeting on Small Arms" (July 7, 2003), http://www.hrw.org/backgrounder/arms/small-arms 070703.htm (accessed December 4, 2003).

21. Bunn, "Preventing Nuclear Terrorism.".

22. John Ruggie, "American Exceptionalism, Exemptionalism, and Global Governance," in *American Exceptionalism and Human Rights*, ed. Michael Ignatieff (Princeton: Princeton University Press, 2004).

23. Stephen E. Flynn, "America the Vulnerable," *Foreign Affairs*, January/February 2002.

24. Matthew Bunn, Anthony Weir, and John P. Holdren, "Controlling Nuclear Warheads and Materials: A Report Card and Action Plan" (Washington, D.C.: Nuclear Threat Initiative and the Project on Managing the Atom, Harvard University, March 2003). As assistant secretary of defense in the first Clinton administration, Dr. Graham Allison of the Belfer Center for Science and International Affairs received the Defense Department's highest civilian award, the Defense Medal for Distinguished Public Service, for "reshaping relations with Russia, Ukraine, Belarus, and Kazakhstan to reduce the former Soviet nuclear arsenal." This resulted in the safe return of more than twelve thousand tactical nuclear weapons from the former Soviet republics and the complete elimination of more than four thousand strategic nuclear warheads previously targeted at the United States and left in Ukraine, Kazakhstan, and Belarus when the Soviet Union disappeared.

25. *International Atomic Energy Agency Safeguards Glossary* (Vienna: International Atomic Energy Agency, 2001), "Guidelines on the Management of Plutonium," sec. 1.30: "Guidelines contained in communications received by the IAEA in 1997 from certain Member States regarding policies adopted by these States, with a view to ensuring that holdings of plutonium are managed safely and effectively in accordance with international commitments, including their obligations under the NPT (and, for States that are members of the

European Community, also under the Euratom Treaty), and with their safe-guards agreements with the IAEA. The Guidelines describe, inter alia, the nuclear material accountancy system, physical protection measures and international transfer procedures applicable to the plutonium subject to the Guidelines. They further specify the information to be published by the participating States in respect of plutonium management, including annual statements of their holdings of civil unirradiated plutonium and of their estimates of plutonium contained in spent civil reactor fuel. The Guidelines are published in [549]."

26. Richard Butler, *The Greatest Threat: Iraq, Weapons of Mass Destruction and the Crisis of Global Security* (New York: Public Affairs, 2000), 128—129. Scott Ritter, *Endgame: Solving the Iraq Problem Once and for All* (New York: Simon and Schuster, 1999), 177.

27. Matthew Meselson, "The Problem of Biological Weapons," *Bulletin of the American Academy of Arts and Sciences* 52, no. 5 (1999): 57; see also M. F. Perutz, "The Threat of Biological Weapons," *New York Review*, April 13, 2000.

28. Barry R. Bloom, "Bioterrorism and the University," *Harvard Magazine*, November–December 2003.

29. F. D. Wormuth, *To Chain the Dog of War* (Urbana: University of Illinois Press, 1989); Brian Hallet, *The Lost Art of Declaring War* (Urbana: University of Illinois Press, 1998); J. H. Ely, *War and Responsibility* (Princeton: Princeton University Press, 1993); see also a discussion of the issue of democratic consent and the war power in my *Virtual War: Kosovo and Beyond* (London: Vintage 2001), 176–84.

30. President George W. Bush's State of the Union Address, January 28, 2003, http://www.whitehouse.gov/news/releases/2003/01/20030128-19.html (accessed December 4, 2003):

> The International Atomic Energy Agency confirmed in the 1990s that Saddam Hussein had an advanced nuclear weapons development program, had a design for a nuclear weapon and was working on five different methods of enriching uranium for a bomb. The British government has learned that Saddam Hussein recently sought significant quantities of uranium from Africa. Our intelligence sources tell us that he has attempted to purchase high-strength aluminum tubes suitable for nuclear weapons production. Saddam Hussein has not credibly explained these activities. He clearly has much to hide. . . . Year after year, Saddam Hussein has gone to elaborate lengths, spent enormous sums, taken great risks to build and keep weapons of mass destruction. But why? The only possible explanation, the only possible use he could have for those weapons, is to dominate, intimidate, or attack. . . .
> And this Congress and the America people must recognize another threat. Evidence from intelligence sources, secret communications, and statements by people now in custody reveal that Saddam Hussein aids and protects terrorists, including mem-

bers of al Qaeda. Secretly, and without fingerprints, he could provide one of his hidden weapons to terrorists, or help them develop their own.

Prime Minister Tony Blair, Speech to the House of Commons, March 18, 2003, http://www.number-10.gov.uk/output/Page3294.asp (accessed December 4, 2003):

What is the claim of Saddam today? Why exactly the same claim as before: that he has no WMD. Indeed we are asked to believe that after seven years of obstruction and non-compliance finally resulting in the inspectors leaving in 1998, seven years in which he hid his programme, built it up even whilst inspection teams were in Iraq, that after they left he then voluntarily decided to do what he had consistently refused to do under coercion. . . . We are now seriously asked to accept that in the last few years, contrary to all history, contrary to all intelligence, he decided unilaterally to destroy the weapons. Such a claim is palpably absurd. . . . Iraq is not the only regime with WMD. But back away now from this confrontation and future conflicts will be infinitely worse and more devastating.

But, of course, in a sense, any fair observer does not really dispute that Iraq is in breach and that 1441 implies action in such circumstances. The real problem is that, underneath, people dispute that Iraq is a threat; dispute the link between terrorism and WMD; dispute the whole basis of our assertion that the two together constitute a fundamental assault on our way of life.

31. Michael Walzer, *Just and Unjust Wars* (New York: Basic, 1992), 80–86.

32. The National Security Strategy of the United States of America, September 2002, http://www.whitehouse.gov/nsc/nss.html (accessed December 4, 2003):

While the United States will constantly strive to enlist the support of the international community, we will not hesitate to act alone, if necessary, to exercise our right of self-determination by acting preemptively against such terrorists. . . Legal scholars and international jurists often conditioned the legitimacy of preemption on the existence of an imminent threat—most often a visible mobilization of armies, navies, and air forces preparing to attack. We must adapt the concept of imminent threat to the capabilities and objectives of today's adversaries. Rogue states and terrorists do not seek to attack us using conventional means. . . . The United States has long maintained the option of preemptive actions to counter a sufficient threat to our national security. The greater the threat, the greater is the risk of inaction—and the more compelling the case for taking anticipatory action to defend ourselves, even if uncertainty remains as to the time and place of the enemy's attack. To forestall or prevent such hostile acts by our adversaries, the United States will, if necessary, act preemptively. . . . The United States will not use force in all cases to preempt emerging threats, nor should nations use preemption as a pretext for aggression. Yet in an age where the enemies of civilization openly and actively seek the world's most destructive technologies, the United States cannot remain idle while dangers gather. . . . We will always proceed deliberately, weighing the consequences of our actions. To support preemptive options, we will: build better more integrated intelligence capabilities to provide timely, accurate information on threats, wherever they may emerge; coordinate closely with allies to form a common assessment of the most dangerous threats; and continue to transform our military forces to ensure our ability to conduct rapid and precise operations to achieve decisive results. The purpose of our actions will always be to eliminate a specific threat to the United States or our allies and friends. The reasons for our actions will be clear, the force measured, and the cause just. (6, 15–16)

33. Leszek Kolakowski, *Modernity on Endless Trial* (Chicago: University of Chicago Press, 1990).